IN THE SHADOW OF THE AYATOLLAH

IN THE SHADOW OF THE AYATOLLAH

A CIA HOSTAGE IN IRAN

William J. Daugherty

Naval Institute Press

Annapolis, Maryland

Naval Institute Press
291 Wood Road
Annapolis, MD 21402

Library of Congress Cataloging-in-Publication Data
Daugherty, William J., 1947-
    In the Shadow of the Ayatollah : a CIA hostage in Iran / William J. Daugherty.
    p. cm.
    Includes bibliographical references and index.
    ISBN 1-55750-169-6 (acid-free paper)
    1. Iran Hostage Crisis, 1979-1981—Personal narratives. 2. Daugherty, William J.,
1947—Captivity, 1979-1980. 3. Hostages—Iran—Biography. 4. United States. Central
Intelligence Agency—Biography.
    E183.8.I55 D37 2001
    955.05'42'092—dc21   2001030449

Printed in the United States of America on acid-free paper ∞
08 07 06 05 04 03 02 01   9 8 7 6 5 4 3 2
First printing

The CIA's Publication Review Board has reviewed the manuscript for this book as
required by Agency regulations, and poses no security objection to its publication.
This review, however, should not be construed as an official release of information,
confirmation of its accuracy, or endorsement of the author's views.

To the sacred memory of the eight courageous men who gave their lives in the Iranian desert so that others could be free; to the Honorable Kenneth Taylor, the members of the Canadian embassy in Tehran in 1980, and the government of Canada for daring to rescue six Americans in need; and to all Canadians for their enduring friendship with the United States and their support during the crisis of 1979–81

CONTENTS

Foreword / ix

Preface / xi

Acknowledgments / xv

List of Abbreviations / xix

Introduction / 1

Part One: Assignment to Tehran

1 The Assignment / 5

2 Retrospective: A History Lesson / 17

3 The Soviet Calculus / 23

4 The 1953 Coup / 29

5 America and Iran, 1953–1977 / 40

6 Revolution / 56

7 Intelligence Failure / 66

8 End of a Regime / 80

9 The Shah Comes to the United States / 94

Part Two: A Guest of Iranian Militants

10 4 November 1979 / 103

11 5 November 1979 / 123

12 6 November 1979 / 125

13 7–22 November 1979 / 130

14 23 November–31 December 1979 / 135

15 1 January–24 April 1980 / 154

16 24 April–22 June 1980 / 179

17 22 June–23 December 1980 / 192

18 The Final Weeks / 202

19 The Rest of the Story / 209

    Notes / 223

    Bibliography / 245

    Index / 251

FOREWORD

Bill Daugherty is one of my most intriguing friends. He has worn many hats during his lifetime, as a Marine Corps aviator, a member of the Central Intelligence Agency, a professor, an author, and, yes, even a hostage. When Bill and I cross paths, I am always reminded of the sacrifices he made for our nation while serving in the CIA, especially while being held hostage in Tehran by Iranian militants.

But my respect and admiration for Bill go beyond his public service. His efforts today as a teacher are just as profound. In today's society, in which education reform plays a large part of the national agenda, it is comforting to know that there are teachers like Bill who exceed expectations and make teaching their passion. When my interns tell me that Dr. Daugherty is one of their favorite professors and I see the smile that joins their remarks, I am also reminded of his dedication and ability to be a great educator.

Although I have never entered Bill's classroom, I considered myself one of his students while reading a draft of this monumental achievement. His personal insight into the events that led to the hostage crisis and the politics involved in the decision making was truly enlightening. Indeed, the details of his nightmarish captivity are unbelievable. After finishing *In the Shadow of the Ayatollah*, I understood clearly why my interns consider Dr. Daugherty an accomplished teacher.

This book will leave you with a better understanding of the issues surrounding a dark period in American history. You will learn the truth about the American hostages' experiences in Iran, especially while reading the bone-chilling accounts that begin in chapter 10. While Bill did not intend to emphasize the weaknesses of the Carter administration, he gives an honest account of the mistakes made by our leaders during that difficult time. Most important, you will gain firsthand knowledge from a selfless patriot who experienced the worst period of his life on behalf of the United States of America.

Congressman Jack Kingston

PREFACE

There are several points the reader should understand about this work. First, this volume tells mainly about one man's experiences during one significant period. I have included just enough information about the relationship between the United States and Iran in the years following World War II to set the stage. There is much more, but it lies beyond the scope of this work. Virtually everyone who was kind enough to review drafts of the manuscript suggested that I include such-and-such an event or discuss so-and-so, or that I contact this or that source for additional insights. They were all wonderful ideas, and truly I wish I could have accommodated. In the end, though, it was necessary to limit the text to the needs of the publisher. This volume, then, in no way constitutes a complete treatment of any element of Iranian or U.S.-Iranian history.

Likewise, this is not the definitive history of the hostage crisis. Many of the principals in the Carter administration have already recorded their memories of the event, and historians and political scientists have written much more. The interested reader should look to the Bibliography as a guide to these resources. Nor is this *the* representative story of the hostages themselves. In the 1950s there was a television program about the New York Police Department titled *The Naked City.* Each episode ended with the voice-over: "There are eight million stories in the Naked City; this has been just one of them." Well, fifty-two Americans have individual stories of their 444 days as captives of the Iranians, and this is just one of them.

I had hoped to accomplish three objectives in this work. First, I wanted to present new material (within the limitations allowed) that would add to the understanding of what occurred in 1979, particularly with respect to the decision-making process in the White House. To this end I was aided immeasurably by individuals who participated in the events described in the text and generously shared what they learned and experienced firsthand. This book reflects the detailed information, unvarnished criticisms, and alternative points of view they passed along.

A second goal was to place certain events in more accurate perspective. Much of America's Cold War foreign policy was informed and founded on intelligence data and activities that, due to security classifications or limited accessibility in open sources, are absent from earlier writings. As more of this material has been declassified, our knowledge of many events that occurred during that era has been expanded. Although this text does not rely on any documentary material that was not already in the public domain when earlier works about the hostage crisis were written, a significant amount of that data had been overlooked, given short shrift, or simply ignored by authors for any number of reasons. I have attempted to collate relevant items in this material to display key events in a truer light. That said, much more remains to be declassified, and history's judgments on some of the issues I have addressed may yet change.

My third goal was to relate the facts and events covered by this book, other than my personal experiences, as objectively as possible. I doubt that I have been completely successful, but I have tried—realizing, of course, that just the tasks of selecting what elements to discuss and what sources to rely on are in themselves a subjective decision. Where I have either deliberately or inadvertently revealed my own thoughts, the reader is welcome to disagree. Nor should the reader take my personal reactions to events of the moment as an attempt to portray the wider issues involved and factors that were beyond my ken. For example, the opinion I expressed on learning of the shah's admission to the United States reflected my concern for my personal safety and that of my colleagues. But the situation looked very different in Washington, despite what I might have thought in Tehran, and I have endeavored to relate those two perspectives as fairly as I can. The reader will easily discern, in these instances, that what appeared simple and straightforward to me was a much more intricate problem for the policymakers.

A word of caution. The majority of the works that examine the actions and decisions of the Carter administration with regard to Iranian affairs seem to be more intent on criticizing the administration or individual participants than objectively reviewing the issues and options. But the hostage crisis was far more complicated than just choosing up sides or criticizing all that went wrong. Developing and executing a national security policy in which Iran played a major role was a complex endeavor for almost all post-1945 American presidents (LBJ being the exception). Iran's geography made it a pivotal player in the Cold War and in Middle Eastern politics. Right or wrong, however, the internal political and social health of Iran were not of much interest or concern to any administration, Democratic or Republican, save John Kennedy's. By the time Jimmy Carter was elected president, his options for dealing with Iran had been seriously limited by the decisions and policies of his predecessors. When the Iranian revolution began to unfold in 1978 he was presented with a continuing series of critical problems, none of which offered easy or clear choices for him.

As for the hostage crisis itself, trying to save fifty-two lives while also preserving America's national interests and honor was an extraordinarily difficult endeavor, and President Carter deserves more credit than his critics have been willing to give. While there were at times serious disagreements within the administration over which of the options to choose, the reader should not assume or think that these differences were motivated by any reason or purpose other than what each participant believed to be the best interests of the country. None of those involved pressed a personal agenda or sought individual gain in deliberations on how to deal with the Iranian revolution, the admittance of the shah to the United States, or the hostage crisis. In a time of humiliation for the United States, the policymakers involved in dealing with the crisis distinguished themselves in their efforts to bring it to an honorable conclusion.

A final point: my occasionally harsh comments about Iranians in general, the Iranian character, and aspects of Iranian culture and history should not be taken as utter condemnation of all things Iranian or of the Iranian people. My personal dislikes of certain Iranians (which are, I admit, still strongly held) extend only to those particular individuals, and for good cause. The insults and criticisms I mention in the text were levied against people who were threatening our lives, arrantly and arrogantly violating long-accepted international norms and values, causing great distress to our families, and bringing about shame and humiliation to the United States. These remarks should not be interpreted in any broader sense.

Prior to publication, the final draft of this text was submitted to the Central Intelligence Agency's Publication Review Board, which I am required to do as a former Agency officer. I support this requirement. The sole purpose of the board's review of the manuscript is to ensure that no currently classified material has found its way into the text. The board has no charge to censor the text by deleting or amending information or positions that may be unfavorable to the Agency or the U.S. government.

I received no assistance from the CIA in writing this book, with the exception of the provision of two documents (out of four I had requested) by the Information and Privacy branch in the CIA's Office of Information Management; both documents had been declassified some years earlier through the Freedom of Information Act. I did, several times and through several channels both official and personal, ask the Agency for help in locating and providing previously unpublished materials. The Agency not only did not provide any of these materials, it lacked the courtesy even to reply to my requests. This despite the Agency's recent statements asserting a new openness and my making it clear that the book would be favorable to the Agency. The reader can thus be assured that this work is strictly my own product with no substantive connection whatsoever to the CIA.

Gary Sick was the Iran action officer for the National Security Council staff during the Carter administration. The failure of the rescue mission and the resulting casualties on 25 April 1980 left Sick tasting "ashes in the mouth." It seems to me that this emotion can also be applied to America's relationship with Iran for the thirty-five years between the end of World War II and the consolidation of the Islamic regime. The United States viewed Iran as essential to the security of the Western democracies, if not to the entire world; the Americans never intended harm to the Iranian people. That is America's tragedy. Likewise, as the shah matured in his leadership, he, too, seemed to have only the best intentions for his country. That his magnificent dreams were never matched in reality is the tragedy of the Iranians. Knowing that so much good was intended by the two countries and yet that so much harm came from the relationship also leaves the taste of ashes in the mouth.

ACKNOWLEDGMENTS

A waggish friend suggested that I begin this section by thanking the Iranian militants, "without whom this story would not have been possible." I'm not going to go quite that far, but there are some wonderful people whose help significantly aided the production of this work. I am deeply grateful for their time, knowledge, energy, and friendship.

This work is a much amended and vastly improved expansion of an article I penned several years ago for the professional journal *Studies in Intelligence*, published by the CIA's Center for the Study of Intelligence. Brian Latell, the center's director at the time, urged me to put my experiences to paper before I left the Agency to add to its historical record. Succumbing to his importuning, I managed to produce a manuscript that was eventually transformed into publishable form by *Studies* editors Paul Arnold (for the classified edition) and Hank Appelbaum (for the unclassified edition). Since my retirement, Paul and Hank have generously continued to give their support and assistance on numerous occasions. I owe these three many thanks for giving me the idea of writing the story in the first place and for their help in turning me into something approximating an author.

I am likewise appreciative of Tom Cutler at the U.S. Naval Institute Press, who believed that my story was worth telling and supported my efforts to tell it. NIP production editor Kristin Wye-Rodney did a wonderful job shepherding the book from raw manuscript to finished work. Mindy Conner copyedited the manuscript, and her professionalism and standards of excellence are evident on virtually every page. This is a vastly superior work because of Mindy's contribution, and I am grateful beyond words.

Many former Agency officers have found university campuses to be unfriendly, if not downright hostile, territory. I am extremely fortunate and thankful to have had the opposite experience. Armstrong Atlantic

State University in Savannah has gifted me with the best job I've ever had and has made it possible for me to work with a truly outstanding faculty. Michael Donahue, my department chair, has my eternal gratitude for believing that I might be a reasonably decent teacher and perhaps even a scholar; Michael has unstintingly supported my work and encouraged me from my first day. Robert Burnett, president emeritus; Frank Butler, vice president for external affairs; Sara Conner, vice president for academic affairs and dean of the faculty; and Joe Adams, dean emeritus, all warmly accepted me on the faculty and made me feel part of the Armstrong family. Many thanks to my exceptionally talented departmental colleagues for their comradeship and assistance, and to others on the faculty with whom I have worked on committee assignments and related endeavors. I particularly wish to acknowledge our department secretary, Linda Hansen, for her unlimited patience and unfailingly cheerful assistance, without which I would be eternally lost; and Hiskia Vanderley, our graduate assistant, who is as gracious as she is efficient (and a fine tennis player!).

Also greatly appreciated is Caroline Hopkinson of Armstrong's Lane Library. Caro's enthusiasm for my project was exceeded only by her professionalism and skill at tracking down published materials for this book. Likewise, Beth Dinnebeil of Lane Library labored in great good humor at the tedious task of locating photographs for the book as well as other useful resources. Their assistance was invaluable and I am very grateful to both for their help and friendship. Sue Brisk of SIPA-USA was quick to respond to my requests for unpublished photos; the results of her help appear in these pages.

Martin Elzy and his staff at the Jimmy Carter Presidential Library kindly assisted this novice scholar in learning to use the resources at the library and provided much-needed assistance. I thank them sincerely for their labors.

I have no words to express my gratitude to the following for the information and insights they contributed by reviewing all or part of this text while in draft form: Ambassador Richard M. Helms; former undersecretary of state David Newsom; Capt. Gary Sick, USN; Gene Poteat, former senior CIA scientific intelligence officer and now president of the Association of Former Intelligence Officers; distinguished intelligence historian Jeffery T. Richelson of the National Security Archives, who not only reviewed selected portions of the draft and then the full document, but also was thoughtful enough to send to me a number of relevant documents and lists of others; and Capt. Richard A. Stratton, USN, a genuine American hero, who reviewed the final manuscript and provided critical insights and corrections.

Zbigniew Brzezinski reviewed the manuscript in full and portions of it a second time. He graciously consented to a candid interview that was especially meaningful to me personally as well as to the accuracy of this work. Ambassador L. Bruce Laingen, senior State Department officers Charles W. Naas and Henry M. Precht, and Mark J. Gasiorowski of Louisiana State University each read one or more drafts and never failed to respond promptly and with good humor when I pestered them (which was far too often) with numerous follow-up questions. Mark also kindly provided several exceptionally useful journal articles and other writings. It has been an honor to have met or corresponded and worked with each of these distinguished individuals and I am grateful beyond words for their assistance. It goes almost without saying that they contributed materially to the positive aspects of this book; any and all errors, whether of fact or interpretation, fall at my own doorstep, no matter how industriously I may try to find a scapegoat.

Sara Behling, an accomplished artist, creative photographer, talented potter, and distinguished teacher, merits very special mention and appreciation for her work on the maps and diagrams in this book. She not only labored diligently in return for absolutely no compensation, she had to put up with me in general. But then, she's my cousin so she's accustomed to this burden. I'm very proud of her.

I am particularly honored that one of America's most outstanding public servants, Representative Jack Kingston of Georgia's First Congressional District, agreed to write the Foreword. Representative Kingston brings the highest standards of personal and professional integrity to his office while faithfully serving the highest interests of the nation. His efforts in building and sustaining a strong military establishment are especially meritorious and deserve the gratitude of all Americans.

During the seventeen years I spent in the CIA's Directorate of Operations, I had the unique opportunity to work with some of America's most dedicated public servants. In acknowledging their friendship and support over the years, I also want readers to know that these men and women willingly make many sacrifices and endure countless hardships in the service of their country; they deserve the nation's thanks and gratitude. Of the Agency officials I can mention, Richard L. Holm and Chris Frederick were role models and mentors (and are now, I am pleased to note, treasured friends) who taught me a great deal more about the intelligence business then either will probably acknowledge. Dick Holm is one of the Agency's genuine heroes and it was a great privilege to have worked for him in Washington and overseas. There are many other valued friends and respected colleagues that I am unable to mention by name; I hope they understand how much I enjoyed working with them and how much I admire their professionalism.

LIST OF ABBREVIATIONS

ACOS	Acting Chief of Station
CIA	Central Intelligence Agency
CMS	Career Management Staff
COS	Chief of Station
CT	Career Trainee
DAO	Defense Attaché's Office
DCM	Deputy Chief of Mission
DC/NE	Deputy Chief, Near East Division
DIA	Defense Intelligence Agency
DO	Directorate of Operations
FBIS	Foreign Broadcast Information Service
IG	Inspector General
INR	Bureau of Intelligence and Research
MAAG	Military Assistance Advisory Group
MCAS	Marine Corps Air Station
MDAP	Military Defense Assistance Program
MFA	Ministry of Foreign Affairs
NE	Near East
NEA	Near East Affairs
NF	National Front (Iran)
NIE	National Intelligence Estimate
NSC	National Security Council
OSA	Operations Support Assistant
PGOI	Provisional Government of Iran
SCC	Special Coordinating Committee
TDY	Temporary Duty

IN THE SHADOW OF THE AYATOLLAH

INTRODUCTION

The embassy had surrendered. Iranian "student" militants were now in charge of an American diplomatic facility, including the Central Intelligence Agency station. Embassy personnel were blindfolded, our hands bound, and escorted to the ambassador's residence, where we were freed of the blindfolds and placed on chairs and sofas located on the first floor. I was situated in a comfortable oversized stuffed chair in the ballroom; the "students" had angrily ordered us to remain silent, leaving each of us to speculate in isolation about their intentions. Early in the evening we were led in small groups to the kitchen where we were fed a light meal. Shortly afterward, a young Iranian carrying a .38 revolver came into the room calling my name. I noticed that his pronunciation of my name was surprisingly good, which I thought curious. I learned later, to my disgust and anger, that the captors had received assistance from several of my colleagues in sorting out who did what in the mission, and obviously one of them had mentioned my name, giving the correct pronunciation. There was no point in hiding: I acknowledged my presence and was curtly advised, "You are wanted in your office." Considering my true position as operations officer for the CIA, being singled out by name and separated from the others did not strike me as a particularly positive development. My bindings were checked, I was again blindfolded, and then I was led out of the residence. It was a frightening walk through a dark night made even darker by the prospect of who might want to see me—and what he might want.

Part One

ASSIGNMENT TO TEHRAN

Don't worry about another embassy attack. The Iranians have already done it once so they don't have to prove anything. Besides, the only thing that could trigger an attack would be if the shah was let into the States—and no one in this town is stupid enough to do that.

Chief, Iran Branch, Directorate of Operations, CIA Headquarters, August 1979

CHAPTER 1

THE ASSIGNMENT

You'd think I would remember the exact moment in which I was offered Tehran, Iran, for my first overseas tour as a newly certified field operations officer for the Central Intelligence Agency. It was, after all, an offer that changed my career, not to mention my life, and somehow it doesn't seem possible that this detail has fled my memory. But it has. I have no recollection today of who made the offer, although the logical person would have been the chief of the Iran Operations branch in the Agency's Directorate of Operations (DO). I do know that I did not hesitate a second to say yes. For the most part I have not regretted that decision, although for some years afterward a certain effort was required to keep it and the events that followed in some sort of reasonable perspective. After all, it is rare, even for an organization in which risk is an everyday part of the business, that a newly minted case officer spends his first tour in jail.

It was only by happenstance that I entered the Agency in the first place. In the spring of 1978 I was in the midst of my last year of doctoral work at the Claremont Graduate School, and although graduation was only eight months away, I had given no thought to life after graduate school. My preference was for public service rather than a job in the private sector, but I wasn't sure I could find a position in California that would allow me to utilize my education. Constitutional law and U.S. foreign policy were my majors, with a minor in U.S. government. My particular interest was the relationship between the Executive Branch and Congress, specifically in the constitutional law of foreign policy and the war powers. I had no interest in working for the State Department and even less in being a civilian employee at the Pentagon. There was always the possibility of a position on Capitol Hill, but I didn't want to deal with the egos that invest that venue. Truth be told, I had enrolled in graduate school simply because I was interested in these subjects and still had nearly three years left on the GI Bill, and I did not really want to leave Southern California. I was content with the notion that I would not find a career in my field of expertise. Rather than dwelling on future employment, however, I was focusing on surviving the next eight months. There was coursework to finish, written and oral doctoral exams to pass, and a dissertation to polish and defend. The postgraduation future was still far away.

Nevertheless, when there came a surprise opportunity to send a résumé to the regional CIA recruiter, I didn't pass it up. I knew what the CIA was and had a good idea of what it did, having read a number of books on espionage in general and the CIA in particular. Although I was intrigued by the work and believed the Agency was making a valuable contribution to the nation, I had never envisioned myself joining up. But if I really was going to go to Washington, this would be the organization to work for. The initial interview with the recruiter went well, and in May I was contacted by Jim, a senior officer in the DO's Career Management Staff (CMS) in Washington, who invited me to an in-depth interview.

Jim was staying at the Marina Del Ray Hotel. I arrived at the appointed hour, unsure what to expect but dressed in a rare (and detested) coat and tie for that important first impression. Jim didn't look like a spy, or a spymaster for that matter—although I didn't have the slightest notion what a spy should look like—but the setting did generate a sense of the clandestine. The drapes were closed tightly, and the medium-wattage table lamp lent an air of secrecy to the affair. For most of two hours Jim asked questions and, when appropriate, provided explanations or background information. I thought I had done well, but Jim said only that he would be in touch. I left, assuming that it would be weeks, if not months, before I heard anything further.

I was not particularly concerned or anxious in any case. Summer school was coming up, and I was committed to reserve duty as the assistant officer in charge of an air traffic control unit at Marine Corps Air Station El Toro; and there was always my dissertation. Odds seemed long that the Agency would actually accept me, and it wasn't anything I had my heart set on, anyway. To my surprise, though, Jim called the very next day and asked if I could again make the hour-long drive to Marina Del Ray, as there was one other issue he wanted to discuss. I didn't mind the drive, but I wasn't thrilled about hauling out the coat and tie again.

In this second interview Jim laid out the basics of a special program managed by CMS in addition to the standard Career Training (CT) program entered by the great majority of DO officers. This CMS program was designed to place a few selected first-tour officers overseas as quickly as feasible, reducing the amount of time the trainee spent in Washington, where one of the favorite pastimes among its more knowledgeable denizens is playing "spot the spook." Participants in this special program (of which there were but one or two per class, if that) were given a more solid background, or "cover," making it harder for observers to discern their true employment. Graduates of the program were expected to be less detectable to host government security services and hostile intelligence services operating in the same locale. The increased operational security was expected to translate into more effective recruiting and handling of sensitive sources. The program sounded fine to me, and the possibility of participating in it served to jump-start my interest in an Agency career. I had been attracted to the Marine Corps in part because of its reputation as an elite, action-oriented, can-do organization, and now I appeared to be on the verge of entering another highly selective organization through an even more demanding program.

In August I flew to Washington for testing and interviews, including a polygraph. The only troubling part was a language aptitude test the first morning. Jetlag had left me sleepless the night before, and I actually dozed off during the test. The ability to learn foreign languages is essential to an overseas operations officer, and I was concerned that a poor showing would sink my chances. Everything else, including the polygraph, went well, however, and I departed Washington in an optimistic mood, a state of mind justified when, in October, Jim called and asked if I could join the January 1979 class. I could.

I entered on duty with the Central Intelligence Agency the morning of 8 January 1979, receiving the oath of office in a safe house in the Virginia suburbs from Jim's immediate boss, with Jim looking on. We then drove through a light snow to CIA headquarters to complete the paperwork. Standing in Jim's second-floor office in C Corridor, looking through the window at the snow dusting the inner courtyard, I was struck by the tranquility of the scene. I thought of this picture often in later years, and it was the image I recalled as I left headquarters for the last time in September 1996. The next morning, feeling odd at being introduced in alias, I joined the new CT class that had also entered on duty the day before, but sworn in as a class at headquarters.

For the next four weeks we shared our introduction to the CIA and the espionage business, lunched together, hit Friday night happy hours at various watering holes, partied on Saturdays, brunched on Sundays, and made lifelong friends. And then, full of piss and vinegar, we left Washington for the Agency's primary training facility three hours away to begin the Initial Operations Course. This training period lasted another four weeks; on the last Friday my CT classmates headed back to headquarters to experience six months of "interims," eight-week rotational assignments with two operational desks and one analytical office in the Directorate of Intelligence. At the end of interims, my classmates would return to the remote training facility for the Field Tradecraft Course (FTC), sixteen weeks of intense instruction and field practicum concluding in their certification as operations officers in the Directorate of Operations.

But I didn't go with them; my program meant forgoing interim assignments and remaining at the training facility as a student in the next FTC. I spent a President's Day long weekend at Chincoteague on the Chesapeake Bay and then met my new classmates on Monday morning. This was the class that had entered the Agency immediately prior to mine; they had just finished their interims and were returning for the FTC. The class had been together for a year and had bonded closely, as CT classes do; it was at first awkward for me and, perhaps, for some of them. But there were also eight "internal" DO employees joining the class, experienced officers who had been serving in operations support or nonoperational assignments and had been selected for the FTC without moving through the CT program. We "outsiders" were grouped together for instruction and we bonded in our own way.

The FTC was challenging and intense, requiring long hours and hard work. Our instructors handed out frank but friendly criticism in response to honest mistakes, and other types of criticism when the mistakes were due to a lack of thought or effort. But it was also a hell of a lot of fun, made more so by the developing friendships with classmates and the positive teaching attitudes of the instructors. Many of the staff eschewed the traditional teacher-pupil relationship, instead interacting with the students more as colleagues working together in a mutual endeavor. This not only enhanced the learning experience but also turned many of the instructors into friends. This burgeoning professional collegiality did not in any way lessen their willingness to let us know in rather explicit terms when we royally screwed up. But it did inspire most of us to work harder for our mentors.

In all, the FTC was much more enjoyable than I had imagined it would be, and, rather to my surprise, I discovered that I possessed a modest talent and some instinct for operations work. I enjoyed it so much that I factored a tour as an instructor into my long-range career planning. Eleven years later, after serving as a CT recruiter, I returned to the training facility as a member of the instructor cadre and had the great pleasure of training many of those whom I had recently helped to hire. And to my joy, several of my former instructors, now retired, were back teaching in the FTC on contract. All of these elements melded to make this tour the very best of my Agency career. But in 1979, that pleasure lay far in the future.

There was one major advantage—and likewise, one related drawback—to my special program. The advantage was graduation, certification as a field operations officer, and a full-grade promotion just six months after joining the Agency while the other CTs labored nearly eighteen months in training. The negative aspect—which actually came to be a blessing in disguise later in my term of captivity—was that I went overseas with an astonishingly small knowledge of the DO and how it did its business. By not sitting on operational desks, not writing cables to the overseas field stations, and not following actual operations in progress, I missed out on a chance to learn a great deal. But the program designers knew this, of course, and had always anticipated that graduates of the program would eventually catch up with their classmates. Our first chief of station (COS) had to be aware of this shortfall, of course, and willing to accept some initial limitations in return for the advantage of having a good officer in deep cover.

Despite my lack of experience I managed to do well in training, even against my veteran colleagues. I was particularly captivated by the stories told by the instructors from the DO's Near East (NE) Division and by the challenging situations found in the Middle East; I decided that I wanted my home base in NE. Just at that point, during a Saturday visit to headquarters, the deputy chief of NE (DC/NE) raised the possibility of assignment to Tehran, currently among the highest national priorities in the intelligence community, even though I possessed no academic knowledge of or practical experience with anything Iranian.

By the time of this conversation in the spring of 1979, the Tehran station was in the midst of coping with postrevolutionary Iran. The shah of Iran had fled the country on 16 January, and soon thereafter—on 1 February

—Ayatollah Ruhollah Khomeini returned from exile in France to oversee a government founded on his perception of a fundamentalist Islamic state. Also of import to later events, U.S. embassy and station personnel had been taken hostage by Marxist guerrillas for several hours on 14 February 1979, in what came to be called the St. Valentine's Day Open House.[1] This event triggered an almost total drawdown of embassy and station personnel, along with a reduction of active-duty U.S. military forces in Iran from about ten thousand to a dozen or so, divided between the Defense Attaché's Office (DAO) and the Military Assistance Advisory Group (MAAG). It did not, however, generate any sentiment at the highest levels of the U.S. government for disrupting or breaking off diplomatic relations with Iran. In fact, it strengthened the Carter administration's determination to reconcile with the Provisional Government of Iran (PGOI). Assistant Secretary of State for Near Eastern and South Asian Affairs (NEA) Harold Saunders explained that "following the 14 February takeover we made a basic decision that Iran was so important that we should maintain a presence there."[2] For the president's national security adviser, Zbigniew Brzezinski, the "central strategic objective" for the United States was to "help Iran preserve its national integrity and independence."[3] There were humanitarian concerns as well, as expressed by Undersecretary of State David D. Newsom: "We particularly wished to maintain a consular presence to be able to assist Jews, Bahais, and other minorities in danger to leave Iran."[4]

Although the United States took the initiative with the PGOI to retain a U.S. diplomatic presence, the Iranian leadership did not object. In what must have been a difficult dilemma, they understood that many Iranians, especially the religious fundamentalists, no longer desired an American presence in Iran, but neither did they want the Americans completely gone. Numerous multi-billion-dollar military sales and assistance programs, as well as equally costly civilian construction projects, had been left hanging from the shah's era, and there remained a range of issues to work out between the Americans and the new regime. Charles W. Naas, director of Iranian affairs at State between 1974 and 1978, and deputy chief of mission (DCM) in the U.S. embassy in Tehran in 1978–79, witnessed the transition from the shah to the PGOI in early to mid-1979. As he saw it, Iran's new leaders wanted to maintain a relationship with the United States, but only if it conformed with accepted diplomatic standards and eliminated the previous unique ties that had bound the United States more to the shah personally than to the country of Iran. One more factor impelled the Iranians to sustain the American presence in Iran: hostile neighbors to the north and west.[5]

Naas understood that Iran's new prime minister, a secular politician named Mehdi Bazargan, and his key advisers (also secularists for the most part) recognized the potential threats posed by the USSR and Iraq and wanted to retain Iran's traditional security arrangements with the United States. Of the two, the USSR was deemed the primary menace. Faced with potential aggression from these foes, Bazargan believed that an American presence would deter any adventurism. Naas held a series of discussions with Bazargan and his advisers in which the Iranians made this point "very clear."[6] And in fact, these fears were borne out more than once after the U.S. embassy was captured in November 1979 and the United States was no longer Iran's ally.

Soon after the embassy takeover in November 1979 the CIA acquired indisputable intelligence that the Soviets were dusting off contingency plans for a military occupation of the northern third of Iran contingent on hostile action by the United States or any other perceived threat to Soviet interests. This was followed by equally convincing intelligence that the Red Army was conducting training maneuvers north of their joint border with Iran. By August 1980 intelligence assessments indicated that the Soviets were training for a large-scale invasion of Iran with the Persian Gulf a potential objective. In a report to the president examining the potential for a political "break-up of Iran," Brzezinski noted that the United States "can't really influence the outcome of an Iranian civil war [should one eventuate], while we do know the Soviets have started training for military operations directed at Iran."[7]

Nor were U.S. government officials the only ones concerned about a possible Soviet move into Iran. A prominent scholar who had long followed U.S.-Iran relations met with presidential assistant Hedley Donavon in late January 1980 to discuss the same issue. In the meeting Professor James Bill appeared to Donavon to be "extremely apprehensive" regarding Soviet intentions vis-à-vis Iran. Bill expressed concern that the Soviets might use Iran's support for Islamic resistance fighters in Soviet-occupied Afghanistan as a "provocation" to move into Iran. If the Soviets did move, Bill projected an airborne assault on Iran's oilfields.[8]

Following the earlier short-lived embassy takeover in February 1979, the Carter administration had reduced the embassy staff to about sixty, including State officers, the CIA station, military attachés and the MAAG cadre, administrative personnel, and Marine security guards.[9] The

Marines were to serve in their traditional role of furnishing internal embassy security and protecting classified materials and U.S. government property. External security—the defense of the embassy grounds and compound from intrusion—was a different matter. The guardianship of every American embassy is vested in the host government, usually in police units, military forces, or, in some locales, contracted private security firms. But after 14 February, "security" at the American embassy in Tehran was courtesy of a ratty, unkempt, undisciplined group of Iranian "revolutionaries" who roamed the grounds at will with automatic weapons, making everyone uncomfortable.[10] Only at the end of the summer was anything resembling a legitimate guard force placed at the embassy gates. When the demonstrators came to the gates on 4 November, these "guards," to the surprise of no one in the embassy, melted away into the crowds.

By March 1979 the Tehran station consisted of case officers rotating in and out on a temporary duty (TDY) basis. But NE Division was looking ahead to the time when the station could again be staffed with permanently assigned personnel and functioning as a station should—recruiting agents and collecting intelligence. And that was the state of affairs when I met DC/NE in Langley on that spring day.

The deputy division chief's decision to assign me to Tehran was, I suppose, a matter of balancing the plusses and minuses. On the positive side of the ledger, my special program had kept my cover clean: I had no visible affiliation with the U.S. government, much less with the Agency or any of its usual cover providers. I did have military service—eight years of active duty with the U.S. Marine Corps—but between those years and my entry on duty with the Agency I had spent five and a half years as a university student. Moreover, it was just eight years since the end of the draft and four years after the conclusion of the Vietnam War, and most male government employees at that time possessed a military background. So this was no reason for a hostile intelligence or security service to suspect automatically that a particular U.S. government official was an intelligence officer.

Second, the nature of my military experience and education weighed in my favor. The majority of my military service was in the aviation community, first as an air traffic controller, and then flying with Marine fighter-attack squadrons, including a Vietnam tour. On leaving active duty in 1974, I returned to academia, earning a B.S. in social sciences from the University of California–Irvine. Next it was off to Claremont for the Ph.D. Thus, at age thirty-two I was not the usual career trainee.

If the positive aspects of my assignment to Tehran were evident, the negatives were at least equally so: I had no actual operational experience in the espionage business; I spoke not a word of Farsi; I knew nothing about either modern Iran or Persian history and had no knowledge of the country's culture and customs; and I had only limited knowledge about the organization that was sending me overseas. These shortcomings may make my assignment to Tehran seem like an act of madness, but in the weighing at that time, the scales apparently tipped to the positive side. My lack of Farsi was mitigated by my cover assignment as the embassy's political–military affairs officer. In that position I would be meeting regularly with officials in the Ministries of Foreign Affairs and Defense, individuals who usually spoke excellent English. In any case, I was pleased with the assignment and confident that I would accomplish what was expected of me.

Near the end of the FTC, however, the offer of the Tehran assignment was withdrawn. When the acting chief of station (ACOS) was offered an inexperienced first-tour officer, he not unwisely rejected me. His position was that Tehran was a hostile operating environment for intelligence officers and their contacts. As most Iranians considered anyone in the U.S. embassy to be CIA, even innocuous encounters with an American official could imperil an Iranian. For recruited agents (who do the actual spying), discovery by Iranian authorities while meeting clandestinely with a CIA officer was a death sentence.[11] The ACOS maintained that our Iranian assets deserved to be handled by experienced officers with proven track records. Further, any operational compromise whatsoever would unquestionably carry severe repercussions for U.S.-Iranian relations, which the Carter administration was striving mightily to preserve and improve. I was offered another station as an alternative. I understood, accepted, and even agreed with the ACOS's decision at the time; and years later its wisdom is still clear to me.

I graduated from the FTC on 7 June 1979 and was assigned another position in NE Division. But in late June or early July I was again offered Tehran. A permanent COS had finally arrived, and when my candidacy was raised with him, he said yes. Later, he told me that given a choice between a well-trained, aggressive, and smart first-tour officer (all of which he apparently assumed I was, sight unseen) who wanted to be there and a more experienced officer who would rather have been somewhere else, he would take the first-tour officer. I thought then, and have ever since, that the COS made a courageous decision—I probably would have decided differently had I been the chief. He earned my respect even before we met, and it has never waned. He was a professionally demanding boss but also scrupulously fair, possessing the highest standards of personal and professional integrity. I was fortunate to be working for him, especially at the beginning of my career.

I accepted the Tehran assignment on the spot, never giving it a second thought. When I am asked today what in the hell I was thinking when I took that assignment, my answer is simple: that's where the action was. I was always disappointed that I never made it to Vietnam as an enlisted Marine, and even more so that I couldn't do more when I was there as a carrier aviator. As the junior officer and least experienced aviator in the squadron, I was not fully combat qualified when we arrived on station and so was limited for some time in the types of missions I could fly. This last circumstance left me perpetually frustrated and, more than a few times, unreasonably angry; Vietnam was to have been my war, probably the only one I would ever experience, and I wanted to make the most of it. It didn't happen that way. Tehran seemed to be a second chance to serve in an assignment that was potentially more meaningful and demanding than routine operations. I was elated at the thought of going to a high-visibility post of significance to policymakers.

Also, I remembered a story recounted to my CT class in the early days of our training by Don Gregg, a senior Agency officer.[12] In the course of making several points, Gregg told us what things had been like after he joined the Agency during the Korean War. While in training, his class was asked if they would be willing to parachute into North Korea and undertake secret missions. Gregg told us that he and his classmates responded in the affirmative without bothering to mull it over, even for a minute. Why? Because if that is what your country and your Agency asked you to do, you did it. There was nothing to think over. That's what the business was about and that's what you did when you made your living serving your country.

When the day came to depart for Tehran, I made the standard courtesy call on DC/NE. He ushered me into his office, chatted a minute or two about my itinerary, and wished me well. Then he walked me to the door, shook my hand, looked me in the eye, and sagely advised, "Don't fuck up." It was a heartwarming send-off.

I arrived in Tehran on 12 September 1979 and began the first of what turned out to be only fifty-three days of freedom. I worked at least eight hours a day as the political–military affairs officer and found that I enjoyed that assignment almost as much as my "real" job—which I was doing in the evenings and on weekends. It made for long days, but it was all interesting and fun. I also discovered that if I knew little about Iran, I knew even less about Iranians.

My entire exposure to Iranian history and culture, beyond the evening television news, came from a three-week area studies course at the State Department and what I had picked up during five weeks on the desk reading operational files and intelligence reports. Virtually all my insights into the Persian mind and personality came from a lengthy memo written by John Stempel, the recently reassigned political counselor, that described in detail (the accuracy of which I would have ample time to confirm) how Iranians viewed the world and why and how they thought and believed as they did. It did not take much effort to discern that even friendly and pro-Western Iranians could at times be difficult for an American to deal with or comprehend.

The thrust of Stempel's memo was neatly summed up by U.S. Navy captain Gary Sick, the Iran action officer on the National Security Council (NSC) staff under President Carter, in the book he wrote about the hostage crisis: "Iranians assume that a simple forthright explanation of events is merely camouflage concealing the devious intricacies of 'reality.' Thus, to Iranians, any significant political, economic, or social upheaval in Iran must be traceable to the manipulation of external powers. As such, events are perceived as neither random nor aimless; rather, they must be understood as purposeful and integral to some grand scheme or strategy, however difficult it is to fathom."[13]

My first encounter with the Iranian elite several weeks after my arrival served as a memorable introduction to this cultural phenomenon. I was meeting with an Iranian woman who, with her husband, owned a successful construction company. This couple was wealthy and highly educated, well traveled and experienced in foreign cultures. This background notwithstanding, the woman insisted that the Iranian government was directly controlled by the CIA—a common perception in Iran ever since the 1953 coup. She was positive the chief of the Iranian desk at CIA headquarters talked every day to the shah by telephone to give him his instructions for that particular day. She asserted that the U.S. government had made a deliberate decision to rid Iran of the shah for some unknown reason. Since the U.S. government had not, in her scenario, decided who should replace the shah as ruler, Khomeini had been installed as the temporary puppet until the CIA could select a new shah. Once the Agency had made that decision, it would manipulate events to place the lucky man on the Peacock Throne. She held no edifying insights into what the CIA's plans were for Khomeini once his utility to the American government had been exhausted.

I was both fascinated and stupefied by this exposition. The woman's unshakable theory did not encompass an explanation of why the United States would have permitted the bloody street riots in 1977 and 1978. Nor did it explain why, if the U.S. government (or the CIA) wanted the shah to leave as early as 1977, he was not just ordered to go, thereby avoiding the enormous problems visited on revolutionary Iran. To an American it was just plain nuts; to an Iranian it made perfect sense.[14]

My initial weeks in Tehran passed quickly. The chargé d'affaires *ad interim*, a courtly and highly respected career Foreign Service officer named L. Bruce Laingen, was both gracious and enormously helpful in seeing that I was included in high-level meetings with Iranian officials, as was air force major general Phillip Gast, head of MAAG.[15] Both of these exceptional gentlemen generously ensured that I participated in substantive meetings at the Ministries of Foreign Affairs and Defense, and at the Iranian General Staff's headquarters. I worked essentially full-time during the day on my cover duties, which were much more interesting than onerous and dealt with issues of genuine import; in the evenings, I reverted to my "true" persona as a CIA case officer. I was thirty-two years old and at the top of my form, physically and, especially, mentally, and during those fifty-three days on the streets of Tehran I reveled in it all. On 21 October, however, I realized that my euphoria would probably be short-lived.

CHAPTER 2

RETROSPECTIVE: A HISTORY LESSON

America and Iran were never natural allies. For much of its modern history the country once known as Persia was like a fish between two cats, the object of unwanted attention from rival imperialistic powers Great Britain and Russia. Each of the two powers attempted to acquire or control, and then exploit, Persian resources and territories, just as other invaders had done for centuries before. Throughout the latter half of the nineteenth century and into the twentieth, America remained aloof from this competition while the Persians maintained their independence by playing each of the rivals against the other.[1] Only with the onset of the Cold War did Iran, as it was renamed in 1935, come to sustain the concentrated attention of the U.S. government. And as a result, the United States eventually moved, in Iranians' view, from a likable and benevolent friend to just another foreign oppressor: "The protector [became] the exploiter" as one Iran scholar states it.[2] But this occurred neither quickly nor—as is popularly now claimed in Iran—because of the role played by the United States in the 1953 coup that restored the shah to power.[3]

From the 1830s, when Americans were first known to have set foot in Iran, until the late 1940s, the United States was content to leave Iran (and all of Southwest Asia, for that matter) to the British, in whose area of influence that region lay. U.S. policymakers studiously ignored periodic importuning from Iranian leaders for closer ties or material assistance, particularly military equipment. When World War II made it necessary for the United States to send troops to Iran in support of the occupation by Great Britain and the Soviet Union, it did so only minimally and withdrew them within six months after the end of the war. What was it about the Cold War that placed Iran "at the vortex of history," as Henry Kissinger has it, and what combination of events finally pushed Iran and the United States into a relationship that created intensely hostile anti-Americanism in Iran?[4] Conventional wisdom holds simply that it was oil, but that is not correct. While oil was indeed a small part of the American calculus, the far better answer is: geography.[5]

Situated between the communist Soviet Union and the warm waters of the Indian Ocean, its southwestern border the oil-rich Persian Gulf, Iran could not fail to become strategically vital to both sides in the Cold War. In the period immediately following World War II, Iranian oil fueled Western Europe's economic recovery; likewise, Iranian oil exports to the West would certainly be consequential in any large-scale conflict with the USSR.[6] Until 1954 that oil was lifted jointly by the British and Iranians, with no American participation.

But there were reasons other than oil for the United States to sustain an interest in the future of Iran at the beginning of the Cold War. Of more immediate concern to U.S. government policymakers was the Soviet Union's resolve to expand its influence throughout the Arab world and Southwest Asia. Iran's location as a port of entry to the Middle East and to historically coveted warm-water ports assigned this ancient country a substantial role in Soviet expansionist goals. And the accident of geography that made it a buffer between the Soviet Union and the oil-rich Middle East made Iran equally important to those seeking to halt Soviet expansionism.[7]

Iran's sixteen-hundred-mile-long border with the Soviet Union was a vital element in Western security considerations after World War II for several reasons. First, the quickest way for the Soviets to reach the Persian Gulf was to head directly south from the Azerbaijan Socialist Republic and through western Iran. Second, the Soviets had occupied Iranian territory south of that border more than once and after World War II attempted to do so again. Third, the contiguity of Soviet territory with northern Iran allowed the Communists to establish covert support bases in efforts to undermine local Iranian authority. Later, American policymakers and intelligence officers found this border vital to U.S. national security programs.[8]

Of almost equal import were the long borders Iran and the Soviet Union each shared with Afghanistan: an invading Soviet army transiting the Afghan frontier and thence into eastern Iran would be unhindered in its pathway to the Arabian Sea, the Strait of Hormuz, and Iranian and Arabian oil reserves.[9] In short, a Soviet invasion of Iran, whether from north to south (through Azerbaijan) or from east to west (via Afghanistan), would find it easy going. Such an invasion would give the Soviets control over the vital Strait of Hormuz, through which passed 40 to 60 percent of the world's oil supplies. Further, U.S. policymakers postulated that if Iran were permitted to fall into the Soviet sphere of influence, American prestige in the region would be severely diminished, perhaps undermining the will of other Middle East countries to resist Soviet expansionism.[10] Finally, in the days before long-range jet transport aircraft, Soviet control of Iran and the immediate region would have created a grave logistics challenge in moving troops and supplies from Europe to the Far East in the event of conflict in that arena.[11]

After the 1953 coup, when the United States became inextricably entwined in Iran's future, additional factors increased Iran's importance to America and the West in general.[12] Iran under the shah commenced an extensive modernization program while adopting a staunchly pro-West, anticommunist political posture. Because of the unusually personal nature of the relationship between the shah and the U.S. government, the two countries not surprisingly came to share similar views of the region's security requirements.[13] As time passed, Iran took on increasing importance as the guarantor of security for the Persian Gulf and Strait of Hormuz.[14] By the 1960s the oil that transited the strait was bolstering the economies of America, Europe, and Japan. If one believes that a strong economy is essential for national security and defense, then Iranian oil was doing much more than simply providing cheap gas and profits for petroleum companies.

One other aspect of Iran's geographic location made it vital not only to the interests of America and the West in general, but to the security of the whole world. Beginning in the late 1950s, the U.S. intelligence community placed signals intelligence listening posts in Iran along the Soviet border. There were ultimately seven sites in the Elbourz Mountains of northern Iran, the most important being the two code-named Tacksman.[15] Tacksman I, located at the southeastern corner of the Caspian Sea near the village of Behshar, was established in the late 1950s. Tacksman II, constructed in 1964–65, was located well into the mountains 40 miles east of Meshad, outside the village of Kabkan. From Kabkan electronic eyes enjoyed unobstructed "line-of-sight" views across the vast open spaces of the Kara Kum Desert and the flatness of the Uzbek plain into the Kazakh SSR (see map 1). There, barely 650 miles north-northeast of Kabkan, near the city of Leninsk (Tyuratam) on the banks of the Sar-Darya, sprawled the Baikonur missile testing complex. (The town of Baikonur was actually a bit more than 300 miles from Tyuratam; the Soviets gave the name Baikonur to the missile complex to disguise its location and confuse Western intelligence.[16] Thanks to U-2 and satellite imagery, this ploy didn't work.)

In the 1950s and 1960s the Soviets tested their liquid-fueled intercontinental ballistic missiles (ICBMs) at Tyuratam, and Tacksman II could monitor every missile launched from that site toward the Kamchatka Peninsula to the northeast. Sophisticated Tacksman II equipment could acquire the telemetry signals almost at liftoff and then continuously record the telemetry through the missile's midcourse trajectory, before the second stage of the rocket fired. This early signal acquisition allowed more precise evaluation of the data with respect to throw-weights, range, reliability, missile dimensions, and so on.[17] It also allowed Tacksman II to inform other signals acquisition sites around the world to activate their equipment in preparation for the missile's arrival within their windows.[18]

The intelligence listening posts could also eavesdrop on Soviet ground and air communications and were vital for monitoring the development of the Soviet Strategic Missile Forces beginning in the early 1960s.[19] More important, they were invaluable in the 1970s for verifying the Strategic Arms Limitations Treaties (SALT) with the Soviet Union and efforts to reduce the prospect of global nuclear war.[20]

The importance of the Tacksman sites to U.S. policy was clearly delineated in an October 1974 memorandum from the Department of State

Map 1. Former Soviet Socialist republics to the northeast of Iran

inspector general to the secretary in response to a National Security Council directive. The secretary was advised that U.S. policy toward Iran should be to "ensure the maintenance and unimpeded use" of the intelligence facilities in Iran, the memo giving clear recognition of the need to sustain a stable government in that country. With that objective in mind, the inspector general "urged" the department to "undertake a long-range study of U.S.-Iran relations and ensure a high level of monitoring" of this relationship.[21] The Tacksman sites thus constituted a crucial element in the U.S.-Iran equation.

It took World War II to create what appeared to be a permanent alliance between Iran and the United States.[22] Although the 1939 Nazi-Soviet Nonaggression Pact apparently raised no concerns in the American legation in Tehran when it became public knowledge, the April 1941 Nazi invasion of Greece did. Two factors were at play: there was an established German commercial and political presence in Iran reaching back several decades under Reza Shah, and the Nazi-Soviet pact left open the possibility of Soviet demands to operate from Iranian airfields, a situation the impotent Iranian army would be powerless to prevent. The geopolitical matrix was further complicated when neighboring Iraq expelled the British in favor of ties with Germany.[23] Because of the war in Europe, British Royal Navy and Royal Air Force units in the Middle East and Persian Gulf were thus forced to rely on Iran even more than previously for fueling stations and replenishment facilities. Then, on 21 June 1941, three German army groups invaded the USSR, one of which (Army Group South under Field Marshal Gerd von Rundstedt) headed for the Trans-Caucasus region in southwestern Russia, toward the Caspian and Iran. The British and the Soviets—suddenly allies—immediately insisted that Iran expel all German nationals, of whom there were some three thousand, among them intelligence agents who had been establishing underground networks in the country.[24] The Iranian monarch, Reza Shah, refused.

With vital trans-European lines of transport and communication to the USSR severed, there remained only two avenues of supply by which vital U.S. Lend-Lease and other materials could reach the Soviets: the treacherous Murmansk run for ship convoys, and the Trans-Iranian Railroad from the Persian Gulf to the Soviet border in northwestern Iran.[25] The solution was the occupation of Iran in the north by Soviet troops and by British forces in the Gulf region to facilitate the movement of Lend-Lease goods.[26] Reza Shah, whose army was exquisitely undistinguished in its efforts to deter the arrival of foreign troops, was forced into exile on the island of Mauritius (later to die in South Africa), and his twenty-one-year-old son, Mohammad Reza Pahlavi, was placed on the Peacock Throne in a figurehead status. During this period Iranians came to view both Soviet and British troops as uninvited transgressors who were looting their country while bringing to Iran's frontier a war in which they had no perceptible stake.

The thirty thousand U.S. troops committed to support the occupation were stationed in southwestern Iran, where they provided logistical support and transport for the Lend-Lease materials arriving at Persian Gulf ports.[27] The tripartite occupation deepened Iranians' suspicions and hostility toward foreigners, feelings entirely merited in the north, where the Soviets used their position to subvert the provinces under their control by supporting the Iranian communist Tudeh party against the central Iranian government. Conversely, the British never received credit for the humanitarian assistance they gave to the Iranian people throughout this period.[28]

The U.S. government's stake in Iran, as well as its diplomatic and military presence, concomitantly increased as a consequence of its support for Britain and the Soviet Union. The war's end found the United States calling on its allies to end their occupation of Iran by 2 March 1946, as agreed to in the 1942 Tripartite Treaty of Albania signed by all three governments.[29] With the onset of the Cold War, however, the Soviet Union had no intention of honoring that agreement. And in the wake of British retrenchment in the Middle East in early 1947, the United States found itself replacing the British lion as the tacit protector of Iran.

CHAPTER 3

THE SOVIET CALCULUS

The Iranian coup of 1953 was a direct consequence of the perceived Soviet threat to Iran in 1953 and its impact on U.S. national security interests. It was this potential menace that ultimately convinced Presidents Truman and Eisenhower to consider replacing the Iranian government with a regime more in line with the goals of Western governments. While some observers blessed with hindsight claim that this danger was overstated, senior U.S. government officials of both political parties had no doubt at the time that the Soviets and communism posed very real threats to U.S. national security interests and to world freedom.

And, indeed, events in the postwar years were alarming. In 1946 and 1947 the Soviets solidified their control over Eastern Europe and local Communist parties attempted to gain control of governments in Italy, France, Turkey, and Greece. In Czechoslovakia, the elected president, Edvard Beneš, allowed Communists to participate in his government. They proceeded to undermine him, gain control of the government, and corrupt it into a Soviet satellite. In 1947, after two years of obstruction and deceit, Stalin initiated serious attempts to force the British, French, and American occupiers out of West Berlin, culminating in the blockade of 1948. In 1949 the Soviets exploded their first atomic bomb, built from plans stolen by spies operating in the United States and Great Britain; these acts of treason helped inspire the anticommunist mania that came to be known as McCarthyism. The Soviet A-bomb also moved President Truman to consider including the thermonuclear hydrogen bomb in the U.S. national security policy; he signed the approval on 31 January 1948.[1] It is also not without significance that in 1946 the Soviet intelligence service (called the MGB at the time) had intelligence officers in London, Rome, Paris, Washington, and New York while there was not a single Western intelligence officer, from any service, in Moscow.[2] That these hostile intelligence officers were obtaining American secrets and recruiting important American officials as well as "regular" citizens became evident with the trials of State Department officer Alger Hiss and those involved in the theft of America's deepest secret, the atomic bomb.

Truman and Eisenhower were further alarmed by a series of Soviet policies between 1945 and 1953 that could or would have threatened Iran. Undeniable evidence of the Soviet mischief that abounded in Europe, on the western approaches to Iran (e.g., Greece and Turkey), and inside and adjacent to Iranian frontiers generated serious worries about the future independence of Iran. Both presidents viewed U.S. security interests, in Jeffery Kimball's words, "in holistic terms: security comprised an interrelated global system of military balances, geographic positions, political stability, ideological unity, national prestige, and economic resources."[3] And both leaders were determined to prevent further communist expansion. Meanwhile, on mainland Asia the victory of Mao Zedong turned the world's most populous nation into a communist dictatorship. In June 1950 communist North Korea, with the (albeit reluctant) assent of Stalin, invaded South Korea, followed six months later by massive Chinese intervention in the conflict. U.S. leaders feared that the USSR would exert its growing influence in other weak spots in the world as well.[4] In the spring of 1953 the Soviets exploded their first hydrogen bomb and commenced a build-up of military forces.

These actions alone were sufficient to stimulate aggressive counterpolicies on the part of the United States and its allies. Neither President Truman nor President Eisenhower could ignore a potential communist challenge in a nation of such crucial strategic importance to the West as Iran. And Ike remembered well the beating the Democratic party had taken following the communist victory in China, gaining the damning label of "the party that lost China"; he had been elevated to the presidency partly because of it. No Republican president (and probably no Democratic president, for that matter) would have been willing to lead the party that "lost Iran."[5]

As for Iran itself, the official record shows beyond doubt that the Soviet Union planned to bring Iran into its camp by dint of programs intended to "establish dominance through subversion and outright military occupation. . . . During the 1940s and 1950s, Soviet operations were freewheeling, blatant—and unsuccessful."[6] In the spring of 1945, even before the end of the war, the central government in Tehran suddenly found itself the recipient of Soviet hostility and threats when Stalin accused the Iranians of planning to assault and occupy the Soviet oil capital of Baku in the Azerbaijan Soviet Socialist Republic, a preposterous imputation in light of the abysmal state of the Iranian military.[7] Next, a pro-Soviet puppet supported by the growing Tudeh party proclaimed the northwestern Iranian province of Azerbaijan to be the "autonomous Democratic Republic of Azerbaijan" and employed Soviet military forces to maintain order. Stalin imperiously informed the Iranian prime minister on 11 March 1946 that Soviet troops would remain in Azerbaijan until Iran agreed to grant the province autonomy (which the Soviets would then easily subvert). Concurrently he proposed a joint Iranian-Soviet company—with the Soviets holding 51 percent—to develop oil resources in all of the northern provinces.[8] If that was not sufficiently ominous to Truman and the West, many in the U.S. and British governments unhappily discerned that the Soviets were additionally obsessed with the possibility that the Western allies might use Azerbaijan as a staging area for incursions into Soviet territory.[9]

Stalin did not withdraw Soviet military units from Azerbaijan by 2 March 1946 as he had agreed to do in the 1942 Tripartite Treaty and had affirmed during the Tehran Conference of 1943. Instead, Soviet agents continued working to undermine the central Iranian authority in Azerbaijan and turn the province into an autonomous entity that could be brought into the Soviet bloc.[10] During most of that year the U.S. government engaged in intensive diplomatic activities to bring about the Soviets' withdrawal.[11] Had the USSR not eventually complied with the treaty and evacuated from Iran, it might have succeeded in annexing most or all of the northern third of Iran, giving the Soviets a decided geostrategic advantage against the West. The situation was so serious that President Truman remarked to Averell Harriman, "We may be at war with the Soviet Union over Iran."[12] To the relief of the Western allies, and the Iranians, the Soviets finally withdrew from Iran in May 1946.

The successful resolution of this crisis convinced Truman that the U.S. support had thwarted the USSR's efforts at imperialism.[13] This conviction was strengthened by a top secret intelligence summary dated 14 June 1946. The summary indicated that the Soviets still maintained a presence in Iran, however, and that their agents would hinder the prime minister's efforts to develop a "unified and genuinely independent Iran." Nevertheless, the UN's diplomatic intervention to resolve the Azerbaijan crisis "apparently helped convince the Soviets that gradual penetration . . . would succeed better" than outright invasion. The summary concluded by noting that the Soviets were confident of their eventual success in that backward nation and believed that the unpopular policies of the British-dominated Anglo-Iranian Oil Company would "forward their cause."[14]

This view was further bolstered by an intelligence assessment of 20 December 1946 that was issued less than two weeks after Iranian troops ousted the Tudeh-supported Azerbaijani provincial government, an action in which the USSR tacitly but reluctantly acquiesced in order to protect an oil agreement signed with Tehran earlier in the year. Calling the denouement in Azerbaijan a "debacle" for the Soviets and noting that it weakened the Tudeh party in Iran, analysts suggested that "the Soviets may now be expected to abandon direct action in favor of intensified infiltration and clandestine activity." This was, of course, precisely what the Soviets were attempting to do in Greece and Turkey and what they would attempt to do the next year in Italy and France. Intelligence assessments of this nature coupled with continuing evidence of Soviet efforts to subvert governments and government institutions (such as the Four Powers Control Commission in occupied Berlin) almost certainly caused worry in the Truman White House when Iranian prime minister Mossadegh's flirtation with the Tudeh party became apparent.

There was more: a 4 June 1947 intelligence analysis entitled "Developments in the Azerbaijan Situation" asserted that while the "collapse" of the pro-Soviet government in Iranian Azerbaijan had eased tensions in the region, continued political turmoil and "persistent Soviet activities and ambitions" would keep the pot boiling. The analysis remarked the geographical value of Azerbaijan, highlighting its 202-mile border with Turkey, 70-mile border with Iraq, and 480-mile border with the USSR. Furthermore, it was a mere 125 miles from the border to the capital of Soviet oil production, Baku. By dint of being located near two diverging mountain ranges, Azerbaijan was a gateway opening Iran to easy conquest. Intertribal strife and the absence of anything approaching a viable governmental structure virtually invited Soviet subversion, and operatives could be easily infiltrated via indigenous groups whose tribal lands straddled the border with the USSR.

Despite the USSR's political setback in the Azerbaijan region, the analysis predicted that the Soviet Union would not "abandon its ultimate objective of controlling Azerbaijan, and eventually all of Iran." After outlining the economic pressures the Soviets could bring to bear on Iran, the analysis opined that continued disorder in the border province could create "a pretext for subsequent unilateral Soviet intervention" on the presumption "that Soviet security was in jeopardy." Control of Azerbaijan by forces unfriendly to the USSR would doubtless be seen as a serious threat to the Soviet oil fields (which produced three-quarters of the USSR's petroleum supplies) and hence a grave threat to Soviet security.[15]

By the spring of 1949 the U.S. ambassador to Iran was convinced that a Soviet invasion of Iran was imminent. The CIA's Daily Intelligence Summary for 17 March 1949 cited a report from the ambassador to the State Department expressing the opinion that "the only uncertainty about Soviet intentions in Iran is the timing of a Soviet move to return" to Iran. Noting recent "setbacks" (probably including the West's defeat of the Berlin blockade and electoral losses for the Soviets' surrogate parties in Italy and France) and "particularly the imminent conclusion of the Atlantic Pact," the ambassador thought it "possible that the USSR may enter Iran in the near future." Expressing its own view, the CIA disagreed that a Soviet incursion was in the offing. An invasion might do more harm to the USSR than good because it would probably "decisively facilitate the rapid and effective implementation of the Atlantic Pact."[16] But the disagreement between State and CIA settled no minds.

A telling document disseminated by the CIA on 27 July 1950 titled "Special Evaluation No. 39, Possibility of Soviet Aggression against Iran" again predicted that the Soviets would resort to clandestine subversion of the Iranian government instead of an open attack.[17] Agency analysts suggested that the Soviet Union would "intensify its efforts to build up subversive forces within Iran and to weaken the country by means of propaganda, border activities, and diplomatic pressure." The assessment went on to review the advantages that would accrue to the USSR should it gain control of Iran. First, the "extension of [the] Soviet frontier to Iraq and Pakistan would facilitate Soviet penetration of the Near East and the Indian sub-continent." Second, the USSR "would be in a more favorable position for extending its control over those areas in the event of global war" and "would gain access to Iran's great oil resources." And, third, the United States "would be denied an important potential base of operations against the USSR [and, conversely,] the USSR would obtain buffer territory between its vital Baku oil fields and the bases from which Baku might be attacked." The evaluation examined several scenarios in which the Soviets could generate pretexts for overt intervention in Iran cloaked with some semblance of legality and finished by declaring that if the Iranian government were to lose faith in the United States, it might "feel compelled to seek an accord with the USSR or at least to attempt a course of neutrality." The consequences of either would leave the Soviets in a "greatly improved position for taking over the country without the use of force."

By June 1951 the Truman administration had concluded that a communist takeover in Iran was a clear and present danger. Thus, President Truman signed NSC-107/2, which determined that "the loss of Iran to the free world is a distinct possibility through an internal communist uprising, possibly growing out of the present indigenous fanaticism or through communist capture of the nationalist movement."[18] A year later, in the waning months of his administration, Truman had come to view Iran as worth defending against Soviet aggression even if it led to global war. NSC-136 and NSC-136/1, signed by the president in late 1952, officially and frankly held that a Soviet invasion of Iran would be cause for war.[19] The two directives authorized overt diplomatic and aid programs for Iran as well as covert operations with the specific purpose of countering Soviet influence (but did not authorize any covert action operations aimed at or against the Iranian government). To counter unforeseen moves by the Soviets, the president's signature also gave contingent authorization for the use of U.S. military forces if warranted by Soviet actions.

From the end of World War II to the final year of the Truman administration, then, a nearly constant series of Soviet provocations directly or indirectly threatening Iran was countered by escalations in American counterpolicies. These policy determinations were shared by Democrats and Republicans, and thus cannot be attributed simply to conservatives attempting to exploit an increasing fear of Communists lurking in the shadows. Senior policymakers of both political parties had no doubt about the seriousness of the situation in Iran. Even now, with the benefit of four decades of history to reconsider, it is difficult to accept an argument that America overreacted to the potential loss of Iran to Soviet control.

CHAPTER 4

THE 1953 COUP

On 19 August 1953 the government of Iran, led by Prime Minister Mohammed Mossadegh, was overthrown as the result of Operation TP Ajax, a covert action program instigated by the British and engineered by the CIA (TP being the digraph that denoted Iranian operations and Ajax the operation code name). It was an act that had enormous political and psychological significance in modern Iranian history and was influential in the 1979 capture of the U.S. embassy in Tehran. One trenchant irony, given the emphasis Iranians placed on the coup during the 1978 revolution, is that it was not of much interest to Iranians at the time.

In fact, in 1953 and for years afterward the reversal of Mossadegh's government was greeted with approbation by a majority of those Iranians who actually cared about or had a stake in their country's government. (Iran was an undeveloped and provincial country at that time, and in the rural areas beyond Tehran relatively few Iranians were affected by, or even had any knowledge of, occurrences in the capital.) Former director of central intelligence (DCI) and, later, ambassador to Iran Richard M. Helms, a man who certainly knows Iran and Iranians, insists that it was only after the onset of the revolution in 1978 that any sizable number of Iranians began to complain about the 1953 coup. Until then, not only had the people for the most part accepted the shah as their leader, there was also a general consensus that—the history of the region being what it is—the method of his return to power wasn't anything much to be upset about, either. Charlie Naas, the career Foreign Service officer and expert on Southwest Asia who served first as country director for Iranian affairs at the Department of State for four years and then as deputy chief of mission in Tehran in the final years of the shah's regime, agrees with Helms. During all of the time he spent observing and participating in Iranian matters, no Iranian ever raised the issue of the 1953 coup with him.[1] In other words, Iranians as a population began to condemn the United States for its part in the coup only when it became politically expedient for them to do so.

The coup has been both condoned and condemned. Critics argue that it was wrong for the United States to overthrow a government of perceived legitimacy for seemingly narrow interests, and insist that the oppressive policies of the shah afterward, particularly with respect to human rights issues and the dictatorship he maintained, prove their point. They claim that the return of the shah ended any possibility that Iran might have evolved into a more democratic form of government with institutions respectful of the civil rights and liberties of its citizens. Indeed, on 17 March 2000 President Bill Clinton's secretary of state, Madeleine Albright, came very close to apologizing for the coup when she acknowledged the role the United States played in it and declared that the coup was "clearly a setback for Iran's political development."[2] The critics also assert that Mossadegh was not a Communist and insist that there was little or no possibility that Communists would have gained control of the Iranian government under his rule. In sum, the coup was an unnecessary (if not illegal or immoral) act of governmental power that was fomented on insupportable grounds.

In rebuttal, there is first the obvious point that the future of Iran with Mossadegh in charge—or Iran without the coup, for that matter, whether Mossadegh or someone else was in power—was and is unknowable. Claims that Iran would have developed into a Western-style democracy or some other acceptable form of government, and that this other government would have been more respectful of human rights and liberties, are speculations, if not wishful thinking. Never in the millennia of its existence had Iran experienced any sustained period of democratic self-government, nor had it demonstrated an adherence to principles that today would be recognized as endorsing human rights and civil liberties. It exceeds mere optimism to postulate that Mossadegh's Iran would have achieved these desirable conditions had the coup not cut short his regime.

Those who see the coup as a necessary act dictated by national and international security concerns deny neither the mistakes of the shah nor the cruelty of his government. Their position is essentially that the benefits to the free world of a pro-West regime in Iran far outweighed the more odious aspects of the shah's rule.[3] Those who support, or at least accept, the necessity of replacing the Mossadegh government point out that there was no assurance that Iran would or could have remained free from Soviet influence had the coup not occurred, and, conversely, that the consequences of the loss of Iran were too adverse to risk. One observer argues that even if the 1953 coup had not occurred, the "intervention would have happened in any case, touched off by some other specific action that Washington took as confirmation of its worst fears."[4] What *is* known, the coup supporters maintain, is that with the shah in power Iran was for a quarter-century a politically stable, pro-West ally in a critical region rent by turmoil and coveted by the Soviets.[5]

One highly important facet often overlooked and inevitably underestimated is the value of the Tacksman sites. It may never be known for certain just how vital to the interests of Western security, or indeed to the security of the world, the Tacksman intelligence was. The full extent of the role it played in enabling policymakers to counter the Soviet threat and bring about arms reduction agreements may likewise remain in the shadows. But it does not require much faith on the part of anyone familiar with intelligence and arms control policy to believe that the world was far safer for two decades because of the Tacksman sites. And these sites would not have existed without the shah in power.

It is not just that the sites collected critical intelligence against the Soviet strategic missile program. A collateral project, code-named Melody, at one Tacksman site provided crucial intelligence on at least two other security concerns: were the Soviets developing an antiballistic missile defense system in violation of a treaty then being negotiated between the United States and the USSR, and if so, was it founded on a modification of the SA-5 antiaircraft missile? There was doubt in some national security quarters that the Soviets actually could upgrade their SA-5 antiaircraft missile to antimissile capability, but it was essential to know for sure. The White House requested a National Intelligence Estimate (NIE) to inform the issue. The Melody equipment was slightly modified to acquire the SA-5 target-tracking radar signals and then used to monitor an SA-5 launch. The system captured signals emitted from the SA-5 that proved indisputably that its target-tracking radar was of the nature demanded by an ABM. When Henry Kissinger, the primary American negotiator, next met with the Soviets in Geneva he was able, he later recalled, to stare "his Soviet counterpart in the eye and read him the dates and time they had cheated on the treaty. The cheating immediately ceased and the Soviets began a mole-hunt for the spy" who was reporting to American intelligence. Melody continued to provide vital intelligence on Soviet missile-tracking radars that were being tested at a key Soviet test range almost one thousand miles distant.[6]

Ultimately, then, judging the appropriateness of the coup distills down to balancing the very tangible suffering of the Iranian people (which could very well have been worse under a ruler other than the shah) against the intangible role Iran under the shah played in ensuring that the Cold War remained that way. Regardless of the security advantages it provided for U.S. foreign policy in the 1950s and 1960s, however, the 1953 coup had far-reaching consequences. Certainly it colored the Iranians' view of U.S. actions and promises during the 1979–81 hostage crisis in Tehran.[7]

The United States made its first sales of military equipment to Iran in June 1947 in consonance with the implementation of the Truman Doctrine and the subsequent Military Defense Assistance Program. As part of that program the shah was asked to submit what was anticipated to be a modest shopping list. What came back to Washington must have confounded U.S. officials: the shah asked for no less than $175 million in advanced weaponry, including heavy tanks and jet aircraft, and supplies enough for 200,000 troops, even though the Iranian army mustered only 120,000 at the time. The supplies eventually provided were valued at just $10.7 million.[8] As the Cold War intensified, however, America's resolve to limit the shah to items that were in his nation's best economic and security interests diminished. From 1946 to 1952 the shah received $42.3 million in economic assistance and $16.6 million in military aid.[9]

The 1950s witnessed the shah consolidating his power and authority and successfully linking his own policy preferences with those of NATO. The U.S. government began to view the shah in a more positive light, and the U.S. ambassador in Tehran decided that the shah was the only Iranian political personage strong enough to forestall a communist takeover. Secretary of State Dean Acheson lauded the shah as the best hope of providing firmness and leadership, even though the monarch was already demonstrating indecisiveness, depression, and a bent for conspiracy.[10] The State Department increasingly backed his pleas for military assistance despite Defense Department objections that the Iranian army had limited technical capabilities and was rife with internal corruption.[11]

As 1951 turned into 1952, Truman became increasingly worried about the support Mossadegh (a wealthy and popular, if eccentric, career civil servant and uncompromising nationalist) was receiving from the Tudeh party. The president was further nettled by the failure of the Iranians and the British to resolve their differences over the British-dominated Anglo-Iranian Oil Company and oil profits. Both sides refused to compromise, which deepened the crisis and eventually led to an international boycott of Iranian oil organized by the British. Truman decreed a harder line toward the Mossadegh government in the spring of 1952, initiating in very small steps policies that would later be attributed to Eisenhower but which clearly originated before he was elected president. Included in Truman's actions was planning for a political action program to prevent a pro-communist government from assuming control in Iran.[12]

While Britain eagerly sought U.S. support for overt military action against the Iranians, preferably as a co-partner, Truman walked a fine line between deterring intervention in Iran and maintaining a positive relationship with America's closest ally. The last thing Truman wanted was any use of force. Military action might push the Soviet Union either to invade and occupy Iran itself or to invoke a 1921 treaty with Iran that permitted intervention in case of foreign invasion, and thus create a casus belli between the United States and the Soviet Union. Although no one doubted that Iran was of vital strategic interest to America, the U.S. military had pressed hard to prevent a policy that might require American military intervention in that country, or anywhere else in the Middle East, for any reason. With U.S. military forces still weakened by the rapid reduction in manpower that followed World War II, and with most of the remaining fighting forces committed to combat in Korea and to the defense of Asia, the Pentagon had no confidence that the United States could fight and win the global war with the USSR that would certainly follow military intervention in Iran in support of British interests.

The vision of an increasingly unstable Iran was nevertheless unsettling to the Truman administration, which feared that the Soviets would exploit the internal unrest and either gain covert control of the Iranian government or, in a worst-case scenario, actually invade and occupy Iran—an understandable worry when the tenor of the times is considered.[13] Thus, in the summer of 1952, with these concerns in mind and in fear that British policies would fail, the Truman White House began drafting options for some type of U.S. intervention in Iran.[14] U.S. military forces were being steadily built up in response to the Korean War and as a by-product of the seminal Cold War document NSC-68 to a point that would enable the United States to match Soviet military power anywhere in the world—and would perforce establish a potential capability to intervene in the Persian Gulf region in addition to meeting other global commitments.[15] The Truman administration was thus poised to pursue a more active stance in resolving the standoff between the British and the Iranians.

Mohammed Mossadegh's rule as prime minister was a brief one. He acceded to the post on 29 April 1951 (a political act essentially forced on the shah) and was ousted less than two years later by dint of a political action operation that was equal parts "romantic intrigue, timing, and luck," to co-opt Evan Thomas's description.[16] Of course, the repercussions of a British oil boycott on the Iranian economy and continuing violence in the streets of Tehran should not be discounted when evaluating the factors that ultimately brought success to the coup plotters. John Stempel argues that the British boycott (which the Eisenhower administration adhered to) was more instrumental in bringing down Mossadegh than the CIA, claiming that the CIA official behind the coup only "encouraged forces who were already restive and prepared to participate."[17] The CIA's official history of the coup details the progression of the coup, and missteps therein, to the point at which CIA officials in Washington and Tehran all thought the operation was a failure. When the coup actually succeeded, thanks mostly to initiatives taken by Iranian army officers and Iranian agents of the CIA, U.S. government officials were as surprised as anyone.[18] The CIA officer who supervised the operation later averred that the coup succeeded because the intended results were desired by a majority of the Iranian people and not because of any CIA derring-do.[19]

The last straw for the Americans was a visit to Washington by an intransigent Mossadegh in the fall of 1952. Immediately on returning to Iran from Washington, Mossadegh broke off diplomatic relations with Great Britain and ordered the official British presence to be out of Iran by 1 November. With this rupture the British opted to pursue a scheme that had been gestating in the London headquarters of the British Secret Intelligence Service (SIS) for some time: the overthrow of Mossadegh. But lacking an official presence in Iran with which to mount a covert program, and with limited financial resources, the British turned to their American cousins for assistance. The original SIS plan, Operation Boot, was a complicated scheme involving tribal uprisings in the provinces coordinated with political moves in Tehran. At the most senior level, the politically appointed CIA officials were generally favorable to the overall goal of the British, if not necessarily the means.

The British raised the idea again in February 1953, by which time the Eisenhower administration had concluded that removing Mossadegh offered the best solution for ensuring that Iran did not turn to the Soviets or otherwise become a communist regime. The White House told the CIA that it should proceed jointly with the SIS to achieve this objective. Although the senior officials at State and CIA (political appointees all) looked favorably on the idea, most officers two or three echelons below the top—in other words, the career civil servants whose day-to-day responsibilities centered on Iranian affairs, including the chief of station in Tehran—held little brief for this intrusion into Iranian politics. Agency and State analysts did not believe that Mossadegh was a Communist or a stooge of the Communists. Nor did they place much credence in the argument that the Tudeh party was poised to take control of Iran.[20] (It wouldn't be the last time that CIA officers who were country or regional experts were directed by political appointees to undertake a covert action that they deemed unwise or foolish.) The American ambassador in Tehran, Loy Henderson (a long-time Soviet expert), was convinced that Mossadegh was simply naive about communism, even as he grew increasingly more reliant on the Tudeh party.[21]

Late in 1952, outgoing secretary of state Dean Acheson briefed the new Eisenhower administration on Iran, highlighting three salient points: negotiations with Mossadegh had failed, with blame falling equally on the Iranians and the British; U.S. policy now included options for unilateral intervention (presumably to replace the Mossadegh regime); and the problems festering in Iran would probably confront Eisenhower sooner rather than later.[22] Sure enough, in early January 1953, even before Ike's inauguration, Mossadegh sent a three-page letter to the president-elect asking for assistance for his country. Eisenhower had been hearing derogatory reports about Mossadegh not only from Truman's people but also from British prime minister Winston Churchill, and so was not an uninformed bystander in the matter. His reply to Mossadegh was noncommittal, expressing hope that "our future relations will be completely free from suspicion."[23] In late January and February 1953 the new U.S. administration watched as the turmoil in Iran increased. A failed attempt in the Majlis (Iran's legislature) to replace Mossadegh through constitutional processes was followed by Mossadegh's move against the leaders of a half-baked plot hatched by retired military officers to establish a separate "Free South in Iran." Finally there came rioting in the streets.[24] The cowed Majlis extended Mossadegh's near dictatorial powers, and soon thereafter, on 28 February, the shah announced that he would abdicate the throne. Rioting broke out anew almost immediately, and the shah retracted his abdication within hours.

The British SIS met with Eisenhower's people and the CIA in February, just two weeks after Ike's inauguration. Kermit "Kim" Roosevelt, chief of the Near East Division of the CIA's Clandestine Service (known at the time as the Directorate of Plans), was named program manager for the coup operation. Operation Boot then became TPAjax. Preparations began in earnest in March, with DCI Allen Dulles authorizing a $1 million budget for the coup (this figure was subsequently augmented by $11,000 for the purpose of bribing members of the Majlis).[25]

Any initial misgivings on the part of the United States eroded through the spring of 1953 as the political and security situation in Iran worsened and Mossadegh became increasingly dependent on the Tudeh party (although he was also popular with many of the middle class, including bazaaris [the merchant class], junior military officers, and clerics).[26] Street demonstrations for and against Mossadegh, which had become common in the opening months of 1953, escalated in violence, with some of the disturbances instigated by the Tudeh party. The Majlis was as chaotic as the country in general and eventually was dissolved by Mossadegh. The Eisenhower team deemed the burgeoning instability in Iran unacceptable, and Ike commented at one point to Republican senator Robert Taft of Ohio that Iran "must in no circumstances fall to communism."[27]

Eisenhower's secretary of state, John Foster Dulles, expressed fears that civil unrest or worse combined with covert Tudeh influence might present the Soviets with the opportunity to gain control of Iran.[28] Thus, as State officials had earlier predicted, the Eisenhower administration was open to the idea of a coup. In fact, top Eisenhower advisers Foster Dulles and his brother Allen had already discussed the idea of a covert reversal of the Mossadegh regime.[29] It was, the two agreed, an opportunity to "turn back the communist tide before it reached the beach . . . please an ally . . . and keep the oil flowing."[30] Eisenhower expressed confidence that the shah would be an effective leader when he resumed full control of the government.[31] On receiving a second letter from Mossadegh pleading for financial assistance, Eisenhower remarked to his advisers that he would not "pour more money" into a country causing its own distress by refusing to negotiate with the British.[32] Intelligence that Mossadegh was soon to receive $20 million from the USSR consolidated, in Ike's mind, the need for a new government in Iran.[33]

In late July, just three weeks before the coup was to occur, the Tudeh party came out openly in support of Mossadegh.[34] The Majlis held new elections in early August, with Mossadegh blatantly rigging the results. In a politically riven country, Mossadegh managed to garner an astonishing 99.4 percent of the popular vote (some two million "voted" for Mossadegh and only a few hundred "voted" against him).[35] Eisenhower was appalled, comparing the electoral manipulation with communist tactics already witnessed in Eastern Europe (and possibly in Ike's mind adding a communist taint to Mossadegh). (This act also undermines later criticism that Mossadegh's government was democratic and legitimately elected.) And if all that wasn't sufficient to convince the Eisenhower administration that Mossadegh had to go, on 8 August Soviet foreign minister Georgy Malenkov announced in Moscow that the Soviet Union had initiated negotiations with Iran to resolve border problems and financial claims.[36] Thus, throughout that spring and summer Eisenhower was certain that Iran was on a steady course toward a "communist-supported dictatorship."[37]

What transpired next was the first successful reversal of a foreign government by the United States in the Cold War. It was an act that would return to confront and confound a future administration in a manner no one could have foreseen.[38] Motivated by a strong determination to contain the spread of Soviet influence, and sincere in their belief that Iran was about to fall under the control of forces inimical to the interests of the free world, the most senior policymakers in the United States ordered the ouster of the government of a sovereign nation. Almost certainly no one in the U.S. government believed that the people of Iran would suffer more under a pro-American government than they probably would have under a Soviet-controlled one.[39]

While it became fashionable in the post-1970 years to assert that the United States prevented Iran from becoming a stable democracy by overthrowing Mossadegh's government, there is little evidence to support this position. It is perhaps true that Iran had been making some small progress toward this end in the half century preceding the coup. It is also true that, under the shah's rule, Iran paid a steep price for twenty-five years of political stability. Authoritarian conditions became increasingly harsh until they finally reached the point at which Iranian citizens were willing to risk death in the street rather than live under them any longer. In the end, the Iranians inherited a dismal legacy: yet another foreign intervention in their nation, yet another lost opportunity to determine their own future for better or worse, and yet more of their oil wealth siphoned off by others, leaving most of them destitute while a privileged elite lived in unimaginable opulence.

Observers of the coup differ on the nature of its long-term outcome, but all agree that it was one of the most important events of the Cold War and perhaps of the twentieth century. Eisenhower believed the results justified the means; he had no second thoughts about the coup and later said that he would use such tactics again to "fight the communists where prudent and possible, with every weapon possible."[40] Kim Roosevelt believed that if the coup had failed, Iran would have fallen to the Soviet Union with disastrous results for the Middle East.[41]

Mark Gasiorowski labels the 1953 coup a "critical event in postwar world history" and a "decisive turning point in Iranian history."[42] He asserts that if the coup had not occurred, the revolution of 1978 might not have followed.[43] James Bill calls the coup a "momentous event" in the relationship between the United States and Iran, a "running wound which bled for twenty-five years."[44] That said, Bill further maintains that while the coup affected Iranians' perception of the U.S. government, it did not make the 1978–79 revolution inevitable, as the United States had ample chances during that quarter-century to "rethink and revise" its Iranian policies.[45]

Former diplomat and now scholar John Stempel says simply that the coup has "assumed a political importance well beyond [its] intrinsic significance."[46] Intelligence scholar and former NSC staffer Gregory Treverton would agree. He thinks that TPAjax receives too much blame for what happened twenty-five years afterward. Nor does Treverton (unlike Bill and others who sympathize with the Iranians) belittle the fact that Iran under the shah was a "pro-West bastion in a turbulent region" for that period, which was "no mean feat." [47]

For fifty-two Americans in 1979, these debates were moot. Although apparently a majority (perhaps a large majority) of Iranians were unconcerned about the coup when it happened, twenty-five years later it began to grate harshly on many Iranians—including untold numbers who weren't even alive in 1953—as anti-American sentiment rose at the onset of the 1978 revolution. Many feared a repeat of the 1953 coup, no matter how inane it may have sounded to Americans. Thus, after lying dormant in the minds of the Iranian population for two and a half decades, the 1953 coup helped precipitate a world crisis and one of the most shaming periods in the history of American foreign policy.[48]

CHAPTER 5

AMERICA AND IRAN, 1953 – 1977

Stability of sorts visited Iran after the coup, principally because the shah, determined to maintain control over his country and government, instituted martial law and proceeded to govern by fiat.[1] Britain lifted the economic boycott and America opened its coffers. The U.S. government continued to assist Iran, sending $23.4 million in technical aid and allocating an emergency aid disbursement of $45 million barely six weeks after the coup; another $40 million was sent to Iran near the end of the year. Unlike assistance in future years, these funds were predominantly to help the Iranian government recover from near bankruptcy resulting from the oil boycott; by 1955, Iran's national economy had rebounded sufficiently for the United States nearly to eliminate this type of aid.[2] The shah cut a deal with international oil companies giving the British only 40 percent of the pie while five American companies received an aggregate 40 percent, the Dutch 14 percent, and the French 6 percent.[3] Politically, the Eisenhower administration designated Iran to be of "critical importance" to the United States and to the West in general (echoing Truman's perception) and signaled its intention two years later to turn America's relationship with Iran into an "anti-communist asset."[4]

To strengthen his control over the country the shah initiated a building program for his army to create a force able to defend the realm not only against attacks from without but—significantly—also from dissidents within. Further, in 1953 he created a security office to monitor internal threats to his regime; in 1955 he enlarged it into a powerful combined security and intelligence organization with few controls and virtually no outside oversight that became widely known by its acronym, SAVAK.[5]

Against all advice from the U.S. government, the shah chose to concentrate law enforcement, internal security, and foreign intelligence collection duties in SAVAK—or at least permitted that to happen. As time passed SAVAK intruded into the realm of domestic law enforcement, blurring and later erasing the separation between criminal activity and true national security violations. Iranians accused of civil crimes were subjected to SAVAK investigations and received the same harsh treatment meted out to those who actually presented (or were perceived to present) a danger to the state. This corruption of justice was not lost on the average Iranian. Aggravating this already abusive situation were two additional misjudgments: SAVAK personnel involved with overseas intelligence collection were permitted to engage in domestic security investigations, which created additional opportunities for mischief; and the shah employed SAVAK as a tool to intimidate, suppress, and eventually eliminate political dissent—legitimate political dissent as differentiated from genuine treasonous, subversive activity.

SAVAK officers initially received training in the requisite investigative, counterintelligence, and intelligence collection activities from the American FBI, CIA, and Border Patrol. In 1961, however, at the shah's direction, the CIA training mission departed Iran and Israel's foreign intelligence service, Mossad, assumed the responsibilities for the professional education of SAVAK officers.[6] Soon afterward SAVAK began earning a worldwide reputation for viciousness because of the cruelty inflicted on many of those arrested, without regard for the seriousness or the nature of the transgression. Despite Persia's three-thousand-year history of rulers notable for their cruelty to the population, many Iranians came to believe—or at least purported to believe—that the FBI and CIA had trained SAVAK officers in methods of torture and encouraged its use on dissidents and opponents of the regime. There was no truth to this. (As I repeated many times to my captors, not only is systematic torture not a part of the American tradition, certainly no one needed to teach Iranians how to torture; they had long been masters of the art.) But Iranians believed it, or wanted to believe it, and this was added to the growing list of reasons to hate America. Eventually, SAVAK reduced its reliance on the CIA and the United States for training in general and initiated similar relationships with security and intelligence services from Britain, France, and West Germany while continuing a multifaceted relationship with Mossad.[7]

That Iran needed a trained counterintelligence service is beyond question. The Soviets, while moving slowly toward cooperation and away from open conflict, did not cease clandestine activities in Iran: the Soviet intelligence services, the KGB and GRU, continued to recruit agents and run espionage operations against the Iranian government while they

maintained their ties to the Tudeh party, supported other nations' training of Iranian dissidents, and maintained infiltration networks to smug-
gle arms and other contraband across the common frontier.[8] To keep
pressure on the shah, in 1959 the Soviets established the National Voice
of Iran, a clandestine radio station in Baku, the capital of the Azerbaijan
SSR, whose broadcasts were both anti-shah and anti-American, albeit
relatively low-key until 1978.[9] The Voice of Iran broadcast inflammatory
demands for the shah's overthrow in Farsi and Azerbaijani and referred
to the Soviet Union as "our friendly northern neighbor."[10] To manage
these continuing threats, SAVAK developed a capable counterintelligence
cadre and gave the USSR pride of place on the list of target countries.

By the early 1960s, political parties in Iran had been either eliminated
or reduced to impotence by the shah, alienating most Iranians who
cared about their country's politics. Although the Majlis still sat as a leg-
islative body, the elections of its members were hardly fair and open.[11]
The shah tolerated neither loyal opposition nor organized dissent, and
SAVAK was the hammer used to beat them down. As for one potential
source of opposition, the clerical leadership, the shah simply co-opted
many of them.

In the meantime, U.S. financial aid kept flowing. From 1953 through
1960 U.S. economic assistance amounted to a staggering $486.4 million;
military aid during those seven years was in the neighborhood of $450
million.[12] Initially the military aid was associated with Iran's adherence
to the Baghdad Pact, but when a revolution in 1958 turned neighboring
Iraq into a Soviet client and potential enemy of Iran, the United States
and Iran signed a mutual assistance treaty further binding the two new
allies. This pact was doubly important in the face of countervailing Soviet
efforts to force Iran to sign a nonaggression treaty with the USSR.[13] The
treaty signed by the shah and Secretary of State John Foster Dulles committed the United States to rise to the defense of Iran if the latter were
invaded. The Iranians were obviously serious about this, for in the wake
of the Soviet invasion of Afghanistan in 1979 the Iranian defense minister told a press conference that if the Soviets invaded Iran, the provisional revolutionary Iranian government would expect the U.S. military
to come to its aid. This, even though American diplomats had by then
been held captive for nearly six months while the Iranian government
broadcast daily diatribes condemning the U.S. government as evil incarnate and labeling the United States "the Great Satan."[14]

During the Kennedy years the president and his foreign policy advisers focused the U.S.-Iran relationship on domestic reforms in the belief that the country would be more stable under a progressive and enlightened government than under authoritarian rule.[15] The Kennedy administration was neither impressed by the shah nor enamored of his craving for a larger army and more advanced arms.[16] Their perspective was no doubt colored by the rise, yet again, of Iranian domestic opposition to political repression and the lack of change in the standards of social justice.[17] Kennedy (as Carter would in 1977) urged the shah to adopt political, economic, agrarian, and social reform; end or at least reduce the blatant official corruption; and rein in his military ambitions.

The shah, likewise, was distrustful of the policies of the Kennedy and Johnson administrations. He believed JFK's attitudes toward Iran to be particularly "intrusive" and resented what he perceived as Kennedy's efforts to impose American liberalism and domestic values on him and on other Third World leaders.[18] Moreover, the shah was not willing to crack down on corruption—in part because it would affect his own relatives, especially his egregiously avaricious and corrupt twin sister, Ashraf, and his closest courtiers, many of whom had been appointed to the official positions that enabled them to plunder Iran in order to ensure their loyalty.[19]

While the shah was not much interested in political or social reforms, he was greatly interested in increasing the size of his army to more than a quarter-million troops and giving them the latest and most sophisticated equipment.[20] A turn to the Soviets in 1963 for military assistance, as a stratagem to play the USSR off against the United States (the classic Persian ballet), instead set off a series of riots across the country. Nevertheless, there was sufficient progress, however modest, for JFK to invite the shah to Washington in the winter of 1962. The shah used the visit to warn Congress about the threat to Iran from the Soviet Union and to ask for more, and more modern, weapons. Although the Kennedy administration deferred the weapons request, it was granted by President Lyndon Johnson in 1964. This represented something of a reversal for LBJ because during an earlier visit to Tehran as vice president he had spoken frequently of the need for reforms and for a balance between military expenditures and a sound economy.[21] Despite the shah's White Revolution—a wide-ranging menu of land redistribution and reforms in agriculture, health, education, and societal issues (e.g., women's rights)—new rioting in June 1963 allowed the shah to declare martial law and again crack down on dissidents.[22]

The clergy were hugely opposed to the White Revolution because it reduced their power and income. A series of demonstrations instigated by radical cleric Ruhollah Khomeini resulted in the deaths of hundreds of Iranians. Khomeini possessed a cornucopia of religious-based grievances against the shah and his regime, including anger over such matters of state as the signing of the U.S.-Iran Status of Forces Agreement providing exemptions from Iranian jurisdiction for U.S. military personnel posted in Iran.[23] The civil disturbances permitted the shah to crack down on dissidents, including religious fundamentalists. Khomeini was arrested and exiled, first to Turkey and then to the Shiite holy city of Najaf, Iraq. By the time of Kennedy's assassination, the streets were again calm, dissent had been stifled, and tightly controlled elections had been held for the Majlis.[24]

The Johnson years were a period of transition in Iranian policy. The U.S. government gradually reduced its focus on political and economic reforms and began to consider the relationship as one of mutual national security interests between the United States and the shah as an individual, rather than the nation of Iran.[25] A briefing paper prepared for Secretary of State Dean Rusk in advance of an official visit to America by the shah explicitly highlighted this change. In it, the assistant secretary for Near East and South Asian affairs informed the secretary that Iran's importance to the United States was increasing—due in part to the Tacksman sites but also because of Iran's propitious location for worldwide communications systems and air transit rights, the latter particularly important now that Turkey and Pakistan had curtailed rights previously granted to the United States and other countries. The assistant secretary closed with the recommendation that military credits and arms sales should be considered "sympathetically."[26]

The association between Iran and the United States was furthered by a simultaneous upswing in Iran's oil revenues and decline in the U.S. economy, which suffered from efforts to finance two enormously expensive programs: the war in Vietnam and Johnson's Great Society.[27] It soon became reasonable (in the eyes of foreign policy and Treasury officials, at any rate) for the United States to reduce its trade imbalance by selling arms overseas. The shah's ability to pay cash from his own treasury for weapons systems provided added incentive for the United States to reconsider his requests, even those that earlier had been deemed excessive or unwarranted. But while these sales provided a boost for the U.S. government's foreign exchange balance, they also quickly reduced any moderating leverage the Americans had over the shah, either for additional reforms or in tempering military sales.[28]

Richard M. Nixon assumed the presidency in January 1969 faced with an abundance of problems. The Middle East was a region of continuing tension and apprehension, not only between Israelis and Arabs but also between the Soviets and the Americans. In that era the United States had no diplomatic relations with Egypt, despite the strategic importance of that country, and the presence of fifteen thousand Soviet advisers there was enormously troubling to U.S. policymakers. The newly concluded Iraqi-Soviet Friendship Treaty that enabled the Soviet Union to send large quantities of military equipment and numerous advisers to Iran's longtime enemy and next-door neighbor also presented a serious threat to regional peace and stability. (Of course, the Soviets were confronting a similar situation with Iran's purchases of American and European military matériel, which they viewed as threatening to their client, Iraq.) Complicating the Middle East equation was the announced withdrawal in 1967 of British forces east of the Suez, to be completed by 1971, increasing Iran's importance as one of the few pro-West powers (along with countries such as Turkey, Pakistan, Bahrain, and Saudi Arabia) in the region.[29]

With the U.S. commitment in Vietnam wreaking economic and political havoc in the United States and generating calls for America's disengagement as world policeman, Nixon initiated a new policy. It proclaimed, in part, that the United States would rely on its allies to defend regional interests rather than sending American expeditionary forces. Explicit in this new doctrine was the promise to provide the allied nations with the necessary means to protect U.S. and regional interests.[30] The shah would play a large role in this regional partnership. Iran was a place of true geographic importance, surrounded by hostile neighbors (Arab as well as the Soviets), sitting astride one of the world's largest oil reserves, and adjacent to the waterway through which much of the free world's oil supplies transited. Iran also possessed seemingly unlimited funds with which to buy arms and was ruled by an absolute monarch not only indebted to the United States but also pro-Western in political and economic orientation.[31] Nixon could not have created a more apposite partner.

His role as America's regional surrogate played brilliantly to the shah's increasing sense of self-importance and consummate desire to be perceived as a world statesman. There was one inherent problem with this concept, however: Iran's foreign policy reflected the shah's personal priorities rather than his country's best interests.[32] Thus, the first three years of Nixon's administration were "watershed years" in which U.S. security interests in the Persian Gulf were linked with the person of the shah rather than with policies developed through the constitutional institutions of the Iranian government. Ironically, these foreign policy measures enabled the shah to complete the consolidation of absolute authority over the internal affairs of his country.[33]

Foreign policy and international relationships between sovereign nations are customarily founded on a government-to-government basis and are intended to survive changes of governmental leadership without disruption. But the Nixon years crystallized the U.S. government's relationship with the shah at the expense of the Iranian nation as a whole. From then until the end of Mohammad Reza Pahlavi's rule, U.S. national security policies in the Middle East were predicated on him and his retention of power. Their commitment to the shah as a person blinded U.S. policymakers to the internal opposition to his regime.[34]

So it was that Iran—the shah, in reality—came to fill one of the starring roles in what was referred to in Washington as the "Twin Pillars" policy, intended to safeguard U.S. security interests in the Middle East (the other "pillar" was to be Saudi Arabia).[35] The purpose of Twin Pillars, in the words of former NSC staffer Howard Teicher, was to "preserve access to oil and the stability of pro-Western regimes, while limiting Soviet expansionary goals."[36] Henry Kissinger, Nixon's national security adviser, thought it was "imperative that the regional balance of power be maintained."[37] If this meant an untraditional relationship with respect to Iran and its leader, so be it.

To ensure that the shah not only sustained the military force to wield power as the "policeman of the Middle East" but also remained a happy friend of the United States, Nixon and Kissinger resolved in 1972 to sell him any nonnuclear weapons system or other military equipment he sought. Concomitant with this policy was the need to provide American technical personnel to support and maintain the equipment. The decision to hand the shah what critics later termed a "blank check" carried with it both positive and negative aspects.[38] The circumstances in which the decision was made are relevant to later events and also showcase the Nixon-Kissinger style of foreign policy.

During a visit to Iran in May 1972, the president agreed to a pact with the shah that held the greatest import for events at the decade's end, for it "radically restructured" the U.S.-Iranian relationship.[39] It was a classic quid pro quo: Nixon wanted to induce the shah to assume the role of regional protector, and the shah desired the prestige, grandeur, and power of the technologically advanced, state-of-the-art military that is so alluring for Third World autocrats. That the shah had been seeking to augment his power and influence in the region for the past several years, and hence needed little inducement to play the role he coveted, apparently didn't register with Nixon or Kissinger. Neither, apparently, did they consider how their policies would affect Iranian society nor concern themselves with questions about the stability of the shah's regime.[40]

Yet, at least a few of those in Washington watching the internal political situation in Iran were starting to worry. A year after the president's Tehran trip, a CIA "Intelligence Survey" profiled Iran's body politic and found pockets of opposition to the shah, "primarily from the intellectual community" but also within the religious community, citing "religious scholars" as "the primary obstacles to social reform."[41]

Evidence that the shah's military forces seriously lacked the technical skills, education, and aptitude to use and maintain the advanced equipment sold to Iran was brought to the attention of the president and his adviser but generated no concern on their part. For a number of years, Gary Sick notes, the Department of Defense "had been required to produce studies and analyses of Iran's security situation; and year after year, through one administration after another, the result was the same. . . . [M]ilitary threats to Iran's northern and western borders could best be addressed by the steady, systematic development and training of its military forces, rather than the rapid introduction of massive quantities of complex high-technology equipment."[42] As Iran observer Barry Rubin describes it, "villagers barely acquainted with the automobile were becoming mechanics" for these complex weapons systems.[43]

When the high-tech matériel began to pour into Iran, the Iranian military was simply unable to assimilate it in anything approaching a timely and systematic manner. In consequence, valuable equipment, some of which had a finite shelf life, was placed in warehouses for months or years while it deteriorated or rusted away. Rubin cites the example of the F-14 program in this regard. The program, desperately desired by the shah, lagged months behind schedule while millions of dollars' worth of electronics and radar equipment rusted into trash.[44]

Additionally, and surprisingly, there seems to have been a studied lack of concern in the Oval Office—which was occupied by a staunch anti-communist president—over the possibility that the technology secrets in the West's most advanced weapons might fall into the hands of its enemies, particularly the Soviet Union, which lay just across the border.[45] That possibility did not escape the Department of Defense, which had tried for three years to limit the shah's arms purchases to less sensitive and complex equipment. At every turn, and especially after literally billions of dollars' worth of orders for America's most sophisticated armaments began to flow to U.S. military contractors, Defense officials (supported by officials at State, CIA, and the military services) tried every means at their disposal to get the administration to reassess the "sell-them-anything" policy.[46]

Nixon informed the Department of Defense on 15 June 1972 that he intended to sell advanced aircraft and laser-guided munitions to Iran, and that he had also promised the shah more "uniformed technicians" to assist the Iranian forces. When they learned of Nixon's agreements with the shah, Defense officials sent a letter to the president (dated 18 May 1972) strongly recommending that the United States not sell Iran F-14 or F-15 aircraft. These fighter-interceptor and fighter-attack aircraft were so advanced that not only had they not yet been delivered to U.S. forces, they had not even been fully evaluated for operational effectiveness. Defense also urged that laser-guided munitions not be sold and that there be no increase in the already sizable number of U.S. military forces in Iran.[47]

The White House ignored all of Defense's recommendations. Further, believing that bureaucratic obstructionism was impeding the president's directives, on 25 July 1972 Kissinger sent a follow-up memo to the secretaries of state and defense giving instructions for implementing the arms agreements with the shah.[48] In this memo, Kissinger directed the Department of Defense to prepare briefings for the Iranian military "as soon as possible" on the capabilities of the F-14 and F-15; informed the two cabinet secretaries that the president intended to sell the aircraft to the shah as soon as they became operationally ready; directed that "within that context, decisions on purchases and their timing should be left to the Government of Iran"; ordered that teams from the U.S. Air Force be made available to brief the Iranians on laser-guided bombs, reminding the secretaries that the president had already approved the sale of these munitions to the shah with the understanding that deliveries would begin within seven months of a purchase order; and required the cost and terms of reference for the provision of "uniformed technicians" to the Iranian forces to be calculated "as quickly as possible" given that Nixon had likewise promised the shah that additional U.S. military forces would be sent to Iran to assist with the advanced-technology materials.

Kissinger closed his memo by ordering the two cabinet departments to "proceed to implement the above as quickly as possible." If any additional impetus was needed, the national security adviser further reminded the secretaries that the "president has also reiterated that, in general, decisions on the acquisition of military equipment should be left primarily to the government of Iran. . . . [T]he purchase of U.S. equipment should be encouraged tactfully where appropriate, and technical advice on the capabilities of the equipment in question should be provided."

A later Senate investigation determined that Nixon had in effect ordered that arms sales be exempted from any review or oversight process by any agency of the U.S. government.[49] This policy overturned the efforts of five presidential administrations to convince the shah to moderate his arms purchases and demanded none of the economic and social development that the previous administrations had required in return for the arms.[50]

Despite this manifest and unprecedented policy, Kissinger later denied vehemently that the Nixon administration gave the shah a "blank check," calling such allegations "hyperbole." To this end Kissinger crafted an entirely unconvincing rebuttal that his memo was intended only to overcome an "obstructionist bureaucracy," as though the national security agencies charged with protecting America's military secrets and capabilities were insubordinate in objecting to the idea that a foreign leader could purchase any weaponry he desired, in whatever quantity he wished, no matter how highly classified the technology.[51] To say that this explanation merely begs the question would be an egregious understatement. The only offense the "bureaucracy" committed was in fulfilling its constitutional, professional, and patriotic duties to ensure that Executive policies are in the best interests of the United States and to safeguard sensitive American military weapons systems and their secrets. After the 25 July memo was distributed, the shah was allowed to purchase whatever he wanted.[52] One expert on U.S.-Iranian relations calls the policy "shortsighted and almost criminally careless."[53] In his memoirs Kissinger asserts that his memo had been forgotten by the time he left office, but one observer makes a convincing case that President Jimmy Carter's Departments of State and Defense continued to treat the shah's arms requests as Kissinger's directive required until it was overturned five months into the Carter administration.[54]

The results of Nixon's "open-handed, blind-eyed" policy were staggering, especially after the OPEC oil hikes in 1974 quadrupled Iran's oil royalties from $5 billion to more than $20 billion in one year. The shah went shopping—big-time. Total arms orders from the shah's military forces from 1972 through 1977 exceeded $30 billion, of which almost $6.8 billion was through U.S. military sales programs. In 1977 alone Iranian arms orders were just shy of $8 billion, with $2.5 billion going to U.S. firms.[55] The shah wanted only the newest high-tech, state-of-the art systems, including *Spruance*-class destroyers, F-14 fighter-interceptors, scores of F-4 fighter-attack aircraft (and later, F-16s), hundreds of Huey helicopters, P-3C antisubmarine and ocean reconnaissance aircraft, F-4G Wild Weasels, and legions of tanks.[56]

By 1975 the shah's army had—at least on paper—"overwhelming military superiority" in the region, even though much of the equipment had yet to be delivered. Nonetheless, purchase orders from the shah continued to flow to U.S. arms contractors.[57] In 1977 Iran's defense budget consumed 40 percent of the overall national budget and reflected a growth rate of 680 percent over the previous five years. The shah's purchases came close to doing what was thought to be impossible—outrunning the country's petroleum revenues.[58] Iran had become simultaneously the world's second-largest oil exporter and the largest purchaser of American arms; in economic importance to the United States it was unrivaled by any other country in the world.[59]

The sale of the Grumman F-14 Tomcats is the best illustration of the relationship between the shah and the Nixon administration. While other U.S. tactical military aircraft developed and brought into service during that period—the A-7, F-15, F-16, and F-18—have been and continue to be sold to numerous countries worldwide, the F-14 and its impressive AWG-9 radar, able to fire six Phoenix missiles simultaneously at six discrete targets at a distance of one hundred miles, has consistently been deemed too militarily sensitive to sell even to our closest allies. There has been only one exception: over the strongest possible objections of the Departments of Defense and State, Nixon sold eighty of them to the shah. Aside from the fact that virtually no military exigency possible could justify this sale, the mechanics of the Imperial Iranian Air Force (IIAF) lacked even the most basic technical skills to maintain airframes, engines, and weapons systems on much less sophisticated aircraft. Nixon and Kissinger nevertheless prevailed.

In the end, the Tomcats were squandered. Fear of crashing or otherwise losing an aircraft and thus displeasing the shah (who tended to promote officers based on favor rather than merit) made IIAF commanders unwilling to schedule aggressive training missions for the F-14s. Likewise, the aircrews were hesitant to fly them in any flight or weather conditions that might be conducive to accidents lest they lose or damage a plane and bear the brunt of the shah's wrath. What was arguably the world's most sophisticated and combat-capable aircraft was flown almost entirely in daylight hours, only when good weather prevailed, and only in low-risk, straight-and-level missions—no dogfighting, no close air support, no armed reconnaissance training missions.[60] And although the F-14 was the U.S. Navy's replacement for the McDonnell-Douglas F-4 Phantom II as the primary fleet defense aircraft, the shah received his Tomcats before the U.S. Navy pilots had received all of theirs. It was an unspeakable waste of one of America's most valuable military assets.

Ultimately, the "obstructionist bureaucracies" were proven correct, although they were never given credit for their foresight. With the shah's fall and the dissolution of the integrity of the Iranian military, Tomcat secrets were soon in hostile hands in Moscow—if indeed they had not been stolen earlier by Iranians working for the Soviet Union's military intelligence service.

The staggering amounts spent on arms sales, yoked as they were with the unrelenting corruption in the royal family and the shah's entourage, were seen by many Iranians as literally stealing their country's heritage. This collective sentiment aggravated in the average Iranian a bitter dislike of the United States far greater than the mild distaste stoked by the 1953 coup. Iranian citizens were at a loss to understand why their petrodollars were being squandered on arms to counter threats they couldn't see or understand; they were enraged to see their precious natural resource—which was finite in quantity—being used (in their eyes) to enrich American corporations and corrupt regime officials while millions of Iranians remained illiterate and ill-nourished, subsisting on the equivalent of $350 per year.[61]

In his "End of Tour" report, departing ambassador Richard M. Helms advised that while the standard of living for many Iranians had increased, a "wide disparity in income" maintained by the shah's "one-man authoritarian government" would militate against political stability.[62] Nixon and Kissinger never understood the enormous fissure between the "haves" and the "have-nots" in Iran and its connection to the arms sales; nor could they as long as they spoke only to the shah and his retinue.

Yet the arms sales were not totally without merit for Iran. In fact, U.S. arms saved Iran from potential destruction less than two years after the shah's regime collapsed. One of the principal threats perceived by the shah, possibly the primary threat in his eyes, was Iraq. This was especially true after the 1958 friendship treaty was signed by the Iraqis and the Soviet Union and Soviet weaponry began arriving in that neighboring Arab state. The shah frequently expressed his concern regarding Iraq's intentions to Ambassador Helms, often in the context of the arms and munitions that would be required to defeat an Iraqi invasion. Moreover, aware of his isolation in the midst of the Arab world, the shah had little confidence that anyone—presumably including the United States—would come to his assistance should an invasion occur. Both Helms and Kissinger have said that the arms sales enabled Iran to repel the initial Iraqi invasion in 1980 and then wage a war of attrition for eight long, nightmarish years before ultimately inflicting appalling losses on the Iraqis and preserving the Iranian nation.[63] Thus, there was a genuine threat to Iran's security that the arms purchases were meant to counter, but it does not seem to have been a threat that many Iranians recognized or believed, and their criticisms of the arms purchases escalated.

The May 1972 agreement between Nixon and the shah also required the United States to provide civilian and military technicians and advisers to maintain the sophisticated equipment and to train the Iranians in maintenance and employment. Eventually, thousands of American workers, along with their families, were living for lengthy periods in Iran. Nixon and Kissinger certainly did not foresee the effects these Americans, through their numbers and their actions, would have on Iranian society and attitudes. In July 1970 there were but seventy-three hundred Americans in Iran; within five years of the 1972 "blank check" agreement more than twenty-four thousand Americans were working in Iran. One company alone had fourteen hundred employees and six thousand family members living in the city of Isfahan.[64] By 30 June 1978 just shy of fifty-four thousand Americans were residing in Iran, and their arrogance and lack of consideration generated intense dislike and antagonism from large portions of the Iranian population.[65] The Americans dressed and acted as if they were back home in Texas, New York, California, or Florida, showing little sensitivity to or appreciation of the very different culture and religion of their host country.[66] They insisted on living in Iran as they lived in America, and literally tons of American food and other goods were delivered to Iran weekly and ostentatiously consumed in plain view of economically deprived Iranians.

In an effort to measure the effect the American population was having on Iranians, in 1976 the U.S. embassy in Tehran and the consulates in Tabriz, Shiraz, and Isfahan undertook the "Survey of Iranian Attitudes towards Increasing Foreign Presence in Iran." As part of the project State Department officers conducted numerous interviews with Iranians in government, business, and academia. The results were remarkably uniform. Interviewees related a range of criticisms about the American workers and their families. They complained that Americans in Iran lacked sensitivity toward the Iranian culture, led "unacceptable lifestyles" for a Muslim country, dressed in a "loud" and inappropriate manner, and did not socialize with Iranians. The interviewees resented Iranian television broadcasting programs that were produced by Iranians and had Iranian casts but used the English language. One study concluded that the behavior of Americans in Iran was contributing to a growth in Iranian nationalism.[67] And the Americans kept coming.

Thus by 1977 the admiration and goodwill evinced toward Americans by earlier generations of Iranians had mostly evaporated, replaced by anger and resentment, and in some, even hatred.[68] To his credit, the shah did try to limit this damage. Mark Gasiorowski notes that for a good part of the 1960s, and certainly through the 1970s, the shah "tried to counter the impression that he was an instrument of U.S. imperialism by maintaining good relations with the Soviet Union, working hard within OPEC to increase oil prices, becoming active in the nonaligned movement and other neutral forums, and frequently criticizing the United States and the West. . . . [R]arely admitted by critics of the shah, these actions left Iran quite independent of the United States, much to the disappointment of U.S. policymakers."[69] In contrast to his neighbors, however, the shah was a political supporter of Israel. During the Yom Kippur War of October 1973 he refused to allow Soviet aircraft to overfly Iran on their resupply flights to Egypt, in stark contrast to several NATO countries (American allies, after all) that did grant overflight rights to Soviet military aircraft. Many Iranians, Gasiorowski notes, "deeply resented the shah's willingness to maintain close relations with Israel . . . [and] began to view the relationship between Iran and Israel as a further manifestation of U.S. imperialism in Iran."[70]

Kissinger claims in his memoirs that the arms sales had little to do with the subsequent overthrow of the shah, holding that "it has become fashionable" to claim that these issues were the proximate cause of the shah's downfall.[71] And in a strict sense, Kissinger is mostly correct—but not entirely so. Certainly the shah's arms purchases were not the sole cause of the revolution; nor did they directly cause his overthrow. But Kissinger's denial should not be taken to mean that the graft and corruption that accompanied the purchases, in tandem with the unrelieved poverty and other social problems in Iran, had no effect on the Iranian population, particularly the multitudes of the indigent.

Iranians' perceptions (correct or not) regarding the purposes behind the sales gave dissidents and militants yet another reason to stir up discontent with the United States and its actions—and more reasons to seek the removal of the shah. So while the arms sales and all that came along with them were not necessarily the primary cause of the revolution or of the antipathy toward America, there is no doubt that they generated a good measure of the hatred and resentment that motivated the dissidents who took to the streets in 1978–79 and supported the takeover of the American embassy in 1979.[72] Scholars and others who know Iran well claim that the senior policymakers in the Nixon and, later, Carter administrations had no knowledge or understanding of the minds and needs of the Iranian people, and a similar understanding of the region's history.[73] Kissinger's apparent inability to see the connection between the arms sales and the attitudes of the Iranian population, and the subsequent effects of these attitudes, goes some distance in validating this allegation.[74]

There were, of course, other serious problems in Iranian society working against the shah's regime. The shah had consolidated his control over the body politic and the armed forces so completely that by 1975 he was an absolute dictator.[75] He brooked no opposition to his policies; made virtually all decisions of state both major and minor; surrounded himself with a retinue of sycophants who catered to his every desire, thought, and whim; turned middle- and senior-grade military officers into weaklings who worked only to seek his favor; both tolerated and provided the foundations for an astonishing amount of corruption on the part of his loyalists and family; and completely lost touch with the needs, woes, and wants of the average Iranian.

The increasing, and increasingly violent, human rights violations by the SAVAK were certainly a major factor in the revolution as well. Although the shah would later disclaim knowledge of SAVAK's acts of torture and inhumanity, it is inconceivable that he was totally unaware of them. Nor did the Nixon administration make any effort to convince the shah to moderate SAVAK's excesses; it would have been unseemly for Nixon and Kissinger to reproach one of their closest allies. Until well into the 1970s, the measures a sovereign nation used against its own citizens to maintain order were not considered appropriate subjects for remedy under international law. Regardless, then, of the reasons why, the Nixon administration was more than willing to leave SAVAK's actions and internal Iranian security measures to the shah.

The election of a new American president in 1977 at first gave the Iranians hope, but that hope was soon transformed into additional resentment and hatred. The incoming Carter administration would find that the true origins of the Iranian revolution of 1978 and the fall of the shah were founded much more deeply in the policies and favors of the Nixon administration than in the 1953 coup.

CHAPTER 6

REVOLUTION

The presidential election of 1976 brought Jimmy Carter to the White House and subsequent changes in U.S.-Iran relations. Where Nixon's policies toward Iran had actively, if unwittingly, created or aggravated divisive issues between the two countries, Carter's policies were predominantly reactionary, developed to deal with the troubles that grew out of Nixon's programs. Nevertheless, early in his administration Carter decided not to alter the relationship with the shah and Iran that he had inherited from Nixon; that did not change until the crisis of 1978 forced him to reconsider. Carter's initial decision to undertake no fundamental changes also meant that there would be no intensive scrutiny of the Iran-U.S. relationship. Without this policy review, the administration missed an opportunity to focus early on the complexities of the Iranian situation and probably rendered it more difficult to recognize the seriousness of the threat to the shah. This is not to say that the new president could have found a way to preserve the shah's regime; that would have been exceedingly difficult, if not impossible. But the Carter administration might have been able to help a moderate, Western-oriented government assume power in Iran, although such was far from a sure thing.

Carter rode into office on campaign promises to enshrine human rights as the centerpiece of America's foreign policies and to reduce the sales of military weaponry to the Third World. These two key issues were arguably more apt for Iran than for almost any other country: Iran was by far the largest purchaser of U.S. arms, and the shah's security forces, particularly SAVAK, were among the most vicious in the world. Yet Carter assumed office without having prepared any new policy initiatives specific to Iran. Nor did he, as noted, conduct an assessment of existing policies once in office. One reason was that there were Iranian contracts and commitments for weapons systems in the pipeline that had been negotiated by previous administrations, with deliveries scheduled into the 1980s. On learning this, Carter concluded that abrupt changes to the U.S. arms policy—and any significant reduction in the flow of U.S. arms to Iran—were impossible.[1] According to Gary Sick, a Carter White House official, Carter realized that "he had no visible strategic alternative to a close relationship with Iran" and therefore there was no decision to be made.[2] Moreover, Carter and his advisers quickly realized that Nixon's policies were firmly cemented in place and that, despite their personal distress over the human rights situation in Iran and their ideological unhappiness with the arms sales, the negative consequences of reversing course would probably be worse than the ills any new policies could cure.

There were, to be sure, benefits in continuity. Newly appointed secretary of state Cyrus Vance noted that the shah had provided generous economic assistance to countries in the region, pursued policies that aided materially in the reduction of tensions in Southwest Asia, deployed military forces to the pro-West Sultanate of Oman to help defeat an insurgency in that country, continued to be a reliable supplier of oil to the West, adamantly refused to join the Arab oil embargo of 1973 or use oil as a political weapon, and remained Israel's primary source of oil despite the condemnation of the surrounding Arab countries.[3] And then, of course, there was the shah's cooperation with the Tacksman sites, which aided U.S. efforts to limit or reduce the risk of global nuclear war. So certain was the new administration that this was the correct course to pursue, and so repetitively reassuring of the shah's capacities were the reports of the American ambassador in Tehran, that no policy review occurred. Ultimately, there would be no high-level White House reconsideration of U.S. policy toward Iran until a Special Coordinating Committee meeting was convened on 2 November 1978—twenty-two months into Carter's term and almost a year after the onset of street violence in Iranian cities.[4]

The exemption of Iran from President Carter's human rights policies was no doubt surprising to many observers. His campaign speeches and policy pronouncements after his election and inauguration had resonated with his intentions to impose sanctions on countries that were systematic violators of human rights. Yet Carter did not actually promulgate such a policy until February 1978, almost fourteen months after his inauguration. Moreover, as the United States was not a party to most of the human rights treaties in the international community, he lacked established mechanisms under international law to enforce global sanctions against human rights violations, leaving little choice but to rely on the inherently unreliable weapons of moral suasion and unilateral sanctions.[5] The USSR and right-wing (mostly Latin American) dictatorships were to be his primary targets, but at first he did not make this distinction clear, leaving the confused leadership in many countries to divine for themselves what the policy meant and to whom it applied.[6]

This was especially true for the shah of Iran, who was baffled by the contrast between Carter's policy pronouncements and policy implementation. But millions of ordinary Iranians failed to see the discrepancy: they saw in the president's human rights declarations the only hope for their future. While previous American administrations had, in the eyes of the average Iranian, actively supported the shah's repression of political, civil, and human rights, Iranians believed that at last there was a president who found these actions unacceptable. Carter's moralistic dicta convinced many Iranians that he would either force the shah to ameliorate his repressive measures or else withdraw U.S. support.[7]

Another policy that confused the Iranians was Carter's stated intention to reduce U.S. arms sales around the globe. Presidential Directive 13 (PD-13), "Conventional Arms Transfer," signed by Carter on 13 May 1977, stated that "arms sales are an exceptional foreign policy implement, to be used only in instances where it can be clearly demonstrated that the transfers contribute to our national security interests."[8] The directive also made it clear that the United States would work to reduce or "restrain" the sales of arms and would urge other countries to sign agreements having the goal of "curbing the proliferation" of arms, and that additional U.S. sales would take into account the "economic impact" to "less developed countries." Under the restrictions cited in PD-13, the shah and the Iranian military should have expected an immediate reduction in overall arms sales and the complete elimination of more than a few advanced weapons systems. But the document had a loophole: it allowed exemptions when such transfers promoted U.S. security and the security of U.S. allies and friends.

Thus it was that, during a May 1977 visit to Tehran, Secretary of State Vance reassured the shah that America would continue to be Iran's principal arms supplier.[9] Although Carter did not reverse the U.S. arms policy toward Iran, PD-13 did tear up the "blank check" so generously given by Nixon and Kissinger, and it permitted appropriate government agencies to review arms sales. Almost by default, then, Carter continued many of his predecessors' Iranian policies. Significantly, this was not fully evident to the shah, who continued to worry about the state of his relationship with the U.S. government and remained uncertain as to Carter's policies for Iran.[10]

A corollary to Carter's lack of new initiatives for Iran was the continuation of the attitudes of previous administrations regarding the shah personally. The plain fact was that, like Nixon and Kissinger, Carter and his national security adviser, Zbigniew Brzezinski, confused the importance of the shah with the importance of his country.[11] Gary Sick, the Iran action officer on the National Security Council (NSC) staff during this period, believes that the U.S. government had "become a hostage to the shah, to his particular view of the world, and in some respects to his concept of Iranian and U.S. interests."[12] There was also the continued assumption, unchallenged by most in the government, that the shah would remain in power and in control of his country at least through the 1980s, if not until the end of the century.[13] This judgment wasn't as ill-advised as it sounds two decades later, for abetting its credibility were analyses from U.S. intelligence organs that, during 1977 at least, indicated that the shah was in control and would be able to remain in control, regardless of the growing domestic unrest.

And it was not just the Americans who believed that. The Soviets also failed to realize the seriousness of the civil unrest in Iran. Interested primarily in protecting their assets in the country, the Soviets responded cautiously and tried to keep their relations with Iran on a normal basis.[14] The Soviet government's certainty that the shah had the political stability of his country firmly in hand was demonstrated by a major administrative decision within the KGB. Until civil war consumed Lebanon in 1976–77, the KGB maintained a staff, headed by Vladimir Golovanov, in its Beirut residency that managed the espionage operations of all "illegals" in the Middle East. ("Illegals" are KGB staff officers who live abroad in non-Russian alias identities recruiting and running agents with no visible connection to the Soviet Union.) When the Lebanese civil war made it difficult for the illegals staff in Beirut to operate, the KGB moved the group to the Tehran residency, headed by KGB colonel Lev Petrovich Kostromin, partly because they saw the country as exceptionally stable. But no sooner had the Tehran residency been revamped in the fall of 1977 to hold the newly arrived illegals staff than the street demonstrations began. As the rioting escalated in scope and intensity, plans for using Tehran as the regional illegals' residency were set aside. Moreover, the KGB took scrupulous care not to contact anyone involved in any of the dissident groups lest the shah learn of their operation in Tehran and sever diplomatic relations with the USSR. Iran was far too important for the Soviets to risk losing their embassy and KGB residency.[15]

U.S. policymakers in Washington had a very poor understanding of the situation in Iran in 1977. This was partly because they continued to focus on the relationship with the shah rather than the polity of Iran, but much more so because the intelligence community had not been tasked with collecting and reporting on the internal Iranian situation. The president and his secretaries of state, defense, and energy strongly supported the shah, and all of them failed to understand the implications when hitherto disparate dissident groups united in opposition to the shah. All failed to see the weaknesses in the shah's reactions to the street rioting, and all comprehended too late that America's options and ability to affect internal events in Iran had evaporated. In these shortcomings, however, policymakers were no more in the dark than anyone else in town.

U.S. officials in Tehran also missed many of the signs. Ambassador William H. Sullivan later referred to the revolution as a "complex event" and claimed that it stemmed from a "broad range of social, political, economic, and religious groups . . . each reflect[ing] their own particular grievances with the Pahlavi system and their own plans to change it."[16] The situation "bred intellectual and political frustration and uncertainty."[17] And as the next chapter explains, there was precious little intelligence on internal Iranian political issues coming from his embassy in 1977 to inform the policymakers.

The intense program of modernization on which the shah had embarked in the 1960s continued to be pursued with vigor in Iran, bringing the (relatively) small but growing middle class economic prosperity and the elite fabulous wealth, often through rampant corruption. But the multitudes in the lower classes—the impoverished, the unemployed, the uneducated, the unskilled—that constituted the vast majority of Iran's population of thirty-five million were left off the gravy train. Moreover, the central government was also egregiously derelict in providing adequate basic social, health, education, and welfare programs. The masses were left adrift while signs and symbols of the great wealth of the few were erected all around them. Resentment and anger, at the regime and at the foreigners whom they considered responsible, mounted steadily among these unfortunate citizens. And the Iranian masses were alienated not just economically but politically as well. The shah by 1975 had acquired absolute power over his government and country: the prime minister and the Majlis were impotent, and the most important of the government organs—the defense ministry and the military, SAVAK, the foreign ministry, the treasury—reported only to him. There was no way for the average Iranian to participate in government, no way to project a voice in the choices of government.

Many Iranians saw the hand of America behind their troubles. America had coerced the shah into spending their oil treasure to buy arms the country didn't need. American corporations were insulting, if not altering, the culture of Iran with their growing presence and their modernization projects. America, in short, was running Iran while the shah was no more than a puppet.[18] The more the Americans became entrenched in Iran, the more the Iranians came to identify America as the villain responsible for their poverty.[19] Nor was the shah himself completely in touch with the reality of the situation. He surrounded himself with sycophants who told him only what he wanted to hear. Zbigniew Brzezinski notes that the shah enjoyed Western-style opulence and wealth while insisting on being treated as a "traditional Oriental despot, accustomed to instant and total obedience from his courtiers."[20] In his isolation and ignorance the shah believed that he was beloved by the people, although he was aware enough to worry (correctly) that Carter and his advisers thought him a tyrant.[21]

Adding to the confusion, and to the detriment of the U.S. position in Iran, were the efforts of the always opportunistic Soviet Union to stir up trouble. But the Soviet Union was wise enough to remain officially (that is, overtly) more or less neutral. Initially, at least, the Soviets did not want to antagonize the shah or alienate him should he survive the growing dissent and remain in power. Later, when there were increasing signs that the shah was going to fall, the Soviets had to take into account that he would probably be replaced by a regime suspicious of communism and the USSR. They opted not to use overt economic or diplomatic pressure to alter events so as not to antagonize whatever new regime followed.[22] Under the table, though, it was a different matter.

As 1977 gave way to 1978 the KGB stoked the fires of anger toward the regime and the United States by instituting a range of covert "active measures" programs intended to influence events in Iran without the Soviet hand showing.[23] For example, in late 1977 the KGB commenced an operation in which batches of letters prepared at KGB headquarters in Moscow and written in fluent Farsi were mailed anonymously to Iranian government leaders, including the shah, and SAVAK officers detailing fictitious allegations of U.S. efforts to destabilize the shah's government and undermine SAVAK.[24]

During the summer of 1978, the KGB intensified the output of the National Voice of Iran. CIA intelligence assessments noted that the tone of the clandestine radio station in Baku "became sharper and more strident as the situation within Iran deteriorated." The radio became an effective source of disinformation and propaganda, inciting hatred of the shah (an "American puppet") and urging the expulsion of Americans from Iran. A former Soviet bloc intelligence officer claims that the radio began providing instructions on organizing demonstrations and similar recipes for rebellion, but a CIA assessment of Soviet involvement in the Iranian crisis disputes this. Agency analysts say that the National Voice of Iran encouraged Iranians to "participate in general strikes, advised soldiers to lay down their arms and support those struggling for liberty, and urged the people in general to use all forms of struggle to overthrow the 'despotic regime.'"[25] Thus the clandestine radio broadcasts did everything possible to contribute to the increasing unrest.

The personality and health of the shah himself at this time also were significant to later events. Those who knew His Imperial Majesty at the time held mixed views. President Carter found the shah "likeable," "modest," and "reticent." He believed the shah to be "a strong ally" and "appreciated his ability to maintain good relations with Egypt and Saudi Arabia, and his willingness to provide Israel with oil despite the Arab boycott."[26] National Security Adviser Zbigniew Brzezinski viewed the shah as a monarch of "obvious intelligence" and possessed of a "keen analytical bent." He once observed as the shah "summarized the geopolitical dilemmas of his region" and was impressed with the performance. But he also saw "megalomaniacal tendencies" in the shah's personality and the obsequiousness with which his retinue treated him. And he was also well aware of the shah's primary character flaw—a lack of personal courage. Clare Booth Luce, who was the U.S. ambassador to Italy in 1953 when the shah fled Iran during the coup, once cautioned Brzezinski to have no illusions about the shah, who, she said, showed up in Rome "frightened, without guts."

In the end, perhaps the fairest assessment of the shah and his rule are those damning words, "he meant well." In many ways, particularly when set against Anglo-Saxon values and ideals of what a "good" government should be and should accomplish, the shah's efforts to modernize his society and move it toward the Western camp were noble. His anticommunist stance, his support of Israel, and his service as a regional statesman were applauded by many, and deservedly so. That he eventually came to realize the harm to the Iranian people caused by SAVAK and other oppressive measures is reasonably evident. Nor was the shah himself venal and corrupt in the way that his family (notably Ashraf) and his closest associates were; in this respect his only shortcoming was in not halting, or at least keeping at an "acceptable level," the avarice of those around him.[27] Even one of his most strident critics, George Ball, notes that the shah "was not an evil man, but had honorable intentions" although he nevertheless "managed to alienate every group" in Iranian society.[28]

As 1977 moved from summer to fall, the opposition movements—plural, for there were many moving in parallel, at first uncoordinated, but less so as time passed—became bolder and more vocal. The shah's responses were weak. He tried to appease the population by reining in SAVAK, but that served only to embolden the dissidents. And the influence of the exiled Ayatollah Khomeini, still in Najaf, Iraq, at that time, grew in volume and reach, gaining him more and more followers. With renewed hope for the future, leaders of the National Front and other prominent dissidents sent a letter to Secretary-General Kurt Waldheim of the United Nations expressing their desire to return to a democratic constitutionalism in Iran that would encompass political freedoms and yet permit the shah to retain his throne as a constitutional monarch. The group sent a similar missive to the American embassy, which forwarded it to President Carter. The NF and its collaborators hoped that the United States would use its influence to help convince the shah to move toward legitimate reform and true democracy. But as Charlie Naas points out, the letter in effect asked the United States "to change the regime of a friendly monarch, one who by that time was a major contributor to our world security policy."[29] There was no chance that the president would agree to the goals expressed in the letter. The Iranians were both demoralized and perplexed at the lack of a reply from a president who, they thought, shared their ideals. Then, at the very end of the year, the Iranians witnessed an event that they interpreted as President Carter's veiled but deliberate response to their letter.

In mid-November 1977 the shah made his twelfth trip to the United

States. The visit was marked by anti-shah demonstrations and pro-shah counterdemonstrations, several of which resulted in violent conflicts. The world was treated to the spectacle of the president of the United States and the shah of Iran at an outdoor ceremony wiping their eyes from tear gas wafting onto the White House grounds from a demonstration just beyond the fence. Iranians back home gave this event a classic Persian ethnocentric interpretation. Not realizing—or, more likely, not believing—that the U.S. government might be different from their own in its response to demonstrations, the dissidents quickly decided that this sort of behavior would not have been allowed to happen if the president hadn't wished it. And based on this hugely erroneous assumption the Iranians then concluded that it meant only one thing: the U.S. government was "abandoning the shah." Thus the tear gas incident served to further inspire them in their opposition.[30]

Six weeks later President Carter reciprocated with a visit to Tehran, arriving for New Year's Eve 1977. Knowing that protocol required Carter to offer a toast at the lavish state banquet being planned, Ambassador Sullivan suggested to the president that he limit himself to "rather anodyne" remarks. To Sullivan's amazement, Carter ignored his suggestion and, in ad-lib comments, lauded the shah as "an island of stability in one of the more troubled areas of the world," offering "tribute" to the shah and to his "leadership, and to the respect, admiration and love" given to him by the Iranian people.[31] This extemporaneous salute was proffered with apparently little thought to the realities of Iranian political life. The president later wrote that he was even more aware of the "currents of dissatisfaction" than the shah, so one must wonder why he was not more circumspect in his remarks that evening.[32]

To the Iranians in the streets this speech was tantamount to an irreversible breach of faith; the final proof to millions of Iranians who had counted on the president to bring human rights to the oppressed. Feeling abjectly betrayed, the Iranians lost faith in President Carter and, with the viciousness of the scorned, came to loathe him with a personal intensity. From that point on, they would consider the president as being in league with the shah and their personal enemy as well.

Within a week began the first acts of a stream of violence and deaths that would prevail until the shah eventually departed his country a year later. The large demonstration in the city of Qom on 8 January 1978 inspired further demonstrations in Iran's other cities and detonated a cycle of escalating violence. At the Qom demonstration security forces shot into the crowd and killed about two dozen participants (some Iranians, rather improbably, estimated as many as one hundred fatalities).[33] In the Shiite tradition, the dead are mourned at the end of forty days. Those who died in demonstrations were mourned as the religion dictated in other large public demonstrations; these gatherings (which of course had an antiregime focus) were challenged by the security forces, leading to more deaths. Soon there were demonstrations against the regime as well as demonstrations related to the public mourning.

As the demonstrations increased in number and intensity throughout the year, so did the number of deaths. On Friday, 8 September, in Tehran's Jaleh Square, soldiers fired on more than one thousand demonstrators. The number killed was probably in the neighborhood of 250 but has been alleged to be anywhere from 200 to perhaps as many as 2,000, with many more wounded.[34] But more important than the number of dead was the impact of the event on Iranian dissident groups and opponents of the shah. The majority of the demonstrators were lower-class residents of Tehran who had migrated to the city during the White Revolution, as opposed to the better-educated moderates who dominated many of the earlier demonstrations; the inability of the moderate clergy to control these people was a clear indication that the moderates were losing control to radical clergy who looked to Khomeini for leadership.[35] Overall, during the revolutionary period from January 1978 to February 1979, as many as ten thousand Iranians may have died in demonstrations and other dissident events.[36]

CHAPTER 7

INTELLIGENCE FAILURE

Official Washington did notice the deteriorating conditions in Iran that spring and summer of 1978, but apparently without great concern; any concern that did exist was insufficient to move the Carter administration to consider reevaluating its basic policies toward Iran. Later, when the shah and his regime collapsed, the president used the national media to blame the administration's surprise on an "intelligence failure," with the underlying implication that policy decisions would have been more effective and outcomes more successful if the intelligence reaching the president had been accurate and timely. Supporting the president's criticism was a 1980 study by the Senate Select Committee on Intelligence. The committee found that "intelligence collection and analyses were weak and that the confidence of policymakers in the shah, which intelligence reporting did not challenge, further skewed the U.S. reading of the situation and contributed to the warning failure."[1] Gary Sick thought the intelligence reaching the president was "dreadful," a description with which virtually everyone in Washington involved with the Iran crisis agreed, both at the time and years later.[2]

Contributing to the intelligence failure was the tendency of policymakers in the Carter administration to disregard intelligence contradictory to their policy preferences. To the extent that this attitude prevailed, the policy preferences and desires of the senior policymakers played a larger role in the "failure" than they might wish to acknowledge. A 1979 House of Representatives review of the intelligence produced prior to the fall of the shah ascertained that "long-standing U.S. attitudes toward the shah inhibited intelligence collection, dampened policymakers' appetite for analysis of the shah's position, and deafened policymakers to the warning implicit in available intelligence."[3] In light of this fact, one scholar believes that "if there was an intelligence failure with regard to Iran, it lay in the relationship between policy and intelligence," not necessarily with the intelligence alone.[4]

When the Iran crisis burst into the news in the late winter and early spring of 1978, it must have seemed to casual observers that the U.S. government had been caught totally unaware by the depth and breadth of the opposition to the shah and his regime. Questions of why and how this could happen were prime material for headlines, editorial pages, and television talk shows. How could U.S. policymakers have been so uninformed? How could the Department of State and the intelligence community have been so inept in the conduct of their duties? How could the shah's opposition have gained so much power and force through the 1970s without U.S. policymakers noticing? These were legitimate questions, and the answers may be surprising.

The intelligence deficit that appeared in early 1978 can be traced directly to presidential policies that began in the late 1960s and lasted well into the 1970s. During that period there was an undeniable shortage—although not a total absence—of intelligence collected on the internal political scene in Iran. This naturally affected the quality of analysis and assessment in later years. But that intelligence deficit was the result of a deliberate decision *not* to collect the intelligence in the first place. Charles Naas was the deputy chief of mission (DCM) in the U.S. embassy in Tehran in the late 1970s; prior to that he had held a series of State Department assignments that involved the staffing of U.S. embassies in Southwest Asia, including Kabul, Ankara, and Tehran. He relates that the political section in the U.S. embassy in Tehran comprised no more than five Foreign Service officers in the 1960s, and sometimes fewer in later years.

Until the appearance of serious civil unrest in Iran at the beginning of 1978, the political section was staffed at such a low level that it was generally unable to follow internal Iranian political issues.[5] (Even in the fall of 1979 there were just four State Department political officers in the mission, despite its continuing importance to policymakers.) Similarly, CIA data collection was minimal from the 1960s though the 1970s. And yet Iran was a country consistently characterized by presidents and senior policymakers as a geographically critical region and one of America's most important allies. Logic, then, legitimately questions why so few CIA and State Department officers were present in the embassy to follow internal Iranian political developments during the 1970s.

There are several reasons why both agencies did little internal reporting until after January 1978—reasons that made good sense at the time
regardless of how feckless they may appear two decades later. The principal determinant was, simply, presidential needs and interest. Iran in the
late 1960s and most of the 1970s—through four administrations led by
presidents of both parties—was believed by policymakers to be politically stable, with the shah in firm command. Thus, none of the four
administrations sought information on the Iranian internal political situation from the intelligence community. The State Department and the
intelligence agencies concurred with the presidential priorities and so
used their collection resources on higher priorities identified by the
White House.

A second, inherently related, cause of the paucity of intelligence during this time was a mundane bureaucratic measure from which the foreign policy and national security agencies are no more immune than are
other government agencies: budget cuts. In the 1970s two cost-reduction
programs at State required embassies around the world to reduce their
staffs. In consequence, the number of officers in the political section in
the Tehran embassy was lowered and the consulates in Meshed and Isfahan were closed. Charlie Naas recalls that "these reductions were made
more palatable by the belief that Iran was stable and that the resources
could be more fruitfully applied elsewhere." Henry Precht makes the
point that if policymakers had considered Iranian internal matters to be
of genuine concern, State (and the CIA) would have been provided with
the requisite funds and personnel: "We did not think [the shah] had a
problem . . . as there were few signs of popular unrest . . . so we didn't
probe."[6]

It wasn't as though State had not tried diligently to cover events in
Iran. The Foreign Service had both a cadre of well-trained young officers
and good contacts within the Iranian opposition in the late 1950s and
early 1960s. But as time passed and U.S. policy came to focus on the person of the shah as opposed to the country of Iran, extensive contacts
with those outside the regime dwindled. In consequence, morale sank
and some of the best officers resigned; others refused assignment in
Iran.[7]

The early 1960s saw a series of riots, a number of which were instigated by the radical cleric Ruhollah Khomeini and supported by the
bazaaris. But with the exile of Khomeini and the security crackdown by

the shah, Naas relates, there was "an implicit assumption that the clergy/bazaar power nexus had been broken. From that time onward little was heard from the embassy or Washington analysis about the clergy." At the beginning of the 1978 crisis, then, there were no experienced Iran specialists serving in the U.S. embassy in Tehran. Naas adds that while many State officers had served in the Islamic world, "none of us were schooled in Shi'ism and [we] did not grasp until quite late in the day what the clergy were up to." In 1978, in fact, there were few in the embassy who had experience in Iran, spoke the language, or understood its culture.[8]

It is also true that U.S. officials in Tehran deliberately chose not to meet with oppositionists during those years. As Henry Precht succinctly explains, "the most radical groups opposed to the shah were shooting us." Six Americans were murdered during the four years Precht served in Tehran (and one more was assassinated after he left). While there were moderate dissidents around, they did not wish contact with American officials in Tehran for fear of coming to the attention of the shah. Neither did State wish to meet with them in Washington lest it send the wrong signals to the dissidents and to the shah. Since SAVAK maintained a presence in Washington, the dissidents were correct to fear that the shah would eventually hear about any dealings they had with the U.S. government. Another opposition group, Precht notes, the "old gentlemen from the 1950s [e.g., former National Front members], didn't seem to count for much."[9] Once during Precht's assignment in Iran, arrangements were made for a visiting U.S. congressman to meet (at the solon's request) with Iranian students; on another occasion a political officer attempted to seek out mullahs close to the bazaaris. Both times the Iranian Ministry of Court stepped in and annulled the arrangements. In short, at no time in the 1970s did an American official meet with a member of the exiled opposition.[10] But there seemed no justification to do so: the stability of the shah's rule; his pro-American, pro-West, anticommunist policies; and his domestic modernization programs were all that Washington could desire. With no interest in seeing a different leadership in Iran and no desire to antagonize the shah, there was no reason for State or the White House to think anything useful could come from such meetings.

The story is much the same for the CIA's intelligence reporting from Iran. According to former DCI Richard Helms, who was also the ambassador to Iran in the Nixon-Ford years, the CIA officers in Iran during the

1960s and 1970s did "little political reporting."[11] The Agency presence in Iran was almost totally related to the Tacksman sites and technical intelligence collection programs. Like State, CIA also went through a series of budgetary reductions in the 1960s, with stations in Southwest Asia directed to concentrate on Soviet and Chinese communist targets and counterintelligence.[12] Thus, policymakers' lack of interest in Iranian affairs affected the assignments of CIA officers just as it did their State counterparts. The end result was sporadic intelligence collection in Tehran and limited analysis in Washington. But nobody in any senior position at the White House complained or expressed a wish to amend the tasking restrictions.[13]

In a classic example of chickens coming home to roost, it was President Carter's DCI, Stansfield Turner, who cut more than eight hundred positions from the CIA's Directorate of Operations, the Agency component responsible for recruiting and managing the assets needed to provide the intelligence desired by the White House. In the view of Carter's national security adviser, this reduction "probably affected" the CIA's ability to acquire intelligence.[14]

Numerous books and articles claim that there existed some sort of agreement, formal or tacit, between the shah and the U.S. government in which the shah demanded—and the United States agreed—that the CIA not collect data on the Iranian political situation. Not only is there no credible evidence that any agreement of that sort ever existed, the most authoritative source available refutes the notion. Dick Helms, as DCI and then ambassador to Iran, is more knowledgeable about the intelligence community's relationship with the shah during this era than anyone, and Helms states without equivocation that there was no agreement. Indeed, as his tenure in Tehran was drawing to an end, intelligence collection against the shah's regime and Iranian military facilities was increasing.[15] While Helms acknowledges that the shah did on occasion pointedly inquire about the activities of the Agency's officers in Iran (in the context of possible operations against the dissidents), he never received a response from Helms. When questioned, Helms would only smile and then deflect the subject.[16]

But while there was no explicit prohibition against acquiring intelligence on the shah's regime in the 1970s, there was a definite sensitivity to the shah's concerns about this and to having contacts with his opponents. This sensitivity almost surely served to some extent as a self-censoring element when it came to internal reporting. Rather than risk angering the shah, as well as senior American policymakers (e.g., Henry Kissinger, who sat atop the relationship for eight years as national security adviser and secretary of state), American intelligence officers turned their attention to other duties and ignored the Iranian political scene. Even the officers in the Military Assistance Advisory Group were so afraid that the Iranian government might view them as spies that they avoided the embassy's military attachés, whose mission was to collect intelligence on the Iranian armed forces. Henry Precht expresses the phenomenon of self-censorship most aptly: "So if there was no formal agreement against delving into Iran's internal policies, there certainly did not have to be one. We regarded the shah as all that mattered in Iran and his opposition as of no consequence."[17]

Yet, occasional intelligence reports on the internal political situation in Iran did dribble into the Washington offices of mid-level policy advisers and analysts, although they seldom went further up the chain. This situation began to change in 1977 near the end of Helms's posting in Tehran, with reporting on the internal scene gradually increasing. Thus there was a modest amount of intelligence indicating that the shah might be in trouble; none, however, provided an unquestionable, all-encompassing picture of the regime's demise. And, of course, these evaluations were usually counterbalanced with contradictory information or were in themselves to some extent ambiguous.

The situation began to change dramatically in January 1978 with the Jaleh Square demonstration and shootings. Intelligence reporting from Tehran began to pick up in the late winter and early spring as embassy officers, both State and Agency, expanded their range of contacts. Yet despite the escalating violence, the policymakers in Washington remained confident in the shah's ability to weather the storm. Few, if any, American officials questioned the shah's ability and willingness to employ SAVAK, police, and a superbly equipped military of nearly half a million troops to maintain control and preserve his regime.

While at least a few mid-level State and Agency officers were skeptical of the shah's determination to remain in power, they faced a singularly difficult obstacle. Anyone of credible reputation in Washington, even as late as June 1978, who predicted that in fourteen months the shah would have been run out of the country and replaced by radical fundamentalists would have been thought daft. And so it remained until a few weeks before the shah's departure. After all, the shah had been in absolute control of his country for most of the decade and he was judged to be strong and decisive by those who knew him best. That the shah could not or would not exercise his powers to halt dissent was virtually incomprehensible to those who were observing the unfolding drama. Nothing in the record points to any open-mindedness to alternative views on the part of any senior policymaker. Henry Precht notes that there is probably nothing harder in the world to change than an established foreign policy that is perceived as having worked for decades. Indeed, a quick peek at U.S. policies toward Vietnam in the Johnson administration and well into the Nixon years demonstrates just how difficult it is to change a policy that *isn't* working.[18] In the case of Iran, almost everyone was certain the policy *was* working and no one perceived the need to change it.

Another consequence of the prevailing sense of stability in Iran that further inhibited coherent understanding of the Iranian picture was the willingness of the foreign policy and national security bureaucracies to forgo staffing their Iranian analytical sections. State's Bureau of Intelligence and Research (INR) had no full-time Iran analyst during much of the 1970s, leaving internal political assessments mostly to the Office of Iranian Affairs and, collaterally, to the Political–Military Affairs Bureau.[19] Nor was INR alone in lacking an Iran specialist. The NSC staff likewise had no expert on Iran—not at the beginning of the Carter administration and not even when events in Iran burst into a full-blown crisis. Navy commander Gary Sick, a specialist on Soviet and Chinese naval activity, particularly in the Indian Ocean area, found himself serving as the NSC's Iran action officer throughout the crisis period of 1978–81.[20] Of the few analysts following Iranian affairs in 1977 and 1978, none detected any sign that the shah would not utilize his security apparatus to maintain control. Even Ambassador Bill Sullivan and DCM Charlie Naas viewed the shah's position as secure.

Further complicating the ability of Washington analysts to understand the situation in 1978 was the simple fact that most of the finished intelligence assessments on Iran were erroneous in their judgments. Until late in the day, reporting from the embassy was inadequate, and little of the analysis that flowed from the reports provided clear insights or consensus regarding the future of the shah. And right up to the end, not one analyst or policymaker predicted that a radical fundamentalist regime would replace the shah's.[21]

Other factors affected the intelligence production and analysis of Iranian political issues as well, of course, and these must receive some attention if the "intelligence failure" is to be fully understood. There is an a priori acknowledgment in intelligence analysis that policymakers rarely receive finished intelligence assessments of crises that completely and correctly identify and explain the underlying causes, accurately predict future events, and yield complete understanding of the effects of each possible alternative course of action. Accurately assessing complex, fast-developing situations that occur in distant lands, in great secrecy, and involve little-known cultures and ethnic factors is among the greatest of intelligence challenges. With the Washington policymakers' unshaken belief in the shah's durability in early to mid-1978, only a unanimous and unequivocal assessment stating that the shah's days were numbered and explaining how, why, and when would have been likely to attract their attention.

But a policymaker who expected such a report would have been unrealistic in his understanding of what was possible. Neither Carter nor others in the White House seemed fully to comprehend this aspect of the limitations of intelligence.[22] In the spring of 2000 DCI George J. Tenent stated concisely what all intelligence officers know and many policymakers don't: for intelligence to be useful, "there must be a realistic expectation of what intelligence can provide. We are neither omniscient nor perfect. We simply cannot provide continuous, contiguous coverage for every issue of concern. And when so much of our mission involves warning and prediction, and when we must carry it out twenty-four hours a day, three hundred and sixty-five days a year, around the globe, we are bound to make mistakes, both in analysis and operations."[23] Nothing in the record indicates that senior policymakers in the Carter administration understood these limitations of intelligence collection and analysis.

Certainly not all Iran observers were so wedded to the belief in the shah's invincibility. Among the first to foresee, in the summer of 1978, a situation sufficiently explosive to perhaps force the abdication of the shah was Henry Precht at State; and for his insights and analyses he was criticized by some in the White House who ultimately attempted to saddle him with much of the blame for the resulting policy fiasco.[24] Precht was also well aware of the dangers of admitting the shah into the United States following his abdication and attempted to convince the administration of those perils—once again to no avail and unmerited opprobrium. He later chaired the Iran Working Group at State for the duration of the crisis and again distinguished himself through his service and expertise.[25]

In 1978, intelligence analysts were hard-pressed to discern, much less to agree on, the precise nature and extent of the civil disturbances in Iran. Most important—and most difficult—was accurately predicting future events, particularly the question of whether or (later) for how long the shah would remain in control of his country. For example, the Defense Intelligence Agency (DIA) issued five intelligence reports in the first three quarters of 1978, and each fell short of comprehending the dynamics of the Iranian revolution and forecasting possible outcomes. Even into September 1978 the DIA was still asserting that the shah would remain in control for another decade.[26]

CIA and State/INR reports were also wide of the mark. An August 1978 CIA assessment entitled *Iran after the Shah,* for example, postulated that Iran was "not in a revolutionary or even prerevolutionary situation," despite eight months of increasing street violence and a range of ineffective or counterproductive responses by the shah. The assessment went on to say that the military remained loyal to the shah and the opposition lacked the ability to overturn the regime. President Carter later cited this report as prima facie confirmation of the "intelligence failure."[27] Indeed, this report was unquestionably a serious miscalculation on the part of Agency analysts, for it not only misled policymakers, it also reinforced the still-prevalent belief in the White House that the shah's grip was strong. An INR assessment of 1 September 1979 indicated that the shah might step down by 1985, but gave the odds of that occurring as "less than fifty-fifty"—which of course implies that the odds of the shah surviving were better than fifty-fifty, an arrantly erroneous prognostication.[28]

But not all of the intelligence was worthless. Amid the erroneous, inconclusive, or ambiguous reports reaching Washington were some that were accurate, or mostly so. The problem was that these reports and assessments were either buried in larger piles of contradictory information, read in isolation from supporting materials, which then diminished their impact, or were insufficiently conclusive in their determinations.[29] Simply put, the chaff overwhelmed the wheat. Yet reasonably accurate and thought-provoking information *was* available. Why, then, did it not have a greater impact on policymakers? And why was no intelligence community consensus reached prior to late August 1978?

There are four salient reasons for these reports' lack of impact in

Washington. First, policymakers and analysts alike were convinced until very late in the day that the shah had the will and the means to confront and defeat the opposition, and were confident that he would do so.[30] Gary Sick comments that while "the president did not invent that view [n]either did he question it."[31] In fact, this attitude was so "deeply ingrained" in the administration that even when the revolution was "raging almost out of control" the intelligence still "continued to receive little attention."[32] This conviction of the shah's invincibility argued against scrutinizing or giving credence to any evidence that might necessitate a labor-intensive and disruptive reexamination of U.S. policies in Iran. Sick also observes that "the implications of such a revolutionary transformation [of U.S. policy toward Iran] extended far beyond the borders of Iran and the bi-lateral U.S.-Iranian relationship."[33]

A second reason why intelligence alone failed to draw the attention of policymakers was the depth of the genuine and legitimate disagreements over the situation in Iran among the foreign policy and national security communities in Washington. With the various agencies reaching some degree of unanimity on the causes of the revolution and possible future outcomes only at the end of the summer, there was precious little for the policymakers to do but to press ahead as before. Certainly, no one wanted to try to dump the shah prematurely and generate the numerous problems that would ensue if he managed to retain the throne. Absent a connective series of intelligence assessments, coordinated by and through the intelligence community and stating in unequivocal language that the shah's time was up, it is understandable that the policymakers distrusted the assessments they were receiving and continued as before.

A third reason has been identified by former undersecretary of state David D. Newsom, who notes that, from the very beginning of the crisis, "policymakers, recalling the Mossadegh period, assumed that the real threat to the shah would come from the National Front and the left." The idea of a religious fundamentalist regime was a part of no one's calculus. Foreign policy leaders, whether in the White House or Congress, "just could not believe that a group of medieval religious leaders had the force to overthrow the shah." Cautioning that "policymakers must always consider intelligence, as well as actions, in light of alternatives," Newsom recalls that there were occasional considerations of alternatives to the shah (e.g., abdication and a regency until the crown prince reached his majority), but there was one dilemma that could not be successfully resolved. As the shah was in sole control of the diplomatic, military, economic, and security institutions, how was the United States to bring about a peaceful change of regime leadership without eroding the structure of the entire regime? No matter how this critical issue was parsed, whether looking at Iran's political left or the right, there were just no acceptable choices. Thus, many in the administration concluded that the United States "should stick with the shah as long as possible."[34]

Finally, in any general situation, but particularly in a crisis, there is always information that is just not "knowable." Complex events can take on a spontaneity and life of their own in which even the individuals in the midst of them are unable to comprehend what is occurring or why; even less are they able to control them. Nor are those attempting to manage some aspect of the crisis at a distance necessarily able to think creatively or reasonably. As the flow of events accelerates, the participants—at whatever level and in whatever location—are forced into reactive measures despite lacking useful knowledge of circumstances and sufficient time to engage in any real planning. Events come to control participants, and not vice versa. In times of rapidly unfolding crisis, intelligence services cannot learn of the participants' plans if those individuals themselves haven't formulated plans. With respect to events in Iran in the last half of 1978 and early 1979, there was probably at least as much "unknowable" information as there was "real" information to acquire and analyze. DCI Turner, in noting that other nations' intelligence services were likewise inaccurate in their analyses of Iranian events, also asserted that "even Khomeini" was in the dark about how and in what direction events were moving.[35] In this the admiral was dead right. And so it was likewise impossible for the intelligence community to ascertain with any clarity the future intentions of the radicals.

Two obstacles to a complete understanding of events in Iran were the partial isolation of the NSC staff from the other agencies, including State and the intelligence community, and the national security adviser's conflicts with the secretary of state and the State Department as an institution. Despite the NSC's lack of an Iran specialist—or any knowledgeable group of specialists working on the problem, for that matter—Brzezinski and others on the NSC staff in some cases deliberately reduced their contact with the career experts at State and CIA. In other instances the NSC staff found their efforts to work with outside analysts stymied by the analysts' parent agencies. For example, Brzezinski was predisposed to ignore State reports in part because he believed that State as an institution did not like the shah or the nature of the shah's regime, and therefore produced skewed and unreliable reports.[36] In late fall 1978, State detailed three Foreign Service officers who had served in Iran and who spoke Farsi to travel around Iran and take the pulse of the country. The report they submitted on their return concluded that the shah and his regime were facing a serious challenge. But Brzezinski, in David Newsom's recollection, "saw this as one more State Department effort to undermine U.S. policy and paid little attention to the survey."[37]

In a no doubt well-intentioned move, but one that further confused the drama and actors, in the fall of 1978 the president "casually" told the shah's ambassador in Washington, Ardishir Zahedi, to "keep in touch . . . through Zbig." With the shah in an increasing state of indecision and confusion over what to do, the president desired another window into the shah's thoughts and decisions. Brzezinski recalls that Zahedi later contacted him "three, maybe four times, by telephone. . . . [H]e gave me rather upbeat and not very credible accounts of the situation, and I would always mention the fact that he called either to the president or to Vance." This communications channel was only one-way, as Brzezinski "did not initiate or convey any messages to [Zahedi] or through him to the shah"; moreover, the Iranian's calls were "neither substantive nor secret."[38] But what Zahedi told the shah (who would then comment on the calls to Ambassador Sullivan) seems not to have been accurate accounts of his conversations with the president's adviser. And so the shah began to lose confidence in the administration: he simply didn't know what or whom to believe.[39]

Brzezinski identifies another sort of "intelligence failure" as well, but this one resided inside the White House. There was, he believes, a "deeper intellectual misjudgment" concerning traditional historical concepts, the effects of rapidly modernizing Iran and the instability inherent therein, and the need to retain religious beliefs as the society was being transformed. In the end, the United States "could not and did not provide effective remedies."[40] Iran in the late 1970s must surely rate as one of the most difficult of all political intelligence challenges of the century.

There was one vital piece of information that no American in Washington or Tehran knew, information that manifestly would have forced a change in U.S. policies as soon as it reached policymakers. The shah had been suffering from cancer of the lymphatic system since 1973, but he had kept it an absolute secret even from his immediate family. Although he saw or talked with Ambassador Richard Helms frequently, the shah always insisted to Helms that his health was fine. Helms believes that his health was the only thing the shah ever lied to him about and confirms that had the cancer become known to the U.S. government, U.S. policies regarding Iran would certainly have changed.[41]

In 1980, a CIA analysis reviewing the U.S. intelligence community's failure to predict the fall of the shah's regime discerned that one reason for this shortcoming was an "insufficient appreciation of the political power of the . . . Shiite movement."[42] But the text also notes that many observers in Washington had expected the shah to exercise "forceful leadership" to save his regime and were baffled by his failure to do so. Knowledge of the shah's potentially fatal disease might have led them to view the shah's feverish attempts to modernize Iran as a response to his mortality and an effort to achieve his dreams for Iran and, ultimately, pass the leadership of a stable and modern nation to his son. The CIA report points to the possible nexus between the shah's illness being diagnosed in 1973 and the shah, in that same year, "initiating the spiraling increase in oil prices" that subsequently yielded the enormous revenues essential to the modernization of the nation.

The analysis recognizes in retrospect what skeptics had argued at the time: that the shah's "zeal" to transport a fourteenth-century country into the twentieth century in a decade was the proximate cause of the revolution. Among other difficulties, the report notes, this rapid move forward generated "major dislocations in the societal structure"; magnified the "discontent" of the lower and middle classes, whose expectations could not be met regardless of the rapidity of modernization; undermined the shah's control of "entrance into the [country's] elite"; created the "conspicuous consumption of the newly affluent [which] in combination with massive social dislocation provided the ideal climate" for revolution; and allowed the shah's "grandiosity to expand exponentially" and his dreams of "future power and magnificence" for Iran to attain "heroic proportions."

The report speculates that by 1978 the shah, realizing that he would be unable to accomplish his goals in the short time left to him, became mordantly depressed and "disfunctional in his decision making." It concludes by stating the obvious: had the U.S. government had prior knowledge of the shah's illness, policymakers' judgments "probably would have been quite different. . . . Serious doubts would likely have replaced the guarded optimism" many in Washington held. And yet . . .

And yet, those who had studied the shah since the early 1950s and were familiar with his behavior in crises were well aware of his inability to act decisively. With this pattern of past behavior, the question screams out: Disregarding for a moment the shah's illness (of which they had no knowledge), shouldn't policymakers in the Carter years have questioned the depth of his determination and steadfastness? What evidence, other than wishful thinking, could have so convinced the administration that the shah was fully capable of acting to retain his regime that they ignored his past history? The question remains unanswered.

CHAPTER 8

END OF A REGIME

From the time of Nixon's first administration, if not before, American policymakers did not seem to give much thought to whether the policies of the United States toward Iran and the foreign policies of the shah were appropriate for the welfare of the citizens of Iran. Thus it should not be surprising that the Westernization programs of the shah and his societal reforms were seen in Washington as measures to be lauded. That these programs might not ultimately be in the best interests of the general Iranian population was not considered.

America's responsibilities as leader of the free world required global considerations to supersede bilateral relationships with many nations, at the expense of local considerations. This policy particularly included Iran. With its lengthy border with the Soviet Union and the intelligence from the irreplaceable Tacksman sites serving a critical role in the SALT negotiations, Iran remained of geostrategic salience in the East-West confrontation. The retention of the shah, who could be counted on to continue serving the interests of the West vis-à-vis the Soviets, was paramount. While not blind to the corruption within the shah's regime, the U.S. government could press delicately and only at the margins on those issues that directly affected the Iranian people. Too much pressure might dilute the shah's pro-West posture or, worse, endanger his regime. The latter point was collaterally important. As former undersecretary of state David Newsom explains, if the United States "was not prepared to save the shah, what did this mean for other royal regimes to which the U.S. had committed itself?"[1]

Carter's national security adviser, Zbigniew Brzezinski, saw "two fundamental questions" for policymakers to resolve: (1) What were America's true national interests and what must be protected as a first priority? and (2) What could the United States do to maintain political stability in Iran?[2] He insisted that the United States should support the shah as strongly as possible, and for as long as possible, for at least three reasons. First, by dint of Brzezinski's natural focus on the Soviet Union, Iran's role in the Cold War equation was of indisputable import to him. In addition to the usual and continuing considerations, such as the Tacksman sites and SALT negotiations, current and potential Soviet misadventures in the region or against Iran proper were bothersome. As events unfolded, Soviet actions vis-à-vis the continuing crisis in Iran from the summer of 1978 through the fall of 1980 measurably justified this perspective.

Second, Brzezinski believed that the only way to ensure that Iran remained a dedicated American client state was to keep the shah on the throne (although a strong and strongly pro-West military government that could assume control in the absence of the shah would also be acceptable). And third, very much in line with Dave Newsom's thinking, Brzezinski believed that the United States had to support Iran because of the damage doing otherwise would effect on its relations with other client states or allies. Such states always "watch what happens when things go sour" in a similarly situated country, he noted. "Credibility and respect and honor are important in international affairs" and can be ignored or discounted only at some peril to other relationships. To Brzezinski, Iran in 1978 was an especially sensitive topic. It had been just fifteen years since the overthrow of Ngo Diem Dinh in Vietnam in a coup that, while not planned and carried out by the United States, was known in advance to American officials. If America was to "just dump" the shah, Brzezinski was certain that regional clients would take note and question America's commitment to them as well.[3] By October, Brzezinski and others in the White House who had been slow to give credence to the potential dangers to the shah had finally realized that he was in jeopardy. Which did not necessarily mean that the extinction of the shah's regime was inevitable. Brzezinski, still certain that the shah held the keys to his own survival and still certain that this regime was the best of the options, advocated encouraging the shah to take any action necessary to suppress the revolution. Brzezinski wasn't completely against any alteration in the Iranian governmental structure, for he did recognize the shah's weaknesses as a leader. If it was necessary or appropriate that the shah's authoritarian rule be replaced, however, order and control must first be restored. Once this was achieved, power could then be shifted from the shah to a more representative governing system.[4]

Arrayed against Brzezinski were most of the senior policymakers in the administration. The president was in many respects in both camps. He supported the shah and at various times informed him that the United States would stand behind him, come what may. Yet the president also was loathe to see the employment of force and did not want the shah to think that the United States had either "directed" him to use major force against the dissidents or would condone such use. The president, in Brzezinski's estimation, "wanted a crackdown but no bloodshed."[5] Brzezinski, on the other hand, felt that any concessions to the opposition would simply beget more opposition (which later proved to be the case). Only force could stop the revolution at this stage.[6] Complicating the understanding and decision-making processes in Washington was the fact that throughout much of the summer and fall of 1978 the shah himself had been at sea in terms of what he wanted to do and how to do it. In attempting to suppress the demonstrations he had tried to walk the almost indefinable line between an acceptable level of violence and excessive force. Too little force and the dissidents would simply gain confidence; too much force and not only would the dissidents be equally inspired, the opprobrium of the world would fall heavily on his shoulders. The shah also tried a government shake-up and dismissed some senior security officers, but nothing worked. By September the moderates were in disarray, the shah's supporters no longer had any organization they could energize to press their agenda, and the radicals were on the ascendancy. But now, rather than calling for a replacement of the regime with a constitutional government, more cries were heard for the establishment of an Islamic theocracy, even though the Iranian middle and upper classes still desired a return to the 1906 Constitution.[7]

Within the U.S. government a growing number of observers had come to the conclusion that, absent the application of a nearly overwhelming level of violence against the demonstrators, there wasn't much hope for the shah. For these people, the debates now centered on who and what was to replace the shah's regime rather than how to save it. And, too, by October 1978 the shah himself had realized that the continued utilization (or increase) of force would be counterproductive, as would be a military coup.[8] Instead of resorting to force the shah began to release political prisoners, by the hundreds, as the U.S. embassy had been urging him to do. But many of the newly released political dissidents joined the revolution, increasing the forces arrayed against him.[9]

Escalating strife and harangues by radical clerics contributed to an even greater cleavage of Iranian society. On the morning of 2 November,

President Carter received a cable from Bill Sullivan relating that the shah had asked him and the British ambassador for advice on how to deal with "the trend towards democracy and a more liberalized society." Another cable from Sullivan that same day reported that the labor situation, a "microcosm of the economic-political situation in Iran as a whole," was deteriorating rapidly and that the problems were spreading in "alarming proportions."[10]

Sullivan's communications convinced Brzezinski that Iran had now "reached the crisis stage and the matter required interagency attention under NSC control."[11] He convened a meeting of the Special Coordinating Committee (SCC). Finally, the administration was holding its first senior-level interagency policy discussion on Iranian internal politics, two years after President Carter was elected, almost a year after the beginning of demonstrations and rioting, and just three months before the shah's final departure from Iran.[12]

At first blush, the lack of senior-level policy meetings on Iran, after ten months of increasingly violent demonstrations and the shah's evident tentativeness in dealing with the unrest, may seem irresponsible. But as is sometimes the case in public policy, what seems on the surface to be a case of neglect proves reasonable and understandable on closer scrutiny. First, in the early days of the Carter administration, at least, no one expected problems from Iran. The country seemed stable and the shah appeared to be in control.[13] Second, the administration and foreign policy bureaucracies universally believed through much of 1978 that the shah would act decisively and prevail. Third (and often ignored by critics), Iran simply wasn't the administration's most immediate foreign policy consideration. During much of 1978 the attention of the president and his senior advisers was almost totally consumed by the SALT II negotiations with the Soviet Union, the Arab-Israeli talks culminating in the Camp David Accords, the normalization of relations with the People's Republic of China and the alteration of U.S. relations with Taiwan, and the Soviet-instigated coup in Afghanistan. As long as Iran didn't erupt, these issues laid stronger claim to the limited time of the president and his senior policymakers.

Sick highlights one other significant reason why policymakers focused on other issues until receiving the second, "alarming," cable from Sullivan: until that time the envoy's cables had expressed nothing but unalloyed optimism regarding the situation in Iran; there had been no sign that the dam was ready to break. Sullivan dutifully informed

Washington of each of the demonstrations or riots, each time suggesting that the shah was quite capable of coping. Nor had the envoy asked for instructions or directions in any of the earlier missives. The year-long string of upbeat cables from the ambassador in Tehran and the impression they gave that he had his house in order with regard to policy direction gave Washington neither reason nor inclination to intervene. Thus, Sullivan's communication of 2 November represented a momentous sea change; Washington responded by convening the SCC. For policymakers in Washington, 2 November 1978 was for all intents and purposes the first day of the Iranian crisis.[14]

The SCC discussed a number of options, each predicated on the shah's retention of power, for all present still had confidence in the shah's ability to handle the civil disturbances. There was no mention of an Iran without the shah and no one doubted that the shah would be able to hold on. After some spirited give-and-take, Carter sent Ambassador Sullivan a cable directing him to inform the shah of four points: (1) the administration recognized the need for "decisive action"; (2) the U.S. government was agreeable to either a civil or military government with the shah still the principal authority; (3) the United States hoped that the liberalization process would continue; and (4) the United States would support the shah in whatever measures he decided to take. The response also stated bluntly that the U.S. government was not telling the shah what to do.[15]

The next day Brzezinski telephoned the shah directly, on the president's instructions, to "buck him up." The call was made precisely because senior advisers knew that "the shah was personally weak" and thought the personal touch would strengthen the president's message.[16] Brzezinski expressed support "without any reservation whatsoever" and informed the shah that the White House was not "encouraging any particular solution." The shah then told Brzezinski that he understood that the U.S. government did not wish him to take "extreme measures"— which may well be the point the president had intended to make. With his reputation invested in his human rights policy, it is highly unlikely that Carter would have condoned bloodshed caused by troops firing into crowds of unarmed demonstrators.[17] (In his memoirs Carter says only that he did not want the shah to abdicate and expressed unconditional support for him.)[18] Brzezinski responded to the shah that the situation was critical and that additional political concessions would probably "produce a more explosive situation." Brzezinski intended to make it clear to the shah that the president and the United States stood behind him and "to encourage him to act forcefully before the situation got out of hand."[19] In the end, both the president's cabled message and Brzezinski's call were insufficient for the shah, who clearly wanted the United States to tell him directly what action to take, including whether or not to use significant force.[20] The reasoning behind the shah's behavior was clear to DCM Charlie Naas: "Part of this was his natural temerity and part was his belief that, if he took action without our approval, we might 'disown' him."[21] The contrast between Sullivan's optimism and the tone of Carter's cable was also a source of some confusion for the shah, who asked the ambassador if he was "familiar with the president's position."[22]

On 6 November the shah dissolved the civilian government and established a military government, although about half of the new ministers were civilians. The shah also directed that the level of violence employed against the demonstrators be reduced, "forbidding the troops to fire except into the air, no matter how badly abused or pressed." This demoralized the army, which constituted the shah's only remaining support base, but the military generally remained loyal to the shah until he left for his last exile.[23] The shah's prime minister told Bill Sullivan, "You must know this and you must tell it to your government. This country is lost because the king cannot make up his mind."[24]

The news split the Washington community. Secretary of State Vance, the State Department as an institution, and Vice President Walter Mondale pressed the president to promote some semblance of a democratic process in Iran regardless of how the chips fell. Brzezinski was "greatly relieved" by the shah's action and thought the reorganization a signal that the shah had "finally faced up to the crisis and was prepared to assert effective leadership." He argued that it was crucial to bolster the shah and take care to do nothing that might loosen the ground underneath him. And he still believed that the best solution would be a crackdown on the civil disturbances. Brzezinski believed throughout the crisis that he and the president should have made key decisions for the shah, including the decision to use the force required to quell the opposition, even though at least Brzezinski knew that doing so would also entail "bloody and uncertain" action.[25] Brzezinski was alone in this position: no one else in the administration wished to place the United States in a position in which it could be blamed for Iranian deaths.[26] The administration's inability to achieve unanimity in policy and the president's indecision were apparently undermined by circumstance: the president, secretary of state, and national security adviser were immersed in critical discussions with the leaders of Egypt and Israel attempting to reach a breakthrough for peace in the Middle East. Thus, a major policy issue (how to handle the deteriorating situation in Iran) with two camps strongly arguing antithetical positions was virtually disregarded at a critical juncture. There was no presidential decision.[27]

The evening of 8 November found Ambassador Bill Sullivan and DCM Charlie Naas in discussion with the generals who had just been appointed to ministerial posts in the shah's new military government. Charlie later acknowledged that the session left him and the ambassador "deeply depressed" and that, for the first time, both "concluded that the shah might very well not survive." The new ministers "showed that they had no concept of the political crisis surrounding them and, hence, no strategy to save the regime."[28] Sullivan thought that the "military government . . . represented the shah's last chance for survival. If it failed to restore law and order, and if it did not succeed in resuming the industrial production of the country," then the revolution's success was "inevitable." After the meeting the two diplomats sat down to draft a cable.[29]

The result was the arrival in Washington, on 9 November, of something akin to a Come-to-Jesus cable from Sullivan bearing the provocative title "Thinking the Unthinkable." Up to this point Sullivan and his DCM had consistently advocated supporting the shah, offering positive opinions on the strength of the shah and his regime. As late as 24 October the envoy had advised against accepting a State Department memo (which the president never saw) that suggested making contact with the dissidents—including the clerics—and opposing a military government. "Our destiny," Sullivan wrote, "is to work with the shah."[30] Sullivan's 9 November cable was thus a radical about-face.

The intent behind "Thinking the Unthinkable" was to stimulate an "urgent policy review."[31] Sullivan laid out arguments challenging the conventional wisdom regarding the shah's survival and what might follow in the near term. He detailed the changes in Iran and in the shah and explored different scenarios that might occur in the near future. Perhaps most important, Sullivan said that in his professional opinion the situation required the U.S. government to begin devising policies and plans for an Iran without the shah. The cable recommended reaching beyond the shah's camp to make contact with the moderate (nationalistic circles, for the most part) elements of the opposition and to think about Khomeini in a role as a "figurehead" in an Islamic state. Sullivan ended by requesting Washington's thoughts within forty-eight hours. He and Charlie Naas then sat back to await the collective wisdom of Washington's officialdom.[32] They waited in vain.

Although this document represented an unexpected—and disturbing—reversal of position by the ambassador and his highly knowledgeable number two, the cable had little impact in Washington. To be precise, it was mostly ignored. Those who were privy to it evinced different responses. Vance saw the ambassador's cable as an enlightened analysis of the actual situation from an astute on-scene observer that "brought home how far the political situation had disintegrated," and he noted how closely it corroborated the assessments of State's experts.[33] Brzezinski interpreted Sullivan's cable as simply one more sign of State's hostility toward the shah. Moreover, Brzezinski concluded that he was being "sandbagged" by the ambassador; after all, if Iran and the shah were rocketing to hell in a handbag, what took Sullivan so long to figure it out and inform Washington?[34] Brzezinski was also quick to note Sullivan's 180-degree reversal, from proclaiming a "destiny" to work with the shah to urging that the shah be allowed to abdicate and replaced with something akin to a coalition. In Brzezinski's view, a coalition was not the answer. "From that moment on," he felt, "the gut question for the shah was not that of reform but that of survival." It was up to the United States to "help the shah regain effective authority—and then to launch the needed reforms."

Carter, too, did not accept his ambassador's recommendations, despite Vance's support, possibly because he at least partially agreed with Brzezinski's evaluation of the cable. Instead, the president thought the best course of action would be to continue supporting the shah as a means to stabilize the situation. Interestingly, the president's memoirs do not mention this cable from his envoy. The cable did serve—at long last—to focus the attention of the administration's most senior policymakers on Iran, but only briefly. Sullivan had expected the cable to stimulate a serious interagency review at the highest policy levels and result in coherent policy guidance for him, and perhaps indirectly for the shah. Instead, he "drifted through the remainder of November," his cable unanswered.[35] Charlie Naas recalls that those waiting in the mission were "deeply disappointed by the absence of a reply."

But the lack of response to Sullivan's missive was neither a deliberate snub nor an unfortunate oversight. In fact, where Sullivan thought he had expressed alarm the State Department saw only moderate concern. Possibly the first official in Washington to find the cable in his in-box was Henry Precht at State's Office of Iranian Affairs. To Precht, the cable was just "the first, faint indication that the embassy was changing its analysis"; in terms of content he judged it "vague" and lacking "hard conclusions." Moreover, Precht notes that "it would have been impossible to devise a meaningful response," given the highly divided positions taken by various officials. Charlie Naas acknowledges that the cable's language and tone "could have been much more forceful," but the embassy personnel were "acutely aware" of the many leaks to the media on anything dealing with Iran. As something of a precaution the ambassador and his deputy used a "soft-shoe approach . . . to avoid immediate knee-jerk reactions." But it appears the language was too soft, for it did not reflect the requisite intensity to motivate action six thousand miles away. Nor did the ambassador send a follow-up cable when there was no immediate reply, as might be expected if one assumed that a significant missive had been misplaced in the bureaucratic maze. As Henry Precht points out, "when there is no follow-up Washington tends to move on. . . . [O]fficials do not think a message is important if no apparent importance is attached to it by its author."[36]

Brzezinski offers another reason why the cable was ignored. He was pressing for a more active role by the Iranian military, believing that they were sufficiently "disciplined, well organized, and powerful" to respond to a "strong display of leadership by the shah [which] would . . . have resulted in effective and relatively bloodless imposition of control over Iran." The problem with this position, which Brzezinski himself recognized, was that the shah was not able to provide that strong leadership.[37] One by-product of the "Unthinkable" cable was to emphasize the near total lack of understanding and communication between the White House and the mission in Tehran. For the president, it was a significant step down the road leading to loss of confidence in his ambassador. As November turned into December, the ambassador's cables and "ruminations" were increasingly out of line with the views of the president and his national security adviser. While Sullivan was perhaps reflecting the division within State over how to deal with the shah, his hedging and questioning also caused the White House to question whether he was presenting the president's positions to the shah. By January 1979 the president was "increasingly troubled" by Sullivan's failure to present an "accurate or balanced" account of events in Iran. Carter was particularly put out by Sullivan's continuing pressure, after 9 November, for the administration to make contact with Khomeini's entourage. When Carter later expressed his intention to relieve Sullivan of his position following receipt of a particularly impertinent missive, however, he was deterred by Vance, who pointed out that it was not a good idea to change envoys in the midst of a crisis.[38]

There are two sides to every story, of course. From the embassy's viewpoint, it was Washington, not Tehran, that was "heaping confusion upon confusion." Brzezinski's personal contacts with Zahedi and the shah, although known to and approved by the president, were most unwelcome in the Tehran mission. Sullivan and Naas viewed the communications as "behind-the-scenes dealings" and a "very disruptive activity" that "gravely muddied the waters."[39] As Washington and Tehran continued talking past each other, it was not surprising that hard feelings developed on both sides that inhibited useful, even civil, exchanges.

In the weeks that followed Sullivan's cable, the situation in Iran deteriorated dramatically, sharpening the contrasting positions of Vance and Brzezinski. The former looked for a political and peaceful solution, with or without the shah, while the latter sought either to retain the shah or to move to a hard-line, pro-American government via a military coup. The disagreement and dissension within the administration grew worse as the situation in Iran deteriorated.[40]

In late November Gary Sick drafted a cable that "represented the clearest and most direct effort to get the shah to do what needed to be done," but before it reached the palace the shah had asked a National Front lawyer named Shahpour Bakhtiar to be the prime minister of a moderate, democratic civilian government of uncertain (but doubtful) future.[41] This act convinced the White House that it was now in the best interests of the United States for the shah to depart.[42] So when, in the first days of January, the shah let it be known that he was leaving "on vacation," the administration was almost relieved. And unlike 1953, no one expected—or wanted—his return. Americans, too, were leaving: more than half of the fifty-four thousand who had resided in Iran a year before had already left; many more were packing.[43]

Bill Sullivan met with Bakhtiar, listened to him enumerate a set of goals that (in Sullivan's judgment) lacked any foundation in reality, and concluded that the Bakhtiar government was going to have a very short life. Charlie Naas remembers the Bakhtiar period as "surreal: Washington spokesmen kept saying that our policy was to support Bakhtiar 100 percent and we at the embassy kept reporting that he had no chance of surviving! It led to some hurt feelings on both sides."[44] Sullivan explained his reasons for believing that the Bakhtiar government could not survive in a cablegram to Washington, but the message received a cold welcome on its arrival; the response stated only that the U.S. position was to support Bakhtiar. Sullivan "wondered just how unrealistic the White House had become."[45] The White House was wondering the same about Sullivan.

By early January, Carter and all of his advisers realized that the shah's rule was over, but the president was frustrated by the embassy's inability to provide sufficient information on the Iranian military's thinking or plans.[46] After consulting with Secretary of Defense Hal Brown, the president directed Gen. Robert E. Huyser, the deputy commander in chief of the U.S. European Command, to make an urgent trip to Iran.[47] A secondary purpose for the Huyser mission would be to "assist the Iranian military in retaining their cohesion once the shah left."[48] Both Sullivan and Huyser's boss, NATO Supreme Commander Gen. Alexander Haig, thought it was an awful idea but lost the argument because Dutch Huyser was exceptionally familiar with the Iranian military and its leaders from previous assignments. Although his superiors in Washington were reluctant to give Huyser written orders, the general insisted: he was told to report back on the status of the military and to encourage the senior military officers to remain in the country and support a civilian constitutional government. But there was also ambiguous language in the orders that could be interpreted as allowing Huyser the latitude to give approval to the Iranian generals if they were leaning toward a coup. Huyser also understood those instructions to be implicit in the verbal briefing he received from Brzezinski.[49]

As 1979 arrived, Brzezinski continued to press for a military government to assume full power. In discussions with the president the evening of 3 January, Brzezinski argued that the United States was "not doing enough" to support the Iranian military and insisted that the U.S. position should be to "encourage the military to stage a coup." Carter disagreed, asserting that the "historical record" (i.e., 1953) would not accept another coup and, besides, there was no identifiable military leader who could assume the reins of power. Brzezinski responded that a leader did not have to be identified beforehand; once the United States gave "a clear signal" a leader "would emerge." For his part the president, although not wishing to see a coup, nonetheless had no desire to cut his ties with the shah and his military.

At the State Department, Secretary Vance and his subordinates continued to support a transition of power to almost any faction *but* the military. There was no attempt to resolve the differences at the highest level of the U.S. government, although the two positions were contradictory and beyond compromise. The president confided to his diary on 4 January that he had to direct his secretary of state "to take action to retain our relationship with the shah and the military—our only two ties to future sound relationships with Iran, since we [don't] know the form of government it might take if the military was eliminated as a major factor."[50]

Aware that he was mostly alone in his belief that a coup was the best, indeed the only, course of action to ensure a pro-U.S. government in Iran, Brzezinski was left to hope that the presence of General Huyser would, in itself, serve as the "signal" to the Iranian military officers.[51] It didn't. The manner by which the shah selected and retained senior military officers virtually ensured that no general officer would possess the requisite independence, courage, and leadership skills to step forward. In choosing his generals, the shah deliberately weeded out officers who were dynamic and inclined to take the initiative in a crisis, for he saw officers possessing those characteristics as potential threats to his regime; instead he preferred timid sycophants in the top positions. When strong military leadership was required, there was no one able to provide it.

Once Dutch Huyser was in Tehran, he began sending reports back to Washington regarding attitudes within the Iranian military leadership that contradicted the embassy's reports. As the month wore on, the president came to place more reliance in the general's reports than in his ambassador's. Of special significance were Huyser's reports in January that senior Iranian military officers were predisposed to leave with the shah, thus ensuring the collapse of the military and of the new government, and that the leadership had done little in the way of planning on how to support Bakhtiar.[52]

While General Huyser was talking with the military Ambassador Sullivan had on his own begun reaching out to the Khomeini camp in efforts to reach a modus vivendi much along the lines he had passively touched on in the "Unthinkable" cable. He did not inform Washington of what he was doing until the first week of January, when he raised the concept of establishing direct contact with Khomeini in general, noncommittal language. The president, on vacation in the Caribbean, agreed with Brze-zinski that Sullivan's proposal was of sufficient import to merit a fuller review in Washington and sent a cable to Sullivan advising him stand down in the meantime. Sullivan was not happy. By then he had "worked himself rather far out on a dangerous limb," operating in a Lone Ranger fashion and neglecting to keep the president and secretary of state apprised of a critical policy action.[53]

The ambassador had concocted his own policy initiative—a decision of such magnitude that it was fully a presidential prerogative—and commenced detailed implementation of it without the approval of any Washington authority. His scheme entailed liaison with the Khomeini forces and "included an agreement to send off the shah's top generals on the shah's plane"—and this when Washington insisted that a responsive, disciplined military was critical to the survival of the Bakhtiar government and maintenance of civil order. And he had not cleared a word of his plan with Washington. By the end of this episode, the remaining trust reposed in Sullivan by the White House and State had diminished considerably. The president's suspicion that Sullivan had not been a reliable conduit of U.S. policy was proved correct. Whether a fully fleshed-out proposal honestly and directly presented to the president by Sullivan would have gained approval is, of course, not known; nor is it certain that such a plan, if actually implemented, would have saved the Bakhtiar government and Iran from the Islamic radicals. But the manner in which Sullivan went about it ensured that "the plan never received the kind of serious examination that it deserved."[54]

On 16 January 1979 the shah left Iran for the last time. Khomeini, the anointed "spiritual leader" of the revolutionary movement, returned to Iran from France to a tumultuous greeting on 1 February. There followed a total breakdown in law, but not necessarily in order. Roving groups of self-appointed revolutionaries called "komitehs" armed themselves with automatic weapons "liberated" from military armories and began to enforce their ideas of Islamic law. They patrolled the streets and established roadblocks, on no authority but their own, arresting anyone whose actions they determined to be insufficiently "Islamic." They detained and abused anyone whose looks or actions they didn't care for, or even simply on whim. Komiteh members further took it on themselves to "confiscate" the possessions of those detained, and their actions soon became little more than highway robbery.

The Iranian workforce was almost completely on strike, the economy virtually at a halt. Iran Air ceased domestic service and threatened to halt international service, the Telecom Industry of Iran was barely functioning, government ministries were closed, and labor action was "increasingly politicized and anti-foreign."[55] The military collapsed within ten days of Khomeini's return. Bakhtiar resigned, and by 12 February a provisional government was forming with a secular prime minister, Mehdi Bazargan, at its head. The Iranian people, including members of the new government, were absolutely "astonished at the rapidity of the collapse": Bazargan told Charlie Naas that he was "very surprised—and hence unprepared—by the quickness of the collapse." That sense of amazement was almost certainly present in the White House as well, for the administration had believed very nearly to the end that the shah could and would survive.[56] Cyrus Vance summed it up aptly when he observed that U.S. policymakers had been "operating with too limited an understanding of Iranian political realities."[57]

CHAPTER 9

THE SHAH COMES TO THE UNITED STATES

In mid-October 1979 the Tehran station consisted of the chief of station (COS), an experienced case officer, an operations support assistant, and me. A third case officer, also with field experience, was due to arrive at month's end. With station operations chugging along in something approaching a normal routine, the COS and the senior case officer scheduled short home leave trips, the chief departing first. So it was that on 21 October the senior case officer was serving as the acting COS. When I came to work that Sunday morning, he shared a cable with me from CIA headquarters advising that President Carter had decided the previous day to admit the shah into the United States for life-saving medical treatment. I simply could not believe what I was reading. My verbal response was an expletive-laden, highly unflattering summation of the intellect, competence, and parental origins of Washington policymakers. It was absolutely the worst thing that could happen for the oh-so-slowly-improving U.S.-Iran relations; and it was the worst thing that could happen for us in the embassy, from a security perspective.[1] With U.S.-Iran relations still lacking stability, and with an intense and growing distrust of the United States permeating the new Iranian "revolutionary" government, President Carter—unbelievably, from our perspective—had decided to allow the shah to enter the United States.

When the shah left Iran on 16 January 1979, it was expected that he would quickly seek asylum in America, the nation that had been his strongest supporter and most stalwart friend. Even Khomeini had voiced no objection to the shah's seeking exile in the United States at this time.[2] But without consulting with the U.S. government the shah first made a one-week stopover in Cairo at the invitation of Egyptian president Anwar Sadat, and then flew on to the household of another monarch, King Hassan II of Morocco, for an indefinite stay. As February rolled in, the shah's invitation remained valid, but the shah preferred to remain as

Hassan's guest. But within just two weeks circumstances flip-flopped for the shah. If he had been loitering in the Near East hoping that there would be a reversal of fortunes in Iran that would result in an opportunity (or call) to return to the Peacock Throne, he was destined for disappointment. Chances were dimming that the PGOI would collapse; nor had Khomeini's support among the masses of Iranians waned. And in a case of rather poor timing for the unfortunate ex-monarch, King Hassan decided he had had sufficient time with the depressed and dispirited shah and asked his guest to leave. The shah sent word to Washington that he was now ready to accept the U.S. government's invitation.

The shah was informed that while the invitation was still officially open, complications had arisen. The takeover of the U.S. embassy in Tehran on St. Valentine's Day had some officials in Washington reconsidering the wisdom of hosting the shah, a potentially inflammatory act that would create a very real threat to American interests and the American officials and citizens still in Iran. The risk to American lives at that time was clear: U.S. intelligence personnel at one of the Tacksman sites had been taken captive only days earlier, and Ambassador Bill Sullivan was at that moment negotiating their release. The entry of the shah would no doubt unleash uncontrollable repercussions against these and other Americans in Iran. In the end, prudence dictated denying the shah's request. Brzezinski concurred, but with reluctance and "personal repugnance" at this insult to America's former friend.[3] Vance, despite his belief that the decision was the only wise one, described his recommendation to the president to deny entry to the shah as "one of the most distasteful I ever had to make."[4] The shah had no choice but to accept the news; he took up residence in the Bahamas on 30 March.

In the next months the Carter administration worked to construct at least a stable, if not immediately productive, relationship with the new revolutionary regime in Iran. As a practical matter, for the health of this relationship, the greater the American distance from the shah, the better, and vice versa. The shah's entry into the United States might unravel the little that had been achieved to date and would render impossible all that might be accomplished in the future. In April, as he grew increasingly discontent with life in the islands, the shah began to evince signs of bitterness, telling the world press that the Carter administration was responsible for his fall. Soon, a handful of powerful people inside and outside the government began to apply unrelenting pressure on the president to allow the shah into the United States. Particularly strident were National

Security Adviser Zbigniew Brzezinski, banking magnate David Rockefeller, former secretary of state Henry Kissinger, and esteemed elder statesman John J. McCloy. In their collective opinion, the admission of the
shah to the United States was "a matter of both principle and tactics."
Brzezinski "felt strongly that at stake were [America's] traditional commitment to asylum and our loyalty to a friend. To compromise those
principles would be to pay an extraordinarily high price not only in terms
of self-esteem but also in our standing among our allies."[5]

Decidedly unhappy in the Bahamas, where he had evolved into a
tourist attraction as he strolled the beaches, the shah again called on his
friend David Rockefeller to assist him in obtaining safe haven in the
United States. After a reassessment of the situation and of U.S. interests,
Carter made it known to the shah through an emissary that this was not
the time, an act that incensed Henry Kissinger.[6] Rockefeller and Kissinger
smoothed the path for the shah to move on to Mexico, where he alit on
10 June 1979.[7] By late July, although he was frustrated by the pressure
being applied on the shah's behalf, Carter still saw no particular benefit
in letting the shah into the United States: "I don't have any feelings that
the shah or we would be better off with him playing tennis several hours
a day in California instead of Acapulco, with Americans in Tehran being
killed or kidnapped," he confided to his diary.[8]

As summer neared its end, the question of the shah's residence-in-
exile faded into the background, although he did gain one more supporter: the vice president. On 25 July Secretary Vance cabled the recently
arrived chargé in Tehran, Bruce Laingen, asking for another assessment
of the PGOI's probable reaction to the shah's entry if he formally
renounced all claims to the Peacock Throne and agreed to eschew any
political activity in the United States. Laingen's reply reprised earlier
comments, citing again the potential harm to U.S. interests and peril to
the embassy staff. But he did hold out hope that the issue might be
resolved in favor of the shah after the current power struggle between the
secularists and the religious fundamentalists had been decided. Laingen
also suggested that formal abdication, which the fallen monarch had so
far refused to do, would "lessen risks to our own interests."[9] Things
seemed to be looking up. But then everything fell apart in October.

What precisely transpired during the next three weeks is uncertain, as the
memoirs of the principals conflict on both dates and details. Later investigative reporting and an interview with former president Carter yielded

additional, and additionally contradictory, details.[10] Put simply, the shah was allowed into the United States on "humanitarian" grounds. All of the president's advisers, including those who had earlier argued against the shah's admission, concurred in this decision. The only dissenter, and then just partially so, was the president himself, who asked his assembled group of advisers, "What are you going to advise me when the Iranians take our embassy hostage?" There was no response, no "Plan B."[11] Despite his obvious misgivings, however, the president also remarked that the shah was "welcome, as long as the medical treatment is needed."[12] The shah entered the United States on 22 October and was immediately admitted to New York University Hospital.

Although the admission of the shah for medical treatment seems a fairly straightforward event, unresolved issues, anomalies, and just plain curiosities linger. These points are worth at least highlighting, if not pursuing, because of the humiliating foreign policy debacle it triggered.[13] First, there is the issue of precisely what illness the shah was suffering from and, collaterally, whether the only place in the world he could be diagnosed or treated was the United States. Memos, statements, and interviews with those involved claim variously that the shah was "seriously" ill with an undiagnosed malady; the shah's health was deteriorating from unknown causes and he could be neither "diagnosed nor treated" in Mexico; the shah had been treated for cancer for most of the decade and was now "in critical condition"; and the shah was at "death's door." Carter himself gives two differing accounts of what he was originally told.[14]

Second, several earlier cables from the embassy in Tehran had explicitly limned serious and continuing dangers both to the mission and to Americans in Iran if the shah were to be admitted.[15] During a home visit in August, Bruce Laingen had advised in strong terms that the shah not be permitted into the United States until the relationship was more stable and the risk to the embassy staff reduced.[16] Once the shah's illness was known, Secretary Vance and his deputy, Warren Christopher, each individually recommended to the president that the embassy in Tehran should be queried anew, before any decision was made, about the Iranian government's reaction to the possibility of the shah's admission. The shah should be granted entry, they said, only if there were no "strongly negative" responses from the Iranian government. Carter initially seemed to agree with both, but then he directed Zbigniew

Brzezinski to admit the shah into the United States forthwith and merely to inform the embassy that it was about to happen.[17] The cable to Laingen made no mention of any "tentative" decision to admit the shah; nor did it say that a final decision on the shah's admission was contingent on a "satisfactory" assessment. And it requested no security assessment whatsoever.[18] (At this point Undersecretary of State Dave Newsom broke ranks with his two seniors, remaining adamant until the end that the United States should assist only in locating "alternate havens" and under no circumstances should admit the shah.)[19]

Third, when Carter gathered his advisers that morning to discuss the shah's entry, the director of central intelligence was absent, represented instead by his deputy, Frank Carlucci. As the discussion progressed, no one asked Carlucci either for an intelligence assessment of the possible repercussions in Iran or for his own opinion.[20] Why not?

Last, and perhaps most serious of all for us in the embassy, all but one of the principals involved have written that Laingen's response to Washington relaying the results of his meeting with Prime Minister Bazargan, Foreign Minister Ibrahim Yazdi, and Deputy Prime Minister Abbas Amir Entezam included a "guarantee" or "assurances" or "promises" that the Iranian government would protect the U.S. embassy and its staff.[21] In fact, however, the cable informed Washington that Laingen had requested protection for the embassy but said nothing at all with respect to the Iranians' response to this request. It simply went unanswered.[22] How so many officials in Washington managed to find such assurances or guarantees in the cable is, to say the least, baffling. The administration then apparently proceeded firm in its collective belief that in the event of any threat to or attack on the U.S. embassy, the Iranians would render all necessary aid forthwith.

One possible explanation for this misunderstanding, although a weak one, is that the absence of a clear warning from the Iranians was sufficient for policymakers to *assume* that the Iranian government would take appropriate measures to protect the embassy. Or perhaps senior officials believed that because the Iranians—and Yazdi personally—had intervened back in February to protect the embassy, they would do so again. And there is yet another possibility: whatever Laingen reported back to Washington simply didn't matter. Both Laingen and Henry Precht understood that the decision to admit the shah had already been made and had concluded that their reports would not affect the president's decision.[23]

One could also ask why the embassy wasn't evacuated before the shah landed in New York. Gary Sick offers one plausible reason: the administration expected the embassy's security measures, including the previous hardening of the chancery, to provide sufficient protection in case of an attack until assistance arrived. No one foresaw that a national government would support, abet, and condone the capture of another nation's embassy and its diplomatically protected staff. Sick believes further that it was a "fundamental mistake . . . to place an unrealistic degree of confidence in the 'moderates' who were nominally in charge" of the PGOI. In fact, the evacuation of the mission was "scarcely discussed at all" in either Washington or Iran. Apparently the principals in Washington placed stock in the mythical assurance of protection and were confident of the "dedication and professionalism" of the embassy staff.[24] This last point is precisely why it was Washington's responsibility to order the evacuation rather than expecting the embassy staff to make that decision. While those us in Tehran could have, at any time between 30 October and 4 November 1979, left Iran for a safe location, it was unrealistic to expect us to willingly desert our posts and unfair to put that burden on us. We were all volunteers, and volunteers are logically the last to concede that their place is elsewhere. And too, most of us volunteered at least in part because we believed that our presence mattered. It was Washington's ultimate responsibility to recognize this and to decide when our presence was counterproductive. But it is also understandable, perhaps, that Washington would place the same faith in us that we had in ourselves.

Whether or not to admit the shah was a dilemma that presented Carter with no good options and no chance of emerging politically unscathed regardless of his decision. He was well aware of the dangers involved, both for the nation and for the Americans in Tehran. His refusal would have generated vociferous political and personal criticism from Rockefeller, Kissinger, and the Republican party and would have been most unwise in an election year. The president's query at that Friday morning meeting about what his advisers would say when Americans were taken hostage in Iran was a rhetorical question. When a real answer was called for, the team came up short.

Part Two

A GUEST OF IRANIAN MILITANTS

Life's like a tea bag. You don't know how strong you are until you're put into hot water and squeezed.

L. Bruce Laingen

CHAPTER 10

4 NOVEMBER 1979

Tehran

Sunday was the first day of the embassy's workweek, for in Muslim countries the "weekend" consists of Friday—Islam's holy day—and Saturday. Of some small significance, this Sunday, 4 November, followed the conclusion of the annual hajj to the holy city of Mecca and was just prior to the Islamic month of Muharram, a commemoration of martyrdom for Shia Muslims. As politics and religion tended to be closely related in revolutionary Iran, we in the embassy might have been a bit more vigilant given that the shah had arrived in New York only two weeks earlier. But I had not the slightest clue about these Islamic markers at the time, and even if this fact had been mentioned to me I probably would have paid no attention; I didn't know enough about Iran and Islam for them to make any sense. Also significant in retrospect was the reopening the month before of Iran's universities, the casks in which political frustration fermented. But I was focused on other things, and, I suspect, so were most of my colleagues.

Iranian students were frustrated, having assessed the Bazargan government as failing "to deliver on the promises of the revolution" and "powerless to defy the self-appointed revolutionary committees [komitehs]" that were taking law enforcement into their own hands. Bazargan himself had carped that his administration was a "knife without a blade."[1] But it wasn't just the komitehs that were challenging the authority of the PGOI; the students themselves were contributing to the government's weakness through their actions: recently, student groups in Tehran had taken to walking into the city's hotels and appropriating them for use as dormitories. Bazargan, faced with defending the interests of the hotel owners against the student revolutionaries, who claimed to be "acting against capitalism and imperialism," was caught in the middle. He did nothing, reinforcing the general impression that the government was impotent.

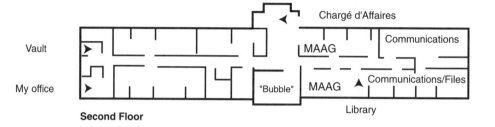

Vault

My office

Second Floor

Chargé d'Affaires

Communications

MAAG

"Bubble"

MAAG

Communications/Files

Library

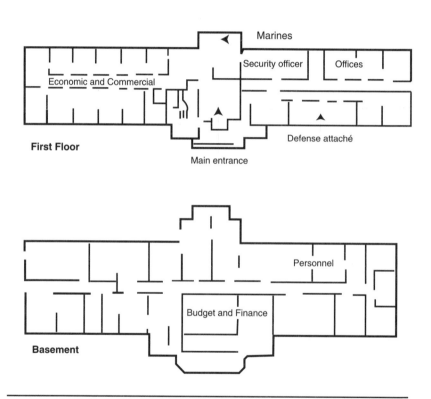

Marines

Security officer

Offices

Economic and Commercial

Defense attaché

First Floor

Main entrance

Personnel

Budget and Finance

Basement

Map 2. The Chancery

The fundamentalists and clerics had focused on another issue: Americans. Americans were still in Iran, still maintaining an embassy, and still, in the clerics' eyes, no doubt trying to influence the PGOI in ways that were inimical to their revolution.

All of these elements combined to brew up a volatile potion that reached its peak potency in November. As I saw it, however, and as many of my colleagues did as well, the real problem was the admission of the shah into the United States. These other aspects were too esoteric, too arcane, for most of us to comprehend. But we did see all too well the danger we faced now that the shah was in the United States.

On this particular Sunday I was in the office by 7:30 A.M. The COS had returned near the end of October and the senior case officer had departed the following day for home leave. At the very end of October the third case officer had arrived. Thus, Tehran station on this sunny, warm autumn Sunday was staffed by the COS, one field-experienced case officer new to Iran, one very junior and inexperienced case officer, and the station's operations support assistant (OSA). We were all in our offices ready to begin the week's work. At about 8:45 I heard the first stirrings of a crowd gathering in front of the embassy for one of the frequent protests, mostly smallish and nonviolent, that had been occurring recently. As we were anticipating huge demonstrations against the shah's entry into the United States, a seemingly minor event like this was unremarkable. Absorbed in work, I was unaware of the exact time when I realized that the crowd noise was becoming louder and closer, but it had to have been about 9:30. I knew it was a different situation when I heard someone in the center hall call out that "they" were over the fence and inside the compound. I looked out the window and saw youngish-looking Iranians swarming about the grounds surrounding the chancery.

The embassy sat on a twenty-seven-acre compound surrounded by a high brick wall. The dominant structure was the chancery, a long, slender, rectangular building of three floors: basement, ground, and top (see maps 2 and 3). On each floor a center corridor ran the length of the high-ceilinged brick building. The chancery had been "hardened" against attacks by welding bars over the tall floor-to-ceiling windows and adding sand-filled bullet traps on the bottom half. The basement was home to the administrative spaces—personnel, mailroom, budget and finance, etc. The ground floor held the economic section (west side) and the defense attaché's offices (east side).

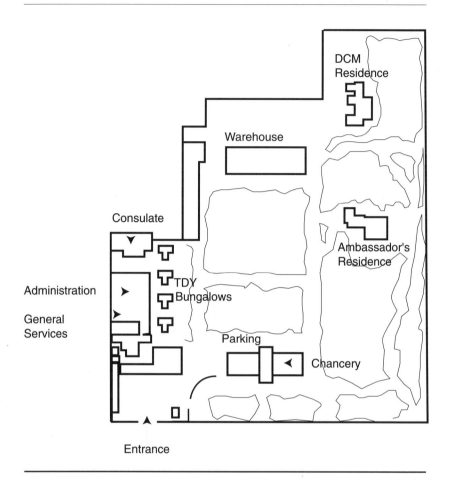

Map 3. The American Embassy Compound

The top-floor offices overlooked either the front lawn or the rear parking lot and, beyond, the athletic field. All but the end suites were entered by doors opening into the corridor. The east end of the corridor terminated at the communications vaults, with entry gained through a cipher-locked door. At the building's center, on the front (south) side of the building, the circular grand staircase rose from an imposing double-door main entrance. The ambassadorial suite lay opposite the stairway on the north (back) side of the building and consisted of an outer secretarial office and the offices of the ambassador and deputy chief of mission. Chargé Bruce Laingen was installed in the ambassadorial office.

At the chancery's west end, the top-floor corridor dead-ended with doors on the left and right opening not into the last offices but rather into the next-to-last ones. The last right-hand door on the north (back) side gave way to the political section. The last door on the left, on the south (front) side of the building, was the entry to the CIA station area. Someone entering from the corridor stepped directly into the OSA's office; facing the windows, the COS's office was to the left, while to the right was the office I had been temporarily assigned. Although the COS's office had its own door to the corridor, it was kept closed and locked. The only entry into my office was via the OSA's. My office had no corridor door. What it did have was a large vault that could be entered only from my office.

The security drill required that in an attack on the embassy, all Americans and local employees in the chancery were to move up to the top floor. There, we were to be protected by a heavy-gauge steel door that blocked entry to the floor from the grand staircase. The door, paneled so that it appeared to be solid wood, was touted as virtually impossible to breach. Thus protected, we were to sit tight and await the arrival of the Iranian police or military—the protection Bruce Laingen and Henry Precht had requested but the Iranians had been unwilling or unable to commit to supply.

With the lower two floors vacated, the top-floor hallway was now full of local employees. Most of the Americans stayed in or near our offices, looking out the windows to gauge what was transpiring. From the political counselor's office at the west end of the chancery we could see embassy staffers who worked in the other buildings on the compound (administrative offices, a warehouse, and four bungalows used by TDY visitors) being marched across the compound toward the ambassador's residence. They were blindfolded and their hands were tied behind their backs. At about 10:30 the Iranians broke into the chancery.

The intruders gained entry by breaching the barred windows in the basement. In moving to the sanctuary of the top floor, the embassy staff had to abandon sensitive files in the defense attaché's office and the economic section, as well as the personnel files that would allow the Iranians to determine who was assigned to the embassy, what our jobs were, and where we lived. All of this occurred without any resistance. Around this time, a tear gas canister was accidentally set off in the area of the central staircase, adding to the confusion and clamor.

When the Iranians entered the compound, the station chief had initiated destruction of the station's files, particularly the sensitive materials in the communications vault. After the Iranians gained the chancery, I returned to the vault in my office, where the OSA was removing what few files we had from our four safes. We began to destroy the materials in the vault while, at the opposite end of the building, the COS continued to supervise the destruction of the highly sensitive cryptographic keys and other materials.

Since early summer, when things began returning to normal, the station had moved from a "read-and-burn" basis, during which no cables or other materials were retained, to a "three-month-retain" status allowing us to maintain skeleton files of essential information for ninety days. An additional proviso was that the materials we did retain were limited to the amount that could be destroyed within thirty minutes. The station vault was a room about twelve feet by twelve feet with a door that would not have looked out of place at Fort Knox. In the vault was a barrel-shaped device about twice the size of a home furnace that was used for destroying classified material by shredding and then incinerating it. It was slow to work and temperamental in nature, subject to jamming at the least provocation.

Ignoring the various sounds from the hallway as well as the mob's shouting outside the building, I began slowly dropping papers into the disintegrator. After digesting just a handful of documents, the temperamental device went *ka-chonk* and shut down. While I was trying, with some desperation, to make it work again, from nowhere that I could discern a small commercial paper shredder magically appeared (its origin still mystifies me). With this shredder we continued to destroy what we could. As we made progress, I noticed the growing pile of shredded paper accumulating on the floor. Rather than completely destroying each document, the machine cut the paper into strips about one-quarter-inch wide. Around noon, just as the last of the documents were going through the shredder (I fleetingly took a bit of satisfaction in thinking that headquarters would be pleased that we had met their "thirty-minute burn time," someone shouted into the vault that our time was up and we had to get out.

As I closed the vault door I was struck again by the sight of the large pile of shredded paper on the vault's floor. As the door swung shut, a placard stating that the vault was secure against forced intrusion for thirty minutes was evident, although in appearance the door looked like it could survive a nuclear warhead. I thought about tossing a match into the pile but reasoned—too optimistically, as it turned out—that the door would hold until the authorities arrived (as they surely would) and dispersed the mob.

I left the vault and made my way to the outer office of the ambassadorial suite. There was a lingering, acrid miasma of tear gas and burning wood—the Iranians were trying to set the steel door afire, not realizing the wood was only a veneer. In Laingen's outer office, political officer Ann Swift was on one phone to State's operations center while Chuck Scott, an army colonel who had replaced Gen. Phil Gast as head of the MAAG, was talking to Bruce Laingen on another. Bruce, in the company of Vic Tomseth, the political counselor, and one of our two security officers, had gone earlier that morning to the Ministry of Foreign Affairs (MFA) on a previously scheduled appointment with the director-general for political affairs. From what I could gather of the latter conversation, Bruce was urging us to hang on while officials at the ministry tried to arrange for security forces to come to our aid.

These two phone conversations carried on for another fifteen minutes or so while the Iranians outside the main door by the stairwell were yelling to us and to each other and trying to force the door. And then one loud American voice was heard over the din: "Open this door right now!" Someone standing close to the door yelled back that Bruce was on the phone and that our instructions were to hold our ground. To this the person on the other side of the door screamed back in a voice shrilled by fear and panic, "You tell Laingen I said to open the goddamn door NOW!"

Earlier that morning, after the embassy grounds had been overrun but before the Iranians entered the chancery itself, the second of our security officers had announced that he was going to go out and "reason" with the mob. Having by then seen a number of our colleagues in the outer buildings marched away bound and blindfolded, none of us who heard this boast had any doubt about what would happen next. No surprise, then, when a few minutes later we saw him, hands tied behind his back, being escorted to the embassy's front entrance by several Iranians. Now, that same security officer was standing outside the door claiming that the Iranians would shoot him if we did not open the door immediately. There was not a great deal of sympathy for him among our group; nor did anyone jump right up and demand that the door be opened to save our defenseless colleague.

Chuck Scott relayed the situation over the phone to Laingen, listened for a moment, and then told us that we were to surrender. The door that would supposedly protect us for as long as it took to get help was to be opened after only three hours. The classified material in the political section and MAAG safes on the top floor, as well as much of that in Bruce's safe, whose destruction the security officer could—and arguably should —have been overseeing had he not chosen to walk out to certain capture, remained intact for the Iranians to recover. The total number of safe drawers holding material that should have been destroyed exceeded fifty. Just before the door opened and the Iranians began swarming about us, Bert Moore, the administrative counselor, looked at his watch and remarked, "Let the record show that the embassy surrendered at twelve-twenty."

I saw no fear on the face of any American at the surrender—after all, the Iranians were just kids and this had happened to the embassy before—but there was naturally an air of concern. There was also understandably intense anger on the part of the Marines who were with us. There is no Marine Corps doctrine or training that teaches Marines how or when to surrender; the word simply isn't in the Corps's lexicon. My brother recounts that when he served in Vietnam as an army officer in the predominantly Marine territory of I Corps, the only two words the Marines knew were *attack* and *kill.* Those words are a far cry from *surrender.* Now, in Tehran, it was agonizing to look at the faces of the Marines who were handing over their arms and allowing themselves to be bound. They had done their duty to the best of their abilities, and now it was their duty to surrender. And they hated it. They really hated it. But they did it. It was wrenching to watch, but I was immensely proud of the way they conducted themselves at this humiliating moment.

That evening, sitting in the easy chair in the residence, my heart pounded when the student with the .38 called my name and told me that there was someone waiting to talk to me in my office. I had not seen this happen to anyone else (although I later learned that several others had, in fact, been questioned about who did what in the mission), which made it even more frightening.

I was walked by an armed guard to the chancery and up the center stairway to the top floor, where I was handed over to another Iranian who escorted me to the station spaces, and then into my office with its impressive-looking vault. At that point it seemed rather obvious that nothing good was going to come from this. Still bound and blindfolded,

I was placed with surprising gentleness against the wall. I heard the escort leave, but, in the silence, sensed another presence. What every intelligence officer at one time or another thinks about and prays will never happen was about to happen to me: interrogation by an agent of a hostile service known for cruelty to those in its custody.

As I waited for the inevitable questions, I had one dominant thought: you are supposed to be an officer in the United States Foreign Service— so act like one! I envisioned how my Foreign Service colleagues would handle questioning. I was sure that none would simply stonewall, refusing to talk, for there would be no legitimate reason for them to do so. It is the nature as well as the work of diplomats to talk, to listen, to negotiate differences, and to reason. Diplomats do not engage in illegal activities in foreign lands, but they do share ideas with, and seek answers and information from, others living and working in their host country. For any Foreign Service officer to stand resolutely mute would be contrary to everything a Foreign Service officer is expected to do. To the extent that I could manage, I decided to engage the interrogator by making him explain and justify the actions of our captors.

Standing with my back to the wall, hands bound, blindfold in place, I waited, determined that I would not be the one to break the silence. The other person let a short but indeterminate amount of time pass and then began to speak. Ultimately, I remained standing for several hours while this first interrogation ran on and on. My interlocutor spoke good English in a deep but surprisingly soft voice that he never raised, despite his growing frustration with me as the minutes passed.

I was confused at first by the direction of the questioning, unsure what the Iranian was after. But after a few minutes that became clear. Because of my large office, executive-style furniture, and especially the vault, the interrogator assumed that I was a senior government official, someone who really mattered. In playing out this line, he even went so far as to postulate that I was the "real" head of the embassy, and Bruce Laingen merely a figurehead. As a GS-11 who had been in the CIA less than a year and was so green that I still got lost in the headquarters building, this construct initially left me speechless. How in the world, I wondered, had the Iranians come up with such an idiotic idea? As I laughed at this assertion, the Iranian began to lay it out.

This suspicion was fed by the Iranians' penchant for conspiracy and their pervasive belief that the CIA controlled at least the State Department, if not the entire U.S. government. As the first element of his "proof," the interrogator noted that Laingen had only a small, two-drawer safe in his office while I had an entire vault. Oops! So didn't I have many more "secret" responsibilities than did the chargé? To the Iranians, it made perfect sense to have the CIA secretly running the embassy in the country that they considered the most important in the Eastern Hemisphere, a country whose former monarch had been nothing more than the CIA's puppet. And how, the interrogator continued, could I be a junior officer when no other junior officer had such a large office or a "personal vault"? Besides, the "real" junior officers were all in their early to mid-twenties, and I was clearly six to eight years older. No, the interrogator said, they were sure I was much more important than I claimed. Why deny the obvious? Why not just tell them about all the spy operations I was running in their country? And, oh, yes, would I mind opening the vault, too?

It was a jolt to the heart when the interrogator suggested I come clean about my "spy operations." Were they guessing, based on their "proof," or did they already know? But how *could* they know? Hope, or possibly desperation, quickly convinced me that they simply could not know that I was CIA so soon into the event. I was wrong; they did know, even though only eight or nine hours had elapsed since we had surrendered. But at that moment it just didn't seem possible to me.

I began explaining why I really was just a junior officer: I had worked for the State Department for only three months, I told him; I had completed graduate studies in January 1979 and then worked for a civilian company before joining State. And I was only temporarily in that particular office because the embassy library down the hall was to be rearranged and I was to move into that space in about two weeks. I tried to explain why I could not possibly have the combination to the vault and why I really didn't know who did. I kept denying that I was anything other than a newly arrived junior officer, so eventually the Iranian decided to focus on the vault. I told him there was one man who would occasionally come in and open the vault, but I maintained that I did not know him, and anyway, he was now in the United States. Having recently arrived in Iran, I said, I did not know many people at the embassy, including this individual.

I held to this story consistently, which was no great struggle as so much of it was true. But the interrogator would not let the vault issue drop. It was evident that the vault would continue to be a problem for me until we were released or the Iranians opened it by force. I had little

hope that the Iranians would actually believe that I was completely ignorant of this vault, which, after all, could be entered only from my office.
During this interrogation session I was directly threatened only a few
times. It was a subtle sort of warning, quiet reminders of firing squads
and SAVAK torture rooms. Also, the interrogator occasionally would
work the action of a pistol and pull the trigger. I was still blindfolded,
but I could hear him playing with the weapon, so the sound of the
hammer falling never came so suddenly as to make me flinch.

I concentrated on staying outwardly calm, answering his questions in
as normal a tone of voice as I could muster. I emphasized that this interrogation was a breach of diplomatic practice and insisted that I be
immediately returned to my colleagues, and that we should all be
released forthwith. Every time he raised the idea that I was the true head
of the embassy, I would laugh and remark that it was a preposterous
idea. Surprisingly, the interrogator never became angry in return; he
would just repeat his "evidence" and continue. At that moment I simply
could not comprehend that the Iranians could actually believe something so farfetched. But it did not take long before I learned enough
about our captors' perspective to realize that they genuinely believed
things that were much more absurd. This realization began to sink in
when they started accusing me of being the head of all CIA operations in
the Middle East.

In more than one hundred hours of hostile interrogation, this particular man was the only interrogator I never saw. I believe that he may
have been trained in interrogation techniques. He exercised abundant
self-control and seemed at ease in this environment. That he was not
harsher may have been due to the Iranians themselves thinking that the
situation would soon be over, and thus that they did not need to press
hard for answers. Later, it would come out that the Iranians captured the
embassy initially intending to hold us captive only for as long as it took
the U.S. government to break off diplomatic relations. They meant to
cause a crisis in U.S.-Iran relations that would put a stop to the U.S.
"plot" to subvert their revolution and turn it in a direction acceptable to
the United States. The takeover was expected to last around four to ten
days, no more.[2] The ultimate length of the hostage crisis astonished all
the participants, Iranians and Americans alike. Having unlimited opportunity to conduct interrogations of embassy personnel was probably not
a factor they considered in their initial planning of the takeover. This
merits explanation.

In February 1979, to the chagrin of many Iranians, the Carter administration had elected to continue with a business-as-usual attitude following the St. Valentine's Day Open House rather than breaking off diplomatic relations. The administration was aware of the stakes involved in maintaining a relationship with Iran and decided that it was worth the effort and risk to continue. In the early summer of 1979, after a period of declining numbers, the U.S. embassy staff began to grow steadily while the secular-oriented government of Prime Minister Bazargan moved toward normalization of relations, to the intense distress of militant students. Student leaders on the campuses began to ponder how to stop this. Secondarily, many of the benefits that Khomeini and the revolutionaries had promised had not come to fruition (or even close), and the people's revolutionary fervor was beginning to weaken. So the students also sought ways to reignite the revolutionary spirit in the country. By midsummer these students began envisioning another takeover of the embassy as a means to accomplish these goals. This time, the militants would hold the embassy staff captive for as long as it took for the United States to sever the relationship and foreclose for all time any opportunity for U.S. interference in their revolution. And their claim that they were doing this for the people of Iran who had been oppressed by the shah and the United States would regenerate popular support for the fundamentalists.

Hovering in the background and adding to the urgency of the students' intentions was the specter of 1953 and the fear that America would subvert another Iranian government. Always suspicious of U.S. motives and sincerity, Iranians now were constantly looking for signs that the United States intended to repeat its actions of 1953. These "signs" appeared most notably with the admittance of the shah to the United States and in a well-intentioned but highly misunderstood meeting in Algiers between the U.S. national security adviser, Zbigniew Brzezinski, and Prime Minister Bazargan.[3] In October 1979 Bruce Laingen learned that both the United States and the PGOI planned to send delegations to the 1 November Algerian national day celebrations in Algiers. In response to a query from State, the chargé advised that a meeting between the prospective U.S. representative, Undersecretary of State David Newsom, and the Iranian delegation might be potentially useful. Henry Precht readily seconded the opinion. Laingen then raised the issue with the Iranians (i.e., Bazargan and Yazdi, who would also be attending) and found them willing. At some point, though, and unknown initially to Precht and others at State, President Carter substituted Brzezinski for Newsom. In Algiers, Bazargan discreetly invited Brzezinski to a private meeting to discuss issues of import to both countries. The meeting occurred in Bazargan's hotel suite, with Brzezinski's assistant, Bob Gates, serving as note taker. The atmosphere was "surprisingly friendly, under the circumstances," Gates recalls, with both parties seeking a better relationship and Brzezinski assuring the Iranians that the United States was "prepared to establish any relationship you want." Brzezinski emphasized anew to Bazargan and Yazdi that the U.S. government had accepted their revolution and that the two nations now needed to cooperate against their "common foe," the Soviet Union. He even left open the possibility of a limited resumption of some military weapons sales (which had been frozen in the wake of the shah's departure).[4]

For their part, Bazargan and Yazdi stressed that the admission of the shah to the United States had led the Iranians to believe that the United States was involved in some nefarious, covert effort to overthrow the Khomeini regime. Yazdi added that the shah's medical treatment was viewed in Iran as a cover to hide this plot. Bazargan suggested (as he had earlier to Laingen and Precht) that an Iranian doctor be permitted to examine the shah in New York, but Brzezinski repeated the administration's position that such was not possible. The Iranians returned time and again to their country's desire for the shah to be returned to stand trial on a number of serious charges related to his reign. Brzezinski held his ground, eloquently explaining America's long history as a place of refuge, and concluded by stating that returning the shah from his safe haven would not be compatible with America's "national honor." Despite the differences, however, the meeting concluded on a friendly note.[5]

The problem with this purely diplomatic meeting lay not in Algiers, Washington, or the Iranian foreign ministry; it resided instead in the minds of many tens of thousands of Iranian citizens. While the session was not in the literal sense "secret," it was held discreetly—which is normal and appropriate protocol in diplomacy—out of the public eye and without media coverage. When word of it filtered back to Tehran, as it did inevitably and quickly, the militant Radio Tehran began broadcasting accusatory "revelations." The announcers maintained that the meeting between the secular Bazargan and Yazdi (who were, as such, not sufficiently "Islamic") and the representative of the Great Satan and the hated Carter could have been only for evil purposes. The secularist Iranians were doubtless plotting with the duplicitous Americans to again initiate a coup that would reverse a popular Iranian government. This was the final straw, the call to action for the militants. The embassy was attacked just three days later while the prime minister and his foreign minister were on their way back from Algiers.

After what seemed like all night but was only a few hours, the interrogator left the room. I was moved by student guards into the OSA's office and my blindfold was removed. I found myself surrounded by a group of about a dozen Iranians, the oldest of whom could not have been more than twenty-two. I was not pleased to see several youths who looked as young as fifteen or sixteen (but were probably a couple of years older) waving Uzi assault weapons. The oldest looking, armed with a .38 revolver (this may have been the same guard who took me from the residence earlier), was also the leader. In good English and making a sweeping gesture about the room, he ordered me to open the vault. I replied that I could not and gave the same explanation that I had given to the interrogator.

We went back and forth on this for some time, with the atmosphere becoming increasingly hostile—the Iranians were growing angry and I was tired, frustrated, and just truly pissed off. The Iranian finally said, "All right, so you can't do it. Now tell me who used this office." I replied that it was "just a secretary," to minimize the OSA's importance to the Iranians, and added that I had never seen her go near the vault, much less open it—just as I had earlier told the interrogator numerous times. But this young Iranian looked right in my eyes and ordered the two youths standing beside him to "find the girl and bring her here." I had been afraid this might happen.

A number of things ran through my mind at that point. One determinant for me, in those days before "political correctness," was my belief that I was paid to take risks and extra responsibilities but that secretaries and OSAs were not. I had no idea what methods the Iranians might use with the OSA to get her to open the vault (which, of course, she was able to do), nor did I know what would happen to her afterward if she did open it. I was also aware that prospects for my immediate future would not be particularly brilliant if I now opened the vault after insisting vigorously for some hours that I could not. In all probability the Iranians would be much less inclined to believe anything I said in future interrogations, thus making it harder to protect what had to be protected. But that also assumed the Iranians believed what I had been telling them up to that point. If not, then I was already in deep trouble.

At the time I had no way of judging how effective my dissembling had been. (Months later, however, when I discovered that the Iranians had learned that I was CIA within a few hours of the embassy's surrender, I realized that what I said earlier had not really mattered.) When they asked for the OSA's name, I told them to leave the woman alone, that she could not open the vault. That had little effect, so then I said that because the guy who worked in the vault had left me the combination in case of emergency, I really could open it. And so I did.

As the door opened I could not keep from laughing at the Iranians' reactions to what they saw inside—or, rather, what they did not see. Up to that very moment they had believed that there were people hiding inside the vault. This notion was based on two factors. First, the staff members in the communications vault at the other end of the hallway were among the last to surrender, if not the last. So it was not necessarily illogical for the Iranians to assume there were people inside this vault as well. Second, and supporting the first factor, was a steady, very audible clicking noise coming from inside the vault, a sound like that of an electric typewriter. I had told the interrogator earlier that the sound was the alarm, which had not been set properly—which was exactly the case. He apparently wasn't much troubled by it. But given the earlier discovery of embassy staff in the communications vault, there was no way the Iranian standing in front of me now was going to believe that the vault was empty.

When the door swung open to reveal the worthless disintegrator, four safes with empty drawers open and extended, and a pile of shredded paper—but no humans—the Iranians who had crowded around the door gave classic movie-quality double takes. They passed dumbfounded looks to each other, at me, and at the emptiness of the vault, as though they had just witnessed Houdini escape. I laughed so hard I thought I'd never stop. All the while, the alarm box inside the vault was emitting its *click-clack*. And then the Iranians became angry—really angry. I was barraged with shouted questions: Who had been in the vault? What had happened to them? Who had shredded the paper? Where was the stuff from the safes? I just shrugged, still trying to stop laughing. I was led to the chair behind the OSA's desk and, to my great surprise, left to sit alone, unbound and without a blindfold.

While I was contemplating the possible consequences of setting the drapes on fire as a means to create confusion, a diversion, or whatever, the parade began. I was soon witness to a steady stream of Iranians— young students, older militants, a half-dozen clerics—sightseers who came to gaze into the vault, and at me. When this spectacle finally waned, and with no more "adults" around to supervise, the gang of young Iranians who had watched the opening of the vault and then vanished reappeared. They took right up where they had left off, yelling and waving Uzis, pistols, and one Marine Corps–issue riot gun. I was propelled out of the chair and shoved up against the wall by the door opening to the center corridor, next to another four-drawer safe. The Iranians now insisted that I open this safe, too. But this time I really didn't know the combination. Nor did anyone else in the station, for that matter. When I had first arrived, I asked the OSA about the safe and she told me that it was thought to be empty, but no one really knew because the combination had been lost. So it just stood in her office, serving as a stand for a houseplant.

The more I denied knowing the combination, the angrier the Iranians became, until I found myself looking down at the muzzle of an Uzi hovering about two inches away from my navel. And it was held by a kid who had probably never held such a weapon before in his life. The situation became even scarier when I noticed that the weapon's safety was off. With all the jostling and shoving, it was just a matter of time before someone knocked this kid's elbow and caused his trigger finger to tighten. I thought there was a good chance I could unintentionally end up with some extra belly buttons, each nine millimeters in diameter. And then, for some reason, all the commotion stopped. I was out of energy, patience, and adrenaline; and I was very tired.

The leader warned me that if I did not give them the combination to the safe, I would be shot at once. I couldn't think of anything to say, so I told him to go ahead and shoot because there was no way I could open the safe. I had no idea whether they actually would shoot me, but I frankly didn't even consider that. I just figured we'd end it one way or another. The Iranians, however, were nonplussed, and the apparent leader, after mulling this over for a moment, said that they were going to have to ask the secretary to open the safe. I said, "Fine." Then I was blindfolded, my hands rebound, and led back to the ambassador's residence. There, instead of a nice, comfy overstuffed chair, I was taken to the dining room and assigned a (very hard) wooden chair around the long table, joining about eight other captives. The Iranians dispensed with blindfolds and bindings that first night, and we slept on the floor under and around the table. The next morning, though, the vacation was over: we were again blindfolded, and this time we were tied to the chairs; as these dining table chairs did not have arms, the Iranians tied our hands to the back of the chair where it met the seat. And there we sat for two more days.

During the next two months the Iranians forcibly opened all the locked safes. The safe in the OSA's office was one of the last, finally drilled open just before Christmas; yet that first night they appeared to be so anxious to get into it that some of them were willing to kill me. Why this safe seemingly lost its priority status is beyond me. When it was finally forced open, it was indeed empty.

Our bewilderment as to why we remained captives was almost more bothersome than the physical discomfort. In the middle of the second day a helicopter landed and took off from the athletic field between the chancery and the warehouse, and our hopes rose that some outside mediator had arrived and that our release was imminent. It was inconceivable to us that we could be held for as long as we had already been held, and by nothing more than a rabble of unshaven (and in some cases unwashed) youths. I overheard my colleagues several times asking the Iranians when we were going to be freed. "When you give back shah," was the reply in fractured English. "When American people force 'the Carter' to give back shah, then you go home, not before." I knew that this was not something the U.S. government would even consider, and I began to wonder if the irresistible force had just met an immovable object.

The end of the day found sixty-six Americans (all government officials save for two visiting civilians who had the great misfortune to be in the wrong place at the wrong time) held captive in the U.S. embassy. In the days that followed, the State Department refused requests from the news media and others to provide an exact number or accounting of the Americans who were being held, or even those assigned to the mission. While it was not greatly popular with news organizations desperately seeking any scrap of information, there was one excellent reason for State's recalcitrance. Unknown to the Iranians, six diplomats had been able to evade the Iranians and had found sanctuary with a small group of intrepid Canadian diplomats led by the resourceful and courageous Kenneth Taylor, Ottawa's ambassador to Iran.

Of course, we in the embassy knew nothing about the militants' efforts to gain the support of the Iranian people and, more important, that of Khomeini for their actions. Without the clear consent of both, the embassy capture might end in the same manner as the previous take-over—with the militants' eviction within hours. The available evidence indicates that Khomeini was not made privy to the takeover plans in advance for fear that he would not agree. And indeed, on learning of the takeover his initial reaction was uncertainty. Within an hour, then, of consolidating their control over the embassy compound, the militants issued two public statements intended to preempt any move to halt the occupation.[6]

First, the students justified the takeover by citing recent statements issued by Khomeini urging students to "expand their attacks" on America and demanding the extradition of the shah to Iran. This student communiqué cleverly put Khomeini on the spot, for rejecting the embassy capture might have been interpreted as a rejection of his own words. Second, the students avowed that the takeover was done for the people, and hence the people must decide what should be done next—whether the diplomats would be held hostage against the shah's return and whether there would continue to be an American embassy in Tehran.[7] These ploys, in tandem with Ahmad Khomeini's positive report to his father that he should support the students, did the trick. They were the first of a progressive series of reasons (and manipulations by the students) that reinforced Khomeini's initial decision not to release the hostages.

Washington

It was about 3:00 A.M. in Washington when the embassy was assaulted, and Ann Swift's call was answered by the watch officer in the State Department's operations center. The watch officer notified Harold Saunders, assistant secretary of state for Near East and South Asian affairs (NEA); Sheldon Krys, NEA's executive director; and Henry Precht's Office of Iranian Affairs. Secretary of State Vance (just back from a trip to South Korea) was also alerted, as was the White House situation room.

Contact was also established between Washington and Bruce Laingen at the Iranian foreign ministry, where he, Vic Tomseth, and the security officer were now, for all intents and purposes, prisoners as well. Laingen was having no success finding anyone in the ministry who could—or would—help: Bazargan and Yazdi were either still en route to Tehran from Algiers or somewhere between Mehrabad Airport and home (or the office, or somewhere else); the minister of defense was in Kurdistan; and the Tehran police chief was supposedly supervising the forces attempting to maintain control at the local universities, where there were also demonstrations. Laingen could do no more than stay in the office of the acting foreign minister and listen to reports of events occurring outside.[8]

When Yazdi finally arrived (it was never certain whether his delayed arrival was unavoidable or instead a deliberate evasion), Laingen quickly and forcefully reminded him that he had proceeded to the U.S. embassy forthwith during the February takeover to resolve the problem and urged him now to do the same. The foreign minister, who expressed no regret at all over the situation, essentially replied, "I told you so." Yazdi limited himself to making a few phone calls, saying that, unlike the February incident, no lives were in danger this time. But perhaps the real reason for his reluctance was Yazdi's realization that he lacked the influence he had enjoyed seven months earlier.[9] When Yazdi asked him at the end of the day where he and his colleagues were going to go, Laingen angrily replied that it was for Yazdi to decide that, since they would be at risk on the streets; indeed, "students" were already at the entrances of the ministry waiting for the American officials to emerge. The three were shown to the ministry's diplomatic reception room, which became their residence until they joined the rest of us some fourteen months later in early January 1981.[10]

In Washington the president and others in the administration waited for the Iranian government to act, believing that Bazargan was working to keep the "firm pledge" he had previously given to Laingen and Precht. When, after a passage of hours, nothing happened, White House staff began attempting to contact anyone they could in the Iranian government and on the Revolutionary Council. Nothing worked. The next step was to began compiling a list of anyone—Iranian, American, or otherwise—who might possess any influence with anyone in the PGOI.[11] Meanwhile, Ahmad Khomeini had visited the embassy and pronounced that the people supported the actions of the militants who were throwing out the "occupiers" (i.e., the Americans). Up to then, the elder Khomeini's thoughts on the takeover had been unknown and there was hope that he would call it off. But when his son, serving as his personal emissary, praised the militants and proclaimed that the takeover was in the name of "the people," any possibility that Khomeini would condemn the action evaporated. This had been our only hope.

While many in Washington and elsewhere were still asking why the students had invaded the embassy, Gary Sick drafted a prescient memo for Zbigniew Brzezinski. The memo correctly recognized that internal Iranian politics were going to play a much bigger role in obtaining the release of the hostages than the shah's return, which, Sick maintained, was another issue Khomeini would exploit for his own political purposes. Sick's memo did contain two "flaws," which were actually errors in prognostication and were shared by the majority of those in Washington working on the crisis. First, Sick thought that once Khomeini's "political point" had been made he would release the captives, and, second, he believed that a menu of different pressures imposed by the United States on Iran would be sufficient to bring the PGOI to its senses.

The hostages for the most part also shared Sick's opinions. The "flaws" were imminently understandable in that no one, Washington policymaker, Iranian militant, hostage, or even Khomeini himself, had the slightest idea that the crisis would last for nearly fifteen months.[12] It was such a bizarre notion, particularly when balancing American economic and military power against Iran's anemic, deteriorating economy and a military that had virtually disintegrated, that no reasonable person would have given credence to the prospect of a lengthy crisis.

From Dave Newsom's perspective, most Washington policymakers appear to have been "blindsided" by their collective memory of the February embassy takeover, when Bazargan and Yazdi were able to gain the freedom of the embassy. Brzezinski's meeting with Bazargan in Algeria certainly did not help the U.S. position, however. Whether, without that event undermining his position in Tehran, Bazargan might have been able to repeat his February rescue is impossible to say.[13]

The author shortly before leaving for Vietnam at age 24. May 1972.

General view of the American embassy compound during the militant student takeover. The chancery is the main building, in the center foreground. Courtesy of Sayad/SIPA Press

Male hostage holders chant revolutionary slogans inside the compound of the U.S. embassy in Tehran, November 1979. Courtesy of Manoocher/SIPA Press

Iranian protesting was not just limited to males. Courtesy of Manoocher/SIPA Press

Iranians cheering during the embassy takeover.
Courtesy of Reza/SIPA Press

A black American U.S. Marine looks away during a press conference announcing the release of all women and African-American hostages at the U.S. embassy in Tehran, November 1979. Courtesy of Reza/SIPA Press

Anti-American propaganda was abundant. Courtesy of Reza/SIPA Press

The author meeting President Reagan. *From left:* political counselor Vic Tomseth, Col. Tom Schaeffer shaking Nancy Reagan's hand, Lt. Col. Dave Roeder,
the author, and Burt Moore. Courtesy of the White House

The author returning for his kiss from the First Lady. Malcolm Kalp stands to
the left of author; Jerry Plotkin is to the right of Nancy Reagan. Courtesy of the
White House

Motorcade proceeds down Pennsylvania Avenue during the homecoming celebration. Courtesy of the White House

CHAPTER 11

5 NOVEMBER 1979

Tehran

We remained bound and blindfolded in the residence, unaware of what had transpired and uncertain of what would follow. None of us could fathom any scenario other than an immediate release. Either the Iranians would come to their senses or the U.S. government would initiate forceful action. The idea that threescore U.S. diplomatic officials would remain as prisoners of a bunch of scruffy kids with body odor and crazy ideas about the shah was simply not within our range of vision. So, we waited.

Meanwhile, other Iranian students decided that one embassy wasn't enough and set about capturing the British embassy in Tehran. The public, apparently not sustaining the same degree of animosity for the Brits as they did the Americans, withheld their approval; the students were out by that evening.

Washington

Policymakers in the national security and foreign policy agencies in Washington were meeting all over town to develop options and responses, immediate and longer term, to this blatant violation of international law and diplomatic convention. The Special Coordinating Committee was convened in the White House under Brzezinski's chairmanship in the first of what was to become a daily session for the next six months. The committee reviewed what was known about events, which of course generated a corresponding list of what needed to be known, and responsibilities were assigned.[1] The first instinct among policymakers in any crisis is to attempt to contact the other side to defuse the immediate situation and to lay the foundation for negotiations. The

SCC quickly realized that direct communication must be established with Khomeini and, understanding the urgency of the situation, decided the fastest and most direct method would be to dispatch an emissary to personally represent the president and the United States. They also began to address one of the more obvious topics: military contingencies.[2]

CHAPTER 12

6 NOVEMBER 1979

Tehran

In the wake of Ahmad Khomeini's recommendation that his father ratify the militants' actions, Prime Minister Bazargan resigned and his government collapsed. Iran was now in the hands of a fundamentalist Islamic Revolutionary Council in thrall to an aged cleric whose ideas seemed to be drawn from the dark ages. During this, the third day, most of us were moved to the basement of the embassy warehouse (quickly dubbed the Mushroom Inn by its denizens for its lack of windows), and some were moved out of the embassy compound altogether and taken to houses in the Tehran suburbs. We were given toothbrushes and toothpaste and, before long, books. The steel floor covered with thin carpeting was only slightly better than nothing as a mattress, and we used our clothing as pillows. We had no news of anything and nothing to do but read and wait.

Student radicals elsewhere in Iran must have been feeling left out of the fun, for on this day groups attacked and took over Iraqi consulates in Kermanshah and Khoramshahr. The Iraqi government responded the way rational people (which apparently excluded these Iranian students) might have been expected to respond: Saddam Hussein ordered the takeover of Iranian consulates in Iraq. Khomeini, having seen a sufficient amount of student activism, ordered the seizures to stop.[1] Apparently, enough was enough.

Washington

The president met with his White House advisers for "crisis resolution" planning three times this day. Like the hostages in Tehran, no one present at these meetings envisioned the hostage problem evolving into a long-term "crisis management" exercise, although all realized that a quick solution was not likely, either.[2] At the day's beginning President

Carter gathered his most senior advisers in the Oval Office, next he chaired the SCC in the White House situation room, and then in late afternoon he met again with many of the same people in the Cabinet Room.[3] It was a full day, committed almost entirely to the nascent crisis.

In the Oval Office that morning, President Carter expressed concern for the safety of the hostages as well as other Americans still in Iran. The idea of issuing a public statement offering a stick-or-carrot solution to the Iranians was explored, but Carter was less than sanguine that this measure would have any effect. The militants had given no sign of interest in the carrot and showed no fear of the stick. The president realized that this episode meant the termination of any relationship with Iran for the foreseeable future. Not only were the two governments manifestly unable to work together, the principal reason for keeping Americans in Iran—as a deterrent to Soviet meddling—was no longer worth the effort. The president asked for opinions on the legality of expelling Iranian students in the United States and leaned strongly toward breaking off diplomatic relations, but he was met with thoughtful resistance. The meeting concluded at 8:30 with the secretary of defense and chairman of the Joint Chiefs discussing contingencies for the application of force.[4]

At the SCC meeting immediately afterward, the usual membership was augmented by the presence of Vice President Mondale, Attorney General Benjamin Civiletti, and Secretary of Energy Charles Duncan (previously number two at the Pentagon until the departure of the Department of Energy's first secretary, James Schlesinger). These men would serve as the primary crisis management team until the summer of 1980. Discussions at this meeting focused mostly on "domestic economic implications" from a possible cutoff of Iranian petroleum production and on potential changes in immigration policies for the large Iranian exile community in the United States.[5]

At 4:30 P.M., a deadly serious president convened the National Security Council in the Cabinet Room. Brzezinski laid out the military options: rescue attempt, retaliation if the hostages were killed, and a contingent military "reaction" in case Iran as a nation began to "disintegrate," with the first two contingencies receiving most of the attention.[6] The group thoroughly examined the idea of a rescue mission. Air Force general David C. Jones, chairman of the Joint Chiefs, provided a "pessimistic assessment" of the chances for any rescue in the near term, as the region's geography would make any such mission inherently complex. Compounding the planning difficulties was a paucity of the reliable intelligence essential to developing a viable operational scheme.[7] General Jones was directed by the president to initiate contingency rescue planning.[8] (At the Pentagon, the response was to establish a joint task force under Maj. Gen. James B. Vaught of the U.S. Army, who immediately set to work.)[9]

With respect to a "punitive" or "retaliatory" use of military force, Secretary of Defense Harold Brown and General Jones produced a list of potential targets with an analysis of, presumably, the risks, gains, and operational concerns for each. Considered in some detail were concepts involving the seizure of Iranian territory, perhaps an island in the Persian Gulf (Kharg Island, with its oil-shipment terminals was no doubt high on the list), and the interdiction of Iranian waterways or port facilities through the laying of minefields. Again, though, any assault and seizure of territory was viewed as unlikely to result in the release of the hostages and very likely to entail a long-term and costly naval and air battle in the Persian Gulf that would damage the interests of both the United States and its allies and the Gulf's oil-producing states. It might also unite the fragmented Iranian society and, possibly, drive the Iranians into the arms of the Soviets.[10]

Mining the harbors was a more attractive option: it could be accomplished quickly with little advance warning to the commanders; it would "impose very high economic costs" on an already suffering Iranian economy; it would cause no permanent damage and the devices could be removed quickly (or programmed to deactivate after a set period of time); it would not constitute a serious and continuing threat to civilians; and it would not place American lives in immediate jeopardy. Mining would certainly be preferable to a full naval blockade, an expensive and complex operation, but both would be manifest violations of international law and would constitute a casus belli—an act of war. The effects of mining or blockading would reach to allies and neutrals and have legal, moral, military, and political ramifications of unknown strength and duration. The policymakers were also worried about the effect mining would have on international oil prices and, again, the Soviets: if the Iranians turned to the USSR for help in minesweeping or other defense measures, the danger that the Soviets might become entrenched in Iran would increase. Nevertheless, the SCC viewed mining as a worthwhile option—it was limited in scope, relatively low in risk, and "afforded a degree of policy control that permitted it to be integrated into a political and diplomatic strategy."[11]

President Carter ordered that operational planning for retaliatory strikes proceed on a contingency basis, but the restrictions and limitations he placed on the planners left them looking at Mission Nearly Impossible.[12] While wanting any punitive strike to be "quick, incisive, [and] surgical," he also required that there be "no loss of American lives . . . minimal suffering of the Iranian people themselves," and "sure success."[13] The latter elements were requirements no military officer could guarantee and on which no president should insist.

The NSC established a framework of policy objectives and guidelines for determining what future actions would be appropriate and when these acts would or could be employed. The guidelines were meant to provide consistency and rationality to the crisis management process but were not to be accepted as carved in stone. According to Gary Sick, they included the following: (1) the actions should make the costs of holding the hostages greater than any present or potential benefit to Iran; (2) attempts to resolve the crisis through diplomacy, negotiations, and other nonviolent means would have to be exhausted before military force would be employed; (3) the previous policy notwithstanding, there would be an immediate and severe military response should the hostages be placed on trial or "physically harmed" (this latter condition was too vague to have much meaning since the hostages were already being physically harmed simply by being held captive, physically restrained, and psychologically abused); (4) military force, if employed, would be "reversible" in degree to preclude a potentially uncontrollable escalating spiral of violence; and (5) the United States would "make no threats it was unable or unwilling to carry out."[14]

This last point was a real problem for the administration. The Iranians viewed Carter with unmitigated contempt and repeatedly maintained that he was either helpless to do anything or that they had no fear of anything he might do. Yet, through the judicious use of credible intermediaries, the administration did finally convince the Iranian power center of America's determination to follow through on any threat. The Carter administration was finally beginning to be taken seriously by the Iranians.

The administration initiated a policy informally labeled "Two-Track" at these meetings. One track was intended to establish some measure of communication with Iran about the well-being and, one hoped, eventual release of the hostages; the second track devised and implemented methods by which the political and economic costs to Iran of holding the hostages would be increased over time. Contacts with a wide range of governments and individuals, overt and covert, from friendly organizations to the Palestine Liberation Organization to nations at odds with America on any number of issues were mobilized to assist in any manner possible.[15] Under no circumstances, however, would the United States return the shah to Iran. The CIA's Foreign Broadcast Information Service (FBIS) picked up a Radio Moscow broadcast stating that the actions of the student militants were "totally understandable" in light of the "disgusting behavior of the U.S. imperialists." Officials in Washington had to face the fact that the Iranian people had expressed their exuberant approbation of the takeover through massive demonstrations and that Khomeini had explicitly praised it from his pulpit. It was, a CIA report noted, now "virtually impossible for any group to act against the militants without his explicit order."[16]

CHAPTER 13

7 – 22 NOVEMBER 1979

Tehran

I spent two more days as a guest in the Mushroom Inn with about forty others, and then I was moved into one of the four TDY bungalows. For the next eight days I was rotated among the bungalows for no reason that I could discern. We were no longer blindfolded, but our hands were continually bound, usually by strips of cloth. On occasion, and just for the hell of it, the Iranians would come in with handcuffs and delight in using them. There was no reason for this, but it did underscore our defenselessness. While this bit of chickenshit harassment was frustrating, life was easier after one of the Marines showed me how to get out of them without the key.

During this time I was taken back up to my office for another interrogation similar to that of the first night. I was blindfolded, placed against a wall, and questioned by the same interrogator. I maintained my cover story, and this man, to my surprise, never pressed to disprove it although he was clearly skeptical. I was politely threatened with summary execution a couple of times, but I did not take it seriously because the interrogator was so casual about it that it sounded like a pro forma exercise.

What was truly frightening were the huge crowds that gathered almost nightly outside the embassy compound walls and were frequently driven to near-hysteria by the demagogic speakers. I think most of us feared that the mobs, whipped into a frenzy, would break into the compound and slaughter the lot of us.

On Saturday, 17 November, Khomeini made two significant announcements: Black Americans and women were to be released because they had already been sufficiently "oppressed" by American society; and any remaining Americans who were determined to be "spies" would be placed on trial before the Revolutionary Courts. Only the return of the shah, proclaimed the ayatollah, could prevent such trials.[1] In keeping with Khomeini's edict, three African Americans and one woman staff member were put on a plane to Germany the next day, and nine more followed on the twentieth. The Iranians now held fifty-three Americans, including one remaining African American and two women who were not released with the others.

On the night of 22 November I was taken back into the chancery and placed in the COS's former office, which was now vacant save for a desk, a chair, and a foam-rubber pallet on the floor. I would remain there until after the first of the year. The room, at the front of the chancery and over-looking the wide boulevard that ran before the compound, was sufficiently close to the street to make the collective roar of several hundred thousand demonstrators a frightening experience for the first several nights, and unsettling thereafter. Eventually I would become so angry and frustrated that I would dream of flying low in an F-4 down this broad expanse of concrete when it was jammed with a half-million screaming and chanting Iranians—and dropping canister after canister of napalm. It may sound mean-spirited, if not worse, twenty years later, but at the time there was no question in my mind that these fanatics deserved exactly that.

Khomeini's approval of the takeover began to manifest itself in overt logistical support of the students by agencies or elements of what was now, for all purposes, Khomeini's regime. The assistance eventually included the use of Revolutionary Guards to protect the embassy compound perimeter; use of the Guards to move the hostages around Tehran and, later, across Iran itself; and help from the public prosecutor's office and the administration of prisons to house the hostages in Evin and Khomiteh Prisons. The Ministry of National Guidance began issuing reports on the crisis to the world news media, including U.S. news outlets.[2] The hostage crisis was truly an act of government-sponsored terrorism.

The KGB-sponsored National Voice of Iran still spewed out virulent anti-Americanism and continued to do so throughout the crisis. It condemned the U.S. government for "massacre and slaughter in the Third World," labeled Brzezinski "this mad dog of imperialism and Zionism," and insisted that the U.S. government continued "to conspire against the Iranian revolution, against Iran's independence and freedom, against the leaders of the revolution, particularly against Imam Khomeini." The broadcasts targeted primarily the young militants, but their ultimate effects are unknown.[3]

Just before Thanksgiving the Soviet foreign minister issued a statement giving notice that the USSR held a "positive attitude" toward the Iranian revolution and cautioning against any "outside intervention" in Iran's internal affairs—a hypocritical position, to be sure, in view of contradictory actions both overt and covert already undertaken or planned by the USSR.[4] Throughout the crisis, while officially disapproving of the takeover, the Soviet Union continued efforts to insinuate itself into Iranian affairs and manipulate public opinion against the United States.[5]

Washington

In setting policies to deal with the crisis, President Carter's overarching objective was to "cause the leaders of Iran's revolution to decide that releasing the hostages was in their interest, but to do it in a way . . . Americans would see as honorable."[6] Unilateral U.S. sanctions began to fall into place on 9 November with a presidential order halting all shipments of military materials ordered by Iran, whether they had been paid for or not, followed by a similar edict banning the importation of Iranian oil on 12 November. On the morning of 14 November the president was awakened by a call from Secretary of the Treasury G. William Miller telling him that Iran was trying to withdraw its deposits from American banks. Just hours later the president signed an executive order freezing Iranian assets—some $12 billion—in U.S. banks, including overseas branches. He also that week issued a directive intended to make Iran pay an escalating price for retaining the hostages, including the deportation of any Iranian student (of the more than fifty thousand) in the United States whose visa was not in order.

At the 16 November SCC meeting task forces were established to deal with four discrete policy areas: oil issues, legal issues, economic issues, and "longer-range" political issues. A "political-military" group was also established, which, for purposes of security compartmentation, was much smaller in membership than the others. It was to oversee planning for military actions against Iran, everything from economic measures (e.g., mining Iranian ports to prevent the exportation of oil or destruction of oil production facilities) to retaliatory attacks to rescue attempts. The group's senior members included Secretary of Defense Hal Brown,

DCI Stan Turner, and Gen. David Jones, chairman of the Joint Chiefs. Brzezinski personally chaired this task force.

One unusual problem in managing this crisis was finding Iranians with sufficient authority to talk to and a method for talking to them. Without an embassy in Tehran and with no other representation, the normal diplomatic lines of communication were severed. The Iranians, on the other hand, had no wish to talk to the U.S. government for any reason, no wish to negotiate.[7] As the crisis wore on and the hostage issue turned into a power struggle with the moderates, the Iranian fundamentalists had even less reason to answer the phone.

Khomeini's pronouncement on the seventeenth that the "spies" in the embassy would be put on trial generated much concern in the White House, particularly because no one seemed to know whether Khomeini had declared that the hostages "could" be tried or "would" be tried. This ambiguity led to a scramble to locate the precise text of his speech. In fact, Khomeini had used both versions in different interviews.[8] This would not be the only time Khomeini would make contradictory claims or pronouncements, and it was just one more sign of the difficulty in finding someone in the Iranian ruling structure with the authority to speak for it.

A statement by the PGOI's new foreign minister (and soon to be successful presidential candidate), Abolhassan Bani-Sadr, was the subject of a debate in Washington on 16 November. Given to the press four days earlier, Bani-Sadr's note made three demands: "return of the shah's assets, an end to interference in Iran's affairs, and an apology for past U.S. 'crimes' against Iran." Policymakers discussing what to make of the pronouncement found themselves divided into two camps. Those who lacked prior experience with other cultures and nondemocratic regimes premised their ideas on the view that the authorities in Tehran, whoever they were and however disorganized, should be held responsible for the takeover.[9] This camp's set of options consisted of pressures to be inflicted on Iranian national interests through economic, political, and, possibly, military actions. In the opposite corner were career government officials and experienced appointees accustomed to dealing with other cultures. Their position, underpinned by three points, was that any solution to the crisis would have to allow the Iranians to save face and declare victory. First, the desirability of holding an outlaw regime accountable notwithstanding, it was important to realize that the Iranian revolution was still unfolding and no one as yet was firmly in power. Second—and exceptionally important to comprehend—the consolidation of political power was by far the most important priority for any Iranian leader or potential leader. Meeting international duties, developing the economy beyond a subsistence level, and other real or perceived responsibilities or needs were far down the list of things to be done. (Indeed, it soon became obvious that Khomeini was willing to permit his country to suffer enormously, even perhaps be destroyed, rather than give up his goal of an Islamic society.) Besides, they argued, Western concepts of law and morality were themselves "targets of the revolution." Finally, regardless of whatever traditional forms of pressure might be applied against Iran, U.S. policymakers would also have to come up with "actions that would play into the internal political dynamics of Iran in ways that might generate internal arguments for the release of the hostages."[10] There were no easy answers, and the administration found itself creating a menu of options, none of which seemed able to surmount Iranian fanaticism and the growing internal political conflict.

On 20 November the president made crystal clear to the Iranians the costs they would incur if the hostages were placed on trial. He issued a policy statement to the world press reiterating his preference for a peaceful solution but warning that military action would follow if trials took place. Placing teeth in this threat was the arrival on station in the Arabian Sea of the aircraft carrier USS *Midway* (CV-41) accompanied by its full battle group of warships. The commander in chief further ordered the deployment of a larger carrier, USS *Kittyhawk* (CVA-63), with its accompanying battle group to the same area. With *Kittyhawk's* arrival in the Arabian Sea the United States had assembled the largest naval force in the Indian Ocean since World War II; two carrier battle groups would remain on station off Iran for the duration of the crisis.[11]

CHAPTER 14

23 NOVEMBER – 31 DECEMBER 1979

Tehran

I passed the next five days adjusting to solitary, or near-solitary, confinement. There was a guard in my room whenever I was awake, and often while I was sleeping. I read books and tried to exercise, but mostly I waited for what seemed inevitable unless we were quickly freed. Time ran out on the evening of 29 November. That night, and for five more through 14 December, I was the guest of honor at meetings I would rather not have attended. Each session commenced after dinner and continued throughout the night until daybreak. A guard would escort me to the "bubble," the embassy's secure soundproof room, where there were always two and often three Iranians intent on learning everything they could about my activities in Tehran. The principal interrogator was Hossein Sheik-ol-Eslam, a mid-thirties, bearded Khomeini loyalist who had previously studied at the University of California–Berkeley, which was appropriate, I thought, given that institution's reputation.

I spent the first two interrogation sessions, and most of the third, in long recitations of my cover story and denials of any activity beyond normal diplomatic work. While frustrating and not a little frightening, these three sittings did give me a valuable opportunity to learn more about the students and their motives in taking the embassy. More important, they were an opportunity to gauge the expertise of Hossein and the two other Iranians as interrogators. In one sense, the confabulations were total-immersion lessons in the workings of the Iranian mind and the Iranian brand of revolutionary theory; and in a detached, academic sense, I was intrigued. I chafed mightily over the continuing confinement, even while in thrall of my own psychological denial that it was happening. But when I could mentally remove myself from the immediate circumstances, I often found the hours and hours of nonhostile discussions and conversations with the Iranians (interrogators and guards alike) interesting, occasionally useful, and not infrequently a source of true amazement. And, probably more than any other benefit, they killed time.

It soon became apparent that Hossein and his friends possessed no training or experience as interrogators, nor did they enjoy any comprehension of the subtle underlying psychological factors used by professional interrogators. While each of them claimed to have been arrested and interrogated by SAVAK at one time or another, serving as the subject of an interrogation is not the same as receiving instruction in how to interrogate. Their elementary efforts, then, mostly emulated the surroundings and trappings of their SAVAK interrogations (that is, times of day/night, room lighting, the good cop–bad cop routine, and so forth). With but a limited concept of what to do and no comprehension of the why of it, they were rendered ineffectual questioners for the most part. As such, Hossein and his cohorts often undermined any progress they might have made in inducing their prisoner to reveal what he wished to conceal. Their unwitting ineptitude also created openings that could be exploited to damage or deter their efforts.

I was able to withhold virtually all of the classified information they sought to learn. Their ineptitude also allowed me to seize control of the interrogations at times and manipulate or disrupt the proceedings. In these interruptions I could protest their uncivilized breach of international law and norms, express anger over our continuing captivity, and register complaints about my treatment. Occasions like these, while perhaps seemingly of little import, yielded valuable psychological victories when I most needed them; the boost to my morale from these episodes was essential to maintaining a positive attitude throughout the ordeal. One small item I hid from the Iranians was that, thanks to the U.S. Marine Corps, I knew more about interrogations and mental stamina than they did. And that was the real key to withstanding their efforts.

Without doubt, my eight years in the Marine Corps played a major role in my ability to endure, if not surmount, the intensive interrogation sessions and to survive captivity in general. Nor was I alone in this regard. Those in the embassy who were in the military or had previous military experience tolerated confinement, interrogation, and abuse—both physical and psychological—far better than those without military experience (with one or two notable exceptions). Just as significant, on our return to the United States, those who were military trained and experienced were in measurably better psychological and physical condition than most of the others in the mission. And this despite the fact that those actually serving in the military or with past military experience were, by dint of their positions in the mission, treated much worse by the Iranians than the others.

The Marine Corps experience was significant for both general and specific reasons. Life in the Marine Corps imparts self-discipline, self-sufficiency, physical stamina, psychological endurance, and intellectual resilience. Above all, every Marine is imbued with a strongly held sense of duty and loyalty to Corps and country, and a corresponding belief in his or her own abilities. What better traits to have or to be able to recover from deep within when confronted by hostile radicals who despise you, your country, and all it stands for? Marine Corps training programs and assignments to the Fleet Marine Force require Marines to deal frequently (if not almost continuously) with physical and mental stress, which again is a relentless presence in captivity, and especially in interrogation. And Marine Corps life at some point, whether through training missions, occupational specialty, or actual combat, exposes the Marine to life-and-death situations—his life and the lives of others. There was no better preparation for my assignment to Tehran than eight years in the Corps.

I had enlisted in the Marine Corps in 1966 at age eighteen, graduating with Platoon 392 from boot camp at Marine Corps Recruit Depot (MCRD) San Diego on 6 June 1966; I subsequently trained as an air traffic controller. While a crew supervisor at Marine Corps Air Station (MCAS) Iwakuni, Japan, I was selected for Officer Candidate School. Commissioned in the fall of 1969 with the Sixtieth Special Officer Candidate Course, I endured the mandatory five months of infantry training at the Basic School and then headed off to Pensacola with orders to flight school. A year later I received the gold wings of a Naval Flight Officer and orders to the F-4 Phantom II fighter/attack training squadron at MCAS Cherry Point, North Carolina, as a radar intercept officer (RIO).

Training and initial qualification flights in the F-4 were followed by a transfer to Marine Fighter/Attack Squadron (VMFA)-251 at MCAS Beaufort, South Carolina, and then transfer to VMFA-333, the only Marine Corps carrier-based F-4 squadron at that time. The squadron was originally headed for a Mediterranean cruise aboard the aircraft carrier USS *America* (CVA-66) when, shortly before deployment, our orders were changed to the Seventh Fleet and Southeast Asia. By the end of the cruise

I had flown seventy-six missions. About half were bombing runs over South Vietnam, with the remainder split between missions over or near North Vietnam (barrier combat air patrols, armed recce, reconnaissance escort, and a few alpha strikes) and strikes against the Ho Chi Minh Trail in Laos. On my return to the United States I attended the Naval Justice School at Newport, Rhode Island, and finished my active duty time as a squadron legal officer.

Of all my Marine Corps experiences, the most demanding was boot camp. I had attended a military school for secondary education and so I went to MCRD San Diego familiar with close-order drill, the manual of arms, how to spit-shine shoes, and the rigors of a military lifestyle—and boot camp was still a nightmare. OCS helped further develop mental toughness, a tolerance for stress, and confidence to handle the unknown. But it was the training as a Marine aviator that directly and specifically helped me survive captivity and resist interrogation. Earning the gold wings of a Naval Flight Officer (deficient eyesight kept me from entering the naval aviator pipeline for pilot training) required several periods of survival training, including instruction in the art of survival in captivity. First, there was a short introductory class in preflight at Pensacola Naval Air Station in the spring of 1970. Next came a longer training period at MCAS Cherry Point. Here, the newly designated aviators were introduced to the psychology of interrogation and methods for defeating hostile interrogation, and to specific techniques for surviving and resisting in a North Vietnamese prison camp. The course included one day in a mock POW compound, complete with interrogations and physical discomfort, mostly in the nature of several cold hours jammed into a metal box four feet long, three feet high, and three feet deep. All of this was, of course, helpful, but I learned the most important lessons of all while my F-4 squadron was in transit to Vietnam.

We embarked on USS *America* in Norfolk, sailing on 5 June 1972 for a thirty-day transit to the Subic Bay Naval Station in the Philippines. During the first week of the voyage the squadron was given training dedicated solely to survival in captivity. Our instructors were a former POW from the Korean War and a civilian named Douglas Hegdahl. I will never, ever, forget Doug Hegdahl.

Hegdahl was a former navy enlisted man who had been more or less blown overboard from his ship while in the Tonkin Gulf several years before through something akin to an unfortunate oversight. A shipmate had mentioned to him that the night firing of the cruiser's big guns was a sight to see; not wanting to miss this spectacle, Hegdahl positioned himself directly underneath the muzzle of one of the ship's 8-inch guns for the best possible view. The gun fired and the muzzle blast propelled him through the air and into the water. North Vietnamese fishermen picked him up and he was soon a resident at Hoa Lo Prison, the "Hanoi Hilton," where he eventually was a roommate of the heroic Lt. Comdr. Richard Stratton. Hegdahl was released after several years, as a propaganda ploy by the North Vietnamese. Although at first he didn't want to leave his comrades, they ordered him to go so that he could carry back information about those in the prison. He returned to the United States with more than four hundred names of American POWs memorized, including many that the enemy had never admitted having captured and which the U.S. government had declared either dead or missing in action.

Seven years later, now in captivity myself, I could recall Hegdahl's lectures with almost crystalline clarity. His comments, advice, examples, and stories, more than anything else, saw me through severe interrogations and helped me keep my sanity, dignity, and secrets intact. Thanks to Doug and the Marine Corps, I was well prepared for the Iranians.[1]

A second factor that helped me cope successfully with captivity was my education. After leaving the Corps in 1974, I lived the next five and a half years in the classroom, moving from second-semester freshman to Ph.D. in that time. I had been away from academia for less than a year when I was assigned to Tehran. With the newly acquired doctorate and the rigors of Agency training still fresh, my mind was sharper than it ever had been before; only the body was captive in solitary, as there were limitless intellectual nooks and crannies into which I could retreat and find stimulation, entertainment, comfort, and distance. Thus, mentally surviving 425 days of solitary confinement was in some ways not as difficult as it might have been.

In short, by the time I was taken captive I had lived through numerous stressful experiences, been shot at a few times (but never hit), and come close to serious injury or worse on several occasions. I had been in threatening situations and had surmounted physical and intellectual challenges. Bolstered by an active intellect developed at Claremont and informed by Marine Corps training, I could not have been better prepared to deal with the rigors, fears, and uncertainties of captivity. It was nothing that I had deliberately planned or trained for, but by exceptional good luck I had a background that allowed me to survive both mentally and physically.

Which is not to say that I was not in serious trouble. I was confronted by angry Iranians who were the declared enemies of my country, who were determined to make me do something I certainly did not want to do, and who—most worrisome of all—seemed to be operating without any oversight or limits on their actions. Through the mixture of fright and anger I was feeling, Hegdahl's lessons flooded my mind. I had decided earlier that if the Iranians learned my true affiliation I would be guided by two principles. First, I would do my utmost to protect classified materials, which included not just documents and information but also intelligence sources and methods. Second, I would do or say nothing that would or could bring harm to any of my colleagues. The exception to this second "rule" was that I would take advantage of any opportunity to escape, even though it might lead to retaliation against the others. Until my cover was exposed, however, I would continue to play the Foreign Service card. And that meant talking as much as I could with the interrogators. Adhering to the traditional military Code of Conduct requirement of "name, rank, and serial number" would only raise the suspicions of the Iranians. Moreover, the code was established for prisoners of war, which, it seemed to me, we were not: most of us were not in the military and none of us was engaged in a war—despite the Iranians' assertions to the contrary.

My decision was supported by lessons learned by POWs in Vietnam and by the frailty of the code's "name, rank, and serial number only" requirement. The most serious problem is that it presents a direct challenge to the interrogator, an attitude of defiance that no serious interrogator can ignore; to do otherwise would jeopardize his credibility and reduce his chances of obtaining information. Thus, when the prisoner remains mute, acquiring information becomes a secondary objective; the overriding objective is now to break the prisoner's will and capacity to defy. After 1967 the military reconsidered the Code of Conduct and began countenancing the same general measures that I relied on in captivity.

The most important objective for the prisoner is to resist. Resistance is critical for several reasons—the most important being to make it more difficult on the captors, to sustain morale, and to protect secrets—but as the prisoner considers how confrontational this resistance should be, he must also recognize that his captors hold absolute control over his health, his welfare, and his life. He must be always aware that the more direct and obvious the resistance, the more serious will be the consequences. For the most part the captive should resist without placing himself in a situation in which his captors will, through their coercive efforts, eventually deprive him of the physical or mental means to resist further. It is instructive to recall that the rule for members of the French Résistance in World War II, if captured by the Gestapo, was to hold out as long as possible to give their comrades time to locate a new hideout. When the captives could take no more, they could do what was necessary to save their lives, including confessing. That many of them never did so while suffering indescribable agony speaks volumes of their courage and hatred of their enemy. But it also led to arguably unnecessary suffering and, worse, to prisoners being completely broken.

The "breaking" process is both a physical and a psychological procedure that renders it mentally harder for the prisoner to resist and physically harder to escape should the opportunity present—or just to survive. The broken prisoner may well carry permanent psychological scars, an unmerited feeling that he is a coward or that he let down his country or comrades, even though he may have suffered horribly and endured the truly unendurable longer than anyone could have reasonably expected. And the physical abuse can be, and often is, such that full recovery (mental and/or physical) after release is not possible.

Prisoners faced with hostile interrogation are confronted with competing priorities: genuine secrets must be protected; the lives of fellow captives must be considered; there is a duty to resist to the limits of one's abilities; one's own health and well-being may be at risk. And there is always, for men and women of character, the necessity to conduct themselves in a manner that will not dishonor the organization and the country they serve, or bring shame upon themselves. It is up to the captives, and to them alone, to balance these competing requirements without failing at any.

There are as many different ways to resist and different tactics to deny cooperation as there are prisoners. Each captive, whether a hostage or a POW, must evaluate the circumstantial variables: the nature of the information he or she possesses, whether the captors wish to learn that information (in many terrorist hostage events, the captors actually don't care), the willingness of the captors to resort to increasingly crueler measures, and his or her physical ability to accept pain. Each of these factors will be different for each person and in each situation.

Regardless of how a captive is treated, the question is not "Should I resist?" It is, rather, "How can I most effectively resist without being self-destructive?" There is never an acceptable reason for refusing to resist, even in the most benign circumstances: why should hostages make it easy for terrorists, thugs, or criminals who have deprived them of their liberty to continue to do so? How subtle or confrontational the form of resistance takes is ultimately the judgment of the captive, but the determination to resist should never be absent. One key lesson Doug Hegdahl taught was that resistance does not have to be confrontational to be effective, and he buttressed this point with stories of his own experiences in the Hanoi Hilton. I recalled these examples and adopted them to my own circumstances. I owe Doug Hegdahl more than I can ever repay.

Some hours into the third interrogation session, on the night of 1–2 December, my carefully crafted story went up in smoke. As with the two previous sessions, I adhered to the cover story I had been spouting since the first night, careful neither to embellish nor to add to it, while seizing or creating opportunities to steer the interrogation anywhere but where the Iranians wanted it to go. The more time we spent talking about neutral or irrelevant subjects, the less time they had to talk about things I hoped to avoid. I had discovered earlier that asking questions about the Shia's brand of Islam, the Koran, the Iranian revolution, the embassy capture, why they continued to hold us, and what was happening in the world would often generate discussions or lectures (some surprisingly lengthy) with Hossein and his two cohorts, as well as occasional tidbits of news of outside events. I took every occasion to derail the questioning. Experienced or trained interrogators would never have allowed this to happen.

For example, I had learned that both of the assistant interrogators had emotional buttons that, when pushed, would quickly turn a structured interrogation into a shambles of shouting and insults. One of the two assistants liked to brag about having spent a couple of years in Florida as a student. He also was highly sensitive about being viewed as a devout Muslim. I found that looking in his direction and asking, in explicit terms, if he had enjoyed boozing it up and performing unnatural acts with young girls on Florida beaches would make him go almost blind with instantaneous rage. By the time Hossein could get him calmed down and the interrogation back on track, fifteen minutes or more would have passed and the subject being pursued just before the outburst would have been forgotten.

This tactic effectively undermined any progress the interrogators had made toward establishing a psychological mood (which was not too great, in any case) that they could ultimately exploit. I could not use this technique too frequently, but it generally worked exceedingly well. There was a physical price to pay, of course, but the penalties were never unbearable and the ensuing disruption was always worth it. And, frankly, I took perverse pleasure in insulting Hossein and his cohorts, whom I had detested from the beginning. It also meant being yelled at a lot, but after the experiences of plebe years at two military schools, boot camp, and OCS, being the target of rabid screaming was not a problem.

I had also discovered that I could ask for a restroom break or for tea or fruit juice and that the Iranians would—amazingly!—stop, fetch the refreshments, and then for varying lengths of time sit and chat almost like next-door neighbors. When the cups were empty, Hossein would say, "OK, back to work," and the questioning would resume. Any mood or intensity that had developed during the interrogations before the break was, of course, dissipated, leaving the interrogators to begin anew. These little timeouts were among a number of features of captivity that always seemed surrealistic. I never did understand why Hossein permitted me to control the sessions to such a degree; it is doubtful that he ever fully comprehended the effects of the interruptions.

On this particular night, we had gone on at length and it was well after midnight. I was tired and, truth be told, feeling a bit complacent. I had successfully, I thought, remained faithful to my cover story while instigating or capitalizing on a half-dozen or so digressions of some length. To my mind, I was holding the upper hand and I was smugly satisfied. After an interlude for tea, Hossein returned yet again to the subject of my general duties in the embassy and my activities since arriving in Iran. Hossein asked if I still denied being a CIA officer. When I said yes, Hossein handed me a sheet of paper. I started to read it, and I swear my heart stopped dead in mid-beat with the same *ka-chonk* sound that the document disintegrator had made when it crapped out. In that moment, I thought my life was over.

The paper Hossein put in my hands was a State Department cable that had been sent through special channels used for State's internal discussions of CIA issues with its ambassadors. This particular cable was about

. . . me! I could not believe what I was reading. The cable gave my true name and stated in plain English that I was to be assigned to the station in Tehran. It mentioned the special program under which I had come into the Agency ten months previously and discussed the need for good cover. When I looked up at Hossein and his stooges, they were grinning like a trio of Cheshire cats. My astonishment quickly gave way to despair and fright. Although I tried mightily not to show it, I was, as Marines are apt to say, scared shitless.

Copies of this cable hit the world press on the morning of 2 December 1979, a few hours after the interrogation session ended. Hossein and a female student dubbed "Tehran Mary" by the American media held a press conference in the Iranian capital attended by several hundred media people and passed out copies of the cable to all present. The cable was subsequently reprinted in newspapers the world over. To my dismay, many American newspapers reprinted the cable again on 21 January 1981 immediately after our release. (And yet, despite this publicity, once I was back at CIA headquarters my division chief of support, who was also responsible for division security matters, couldn't understand how I could think that anyone might know I was CIA since the Agency hadn't officially admitted it.) The sight of Hossein and his cronies giggling and punching each other like schoolgirls over catching the spook made me so angry that I forgot my fear and was able to get my addled mind moving again. It somehow got through that I had essentially two options: I could try the old "this is a fake piece of crap" ploy, or I could try something—anything—else. It just wasn't clear to me at that precise moment what "anything else" could be. But certainly the document was real, and, more to the point, it looked real, identical with other State Department traffic in terms of format, routing lists, appended comments, special printer paper, State's unique argot, and so forth. As even the KGB had never been able to create accurate reproductions of State documents in disinformation operations, there was just no way that this rabble of punks, barely semiliterate in normal English much less bureaucratic jargon, could fabricate such a convincing document. (Nor did State, as far as I know, ever deny that the document was genuine.) Thus, denying the document's provenance, which the Iranians were probably expecting, did not seem a realistic or useful response. With my still rather staggered brain cells generating no ideas, brilliant or otherwise, I just looked up at the gloating Iranians and, for want of anything smarter, said, "OK, so what?" The three interrogators stopped smirking and exchanged bemused looks, much as the Iranians had done the night I told them to shoot me because I couldn't open the second safe. Hossein and company were not expecting this sort of reaction and didn't know what to do for a moment. But that little respite lasted only a few seconds.

For the next few hours the Iranians tried to confirm that their previous suspicions of my activities were correct. Resurrecting the themes from my interrogator the night of the capture, Hossein "encouraged" me to confess that I was the head of the CIA's entire Middle East spy network, that I had been planning Khomeini's assassination, and that I had been stirring up the Kurds to revolt against the Tehran government. They accused me of trying to destroy their country. Most of all, my interlocutors told me they did not believe anything I said. They ranted and screamed at times; and with all kinds of emotions flooding my mind (not to mention gallons of adrenalin) I yelled insults right back.

We traded accusations of lying, which led to a semicoherent digression about whether the Iranian militants holding the embassy, especially the three in front of me, were "bad" Muslims, and what the Koran said about lying and hostage taking and so forth. Because I had never read the Koran and knew next to nothing about Islam, I wondered later how idiotic I would have sounded to a Muslim in a different situation. Ignorance notwithstanding, I alleged their perfidy as loudly and authoritatively as I could. They screamed that I was evil and I screamed back that they were bad Muslims until we all ran out of steam. Then—amazingly—it was teatime.

In a somewhat less intense state we spent an indeterminate number of hours discussing why I did not speak Farsi and knew next to nothing about Iran. The Iranians found it inconceivable that the CIA would send to such a critical place as Iran someone who was so ignorant of the local culture and language (not an illogical question, to be sure). It was so far beyond them that weeks later, when they at last acceded to the truth, they were personally offended. It had been difficult enough for them to accept that the CIA would post an inexperienced officer in their country. But it was beyond insult for that officer not to speak the language or know the customs, culture, and history of their land.

I strung out this train of conversation as long as I could. Finally, seeking a small psychological victory, I said that there were many Iran specialists in my government who could have come here, but all had refused the assignment and so I was sent instead. This rather mild insult took them aback. The younger Iranian, the one from Florida who was so easy to set off, asked why U.S. government officials who specialized in Iranian affairs would be so reluctant to come? "Because they are afraid," I responded. Perplexed, he asked, "What could they be afraid of?" I held up my bound wrists. "They are afraid of this," I said.

We spent the remainder of the night, what little there was left of it, in a (relatively) calmer atmosphere with the Iranians making the same outlandish accusations and some that weren't so outlandish. I tried to refute the more reasonable charges with a mixture of the truth, when appropriate, and logic, which at times was not founded in truth. The more bizarre things I could only laugh or snort at, or otherwise ridicule. Some of their charges were tossed on the table only once or twice, and it thus became possible to discern the ones about which they were really serious. There was one point that night that Hossein did make chillingly clear. "This is our country," he declared, looking into my eyes, "and we intend to find all the spies and foreign agents who have been disloyal and who are trying to stop the revolution."

In the three nightlong sessions that followed, Hossein and his comrades pressed hard to learn whom I had been in contact with in Tehran and what these Iranians had told me. In fact, I had only one genuine agent who was providing sensitive material, but to the Iranian revolutionary mind, simply meeting privately with an American embassy official, much less a CIA officer, was evidence of perfidy and grounds for severe punishment, including death. A dozen or so Iranians were now in jeopardy merely because they had had dinner with me or had invited me into their homes. During these interrogations, I continued to play the "new guy" card as often and as forcefully as I could, denying that I knew any Iranians and offering logical-sounding (to me) explanations as to why I could not have known or done whatever it was they were asking me about.

I maintained that it had taken me several weeks after arriving to learn my way around just a part of the city and that, as a new and inexperienced officer, I was an unknown quantity to the station chief in terms of my capabilities, competence, and judgment. Given the serious security situation in Tehran, I told Hossein, the chief had been reluctant to assign me any significant responsibilities so soon after my arrival. I had thus been spending most of my time doing my State cover job, familiarizing myself with the city, and performing only a bit of elementary "spy stuff" like finding discreet meeting sites and so forth. I did not vary from this simple story, hoping that it sounded plausible and that in its consistency it would also be convincing.

Unfortunately, the shredded documents that I had left with misgivings in the vault returned from the beyond to make an even bigger liar out of me. The Iranian students had industriously set about reconstructing the shreddings (I heard they employed rug weavers); by early December they were able to read portions of most of the documents. They would eventually manage to piece back together virtually all of what we had tried to destroy. When Hossein began asking about specific nights or people, I knew with certainty that he was no longer fishing for information. Whatever the source(s), he was focusing on exact events that he already knew about. When Hossein showed me one of my own cables—strips of paper carefully taped together—about a meeting I had had with a contact, everything became clear.

For the remainder of that interrogation and for the next two sessions, my goals were to limit the damage and to determine how much other information they had. I refused consistently to give accurate answers to any question until, in a fit of pique, Hossein would haul out a reconstructed document and show me that he knew I was dissembling; and then off we would go again. In the midst of intense questioning about one Iranian I had met more than a few times—a former agent whom I had been attempting to re-recruit—Hossein related information about our meetings that only that person could have known. Obviously, this person had been arrested and interrogated. (When I confronted Hossein about this, he did not hesitate to tell me that my surmise was correct; two months later he told me that this unfortunate person had been executed.) Once I was proven anew a liar, they would bring up another person or event and we would go through the whole rigmarole again. And on and on we went, until they got tired of it and began to use physical means of persuasion, as much out of frustration as for any other reason.

The last two interrogations were, I believe, potentially the most dangerous for me in terms of deliberate physical harm: the Iranians definitely knew that I had been trying to recruit and run spies in their country, but they did not know how effective or successful I had been. At that juncture they had no reason to believe anything but the worst about my activities. Ironically, it was (I am convinced) the reconstructed documents, the shreddings I had neglected to destroy, that made further

interrogation of me a waste of their time. The final all-night interrogation, on 13–14 December, was also the hardest. When I was returned to
my room that morning, aching and tired, I was as despondent as I would
ever be.

By mid-December, however, enough of the shredded cables and documents had been reconstructed to convince the Iranians that while I had
done more than I was admitting to, I had not done nearly as much as
they had suspected. But it was enough to justify (to them) keeping me in
solitary confinement throughout my captivity—as they did the station
chief. The third case officer, who had arrived on post just a few days
before the takeover, apparently had not angered the Iranians to any great
extent, at least in terms of being a "spy" in their country. He did, however, make quite a nuisance of himself. His method of expressing anger
over his captivity and his resistance to their goals was to provoke them
frequently by trying to escape, assaulting the guards, levying debasing
insults, and in general causing the Iranians as much trouble as possible.
His reward was occasional physical abuse and something like 360 days
or so in solitary parceled out during the fifteen months of the hostage
crisis. If resistance can be at least partially defined as making it difficult
or unpleasant for your captors to hold you against your will, this officer
succeeded admirably.

With the reconstruction of the station files, the Iranians had a fairly
clear picture of my limited operational activities. After this point they
mostly left me alone and concentrated on the chief, who had no easy
out.

Washington

Khomeini's threat to put the hostages on trial created genuine alarm in
the White House that the Iranians might execute some of us, particularly
the CIA officers, with or without a trial and then release the rest, perhaps
in stages. Hoping to deter trials, executions, or serious physical abuse,
President Carter sent word to the Iranians through several intermediaries that the death of or serious harm to just one American hostage, no
matter which one, would provoke the same response from the United
States as if all had been killed or harmed. And the U.S. reaction would
be severe and devastating.[2] The intensity of the president's threat must
have been sufficiently underscored by the intermediaries, as the Iranians
had previously been not simply skeptical but outright scornful of Pres-

ident Carter. Fully expecting the Americans to react to the embassy capture with immediate military force, the Iranians had become more and
more convinced that Carter was a weakling as time passed. Somehow,
however, the president's threat was transmitted to Khomeini's representatives with enough gravity to overcome the Iranians' arrant contempt.

While no Iranian official ever mentioned or referred to this warning in
any public forum, there were signs that they were suitably impressed
with its seriousness. As time passed, freely issued threats to execute the
hostages were for the most part replaced by assertions of the Iranian
people's willingness to "suffer martyrdom" from an American attack,
although Khomeini continued to warn that an attack would result in the
deaths of the captive American officials.[3] The last time a trial was mentioned to me was the night of 22 February 1980, although there were
occasionally comments in the Iranian press that appeared to be for
propaganda purposes. Even these statements had evaporated by May
1980.[4]

The ultimate effect of the warning on the Khomeini regime was yet to
be realized. Meanwhile, with the prospect of Americans on trial in Iran
still a genuine possibility, President Carter convened his advisers on
23 November at Camp David to map out a course of action if the trials
(or summary executions of any Americans) should actually occur. Those
gathered around the table at the presidential retreat reviewed the list of
options developed in the early days of the crisis. The group was able to
reach consensus on several proposals—contingent, of course, on the
hostages being subjected to trial or harm.

The first step would be for U.S. forces to close Iranian ports and harbors by laying minefields, essentially foreclosing Iranian commerce with
the world. A naval blockade was considered again, but fear of repeated
and escalating confrontations with vessels belonging to Iran's allies, as
well as those of neutral nations, militated against this measure. The
group recognized that even mining the harbors would cause problems
with other countries, but the consensus was that its positive aspects outweighed its liabilities.[5] Punishment of any of the hostages in response to
the minefields would generate a U.S. attack on "strategic targets" in Iran,
including oil refineries. The United States might even close the Strait of
Hormuz to convince nations that relied on that waterway for oil shipments to bring pressure on the Iranians to forgo punishment of the
hostages.

No doubt frustrated with the Iranians' unwillingness to negotiate for the hostages, much less to release them, three days before Christmas Zbigniew Brzezinski drafted a memo for the president offering a new military option. Acknowledging that Khomeini would probably be moved neither by the increasingly restrictive economic sanctions nor by the prospect of conventional military action, Brzezinski argued for military actions that would lead to the ayatollah's downfall and to the ultimate release of the hostages. In short, Brzezinski recommended that the president begin planning clandestine military special operations to work in concert with a covert political action campaign of some unspecified nature with the goal of removing the de facto leader of Iran.

Brzezinski added that Khomeini had apparently been influenced by the president's threat of 23 November and that taking a piece of Iranian territory such as one or more of the Iranian islands in the Persian Gulf "might inject a humiliation on Khomeini which could effect the release of the hostages." Carter responded to Brzezinski's memo with a note handwritten in the margin: "We need to list everything that Khomeini would not want to see occur and which would not invite condemnation of the U.S. by other nations."[6]

In light of the Khomeini regime's intransigence to date, Brzezinski believed that the administration needed to apply direct pressure on the regime—and on Khomeini himself. Furthermore, Brzezinski had never shared the opinion of the former U.S. ambassador in Tehran, Bill Sullivan, that Khomeini was a "Gandhi-like" figure; now, seven weeks into the crisis, Brzezinski thought it essential that the president at least contemplate more forceful action.[7]

Brzezinski was absolutely correct in his basic assessments: Khomeini had no interest in negotiating the release of the hostages, nor was he personally moved by any threat. Simply put, Khomeini was perfectly willing for the Iranian population to endure deprivation and hardship, even large numbers of casualties from a military strike, if it would aid in the establishment of an Islamic society. Planning U.S. military attacks against strategic targets to be used on appropriate provocation (e.g., trial and punishment of any of the hostages) made good sense. And even though I would have been a recipient of any penalty imposed in retaliation for a military strike, the application of military power would have received my complete support. Even two decades later the idea of a military strike under the conditions specified still seems imminently sensible.

Brzezinski was also correct in conceiving such a document, for deriving imaginative solutions to seemingly intractable problems is an intrinsic part of the national security adviser's duties. Perhaps more to the point, he had long ago anticipated the chaos that would follow the shah's downfall and, with his prognostication borne out, he believed it was time to act.[8] But given the nature of the objectives and methodology it advocates, the memo is worth examining from perspectives beyond the conceptual.

Despite the positive, even desirable, goal of employing the might of the U.S. military against Iran in the contingencies specified, the ancillary covert political action mission to overthrow the regime and its prospects for success are another matter entirely. First, Bruce Laingen had made serious efforts during his tenure in Tehran to convince the new Iranian regime and its supporters that the U.S. government had accepted their revolution and the change of government. Thus, while the fear of another coup à la 1953 was uppermost in the minds of the revolutionaries, Laingen and the rest of the embassy staff (including, it must be stressed, those in the CIA station) faithfully served the president's policy of working with the new Iranian government. Beyond that, during my interrogations I repeated consistently and forcefully to Hossein that the U.S. government did not plan to oust the Khomeini regime. Had Brzezinski's memo or its contents somehow become public, there is no doubt that the Iranians would have seen it as proof both that the U.S. government had never accepted or ever intended to work with the revolutionary government and that the shah's admission into the United States was simply a hoax. The lives of the hostages would probably have been much more difficult and our safety much less assured. It would also have made any negotiations, if and when they began, more difficult as Iranians would have held no faith in any U.S. government assurances or agreements.

Second, the memo carries an implicit belief that Iranians would turn against the "humiliated" Khomeini when Iranian territory was occupied by the American forces, creating an opening in a divided society for an overthrow of the regime. It is a mistaken belief: there was not then, nor is there yet, any indication that U.S. military action against Iranian territory would have done anything other than unite the Iranian people and strengthen the hold of the revolutionaries on the reins of government. The bombings of Germany and Britain and the attack on Pearl Harbor in World War II, as well as the air attacks on North Vietnam during that conflict, all unified the societies at which they were aimed rather than doing otherwise.

Thus, it was probably unrealistic to expect the application of military power—most likely accompanied by Iranian casualties—to create significant rifts in Iranian society. Moreover, the Iranians were always expecting some sort of military response to the hostage taking, and the population and the government were psychologically prepared to be "punished" by the Great Satan.

There were also serious deficiencies from a purely operational perspective. Covert action operations—as opposed to those intended to acquire information or to counter the activities of hostile intelligence services—are intended to influence the actions of a target audience in a direction favorable to U.S. policy interests. The audience is often a government but may also be a population, a discrete group such as a terrorist or drug gang, or an individual, in the case of an absolute dictator. These operations are in general categorized as propaganda, political action, or paramilitary, depending on their objectives and methodology.

There were numerous operational problems standing in the way of covert actions in Iran. By December 1979, the CIA had no staff officers or recruited agents in Iran who could initiate, conduct, or support a covert action operation. Indeed, the Agency was fortunate to have assets who could simply report basic intelligence to U.S. government representatives. There was no resistance group or organization within Iran's borders capable of moving against the regime. There were no exile opposition groups capable of acting, with or without American assistance. Nor was there any facility in Iran that American intelligence could use as a base of operations to support a covert action program of any ilk.

For the most part, covert action programs do not produce the desired results quickly; by nature and design they are long-term activities. Military force could have been applied against Iran with reasonable speed, but it would have taken much longer just to find, validate, and recruit Iranian assets to undertake a political action program, much less to begin actual operations. By this time Iran was essentially a police state, with official and—at least as significant—numerous unofficial security groups (the komitehs) operating almost without constraints or oversight. The internal security situation was sufficiently oppressive that Iranians who had been recruited in the United States in 1978 and 1979 and returned to Iran as intelligence providers uniformly failed to initiate contact with station officers after a good look at the pervasive security situation. Thus, the odds of recruiting Iranians willing to participate in a political action program inside Iran to destabilize the Khomeini regime would have been extremely small. And, of course, it would have been impossible to do any recruiting inside Iran proper.

In sum, there was no foundation inside or outside Iran on which to construct a covert action program—either in concert with the military or by itself—having the goals expressed by Brzezinski. President Carter's marginalia may be accurately interpreted as voicing his understanding of the complications involved while also leaving the door open for "direct action" in the "most extreme circumstances."[9] But the "extreme circumstances" never arrived; instead, shrinking diplomatic options and the belief that there was little alternative led policymakers not to a plan for covert action or a military strike to "alter the regime," but instead to a plan to end the crisis by rescuing the hostages.

Iran's terms for the release of the hostages had been clearly stated by Khomeini's representatives: the shah was to be returned for trial, the United States was to apologize for "crimes against the Iranian people," the monies "stolen" by the shah were to be returned to Iran, and the United States was to pay unspecified financial damages.[10] The Carter administration had no intention of meeting any of these desiderata. But in any case, by the spring of 1980 these demands had become irrelevant to the negotiations process—the hostages had become instrumental in an internal battle for power between the moderates and the radicals or fundamentalists. Khomeini had no intention of relinquishing control of the hostages, much less returning them to the United States, until his vision of an Islamic state in Iran was assured.

CHAPTER 15

1 JANUARY – 24 APRIL 1980

With the interrogations over and the Iranians no longer interested in me, life assumed some sense of normality. My routine was to wake sometime after daylight and then await the usual breakfast of Iranian bread or Afghan barbari bread with butter and jam or feta cheese, and tea. It doesn't sound like much, but the barbari bread with feta was actually pretty good. Sometimes the bread would come with butter and jam, which was also rather tasty. I would then prop my sleeping pallet against the wall and take my morning walk, which consisted of striding from one corner of the room eight to ten paces to the opposite corner, reversing course, and repeating until I became tired or my feet grew sore. During the walk I would "teach" my imaginary class or do other sorts of mental gymnastics to keep my intellect exercised and to make the time pass more quickly. (Nevertheless, after my return to America I found it very hard to concentrate for a number of months, apparently a common problem among long-term hostages and POWs.) I would read until lunch, after which the morning agenda would be repeated until dinner. After dinner, I would again walk and read until I was able to sleep.

During the initial months when we were kept in the embassy compound, our noon and evening meals were American-style food prepared by Iranian students who had been trained by the chargé's cook. Most of the meals were adequately nourishing and palatable, with the food coming mainly from local U.S. military commissary stocks seized by militants during the withdrawal of the nearly ten thousand military personnel who had been in Iran as part of the MAAG. By the fall of 1980, however, some of the foodstuffs clearly were suffering from old age. Chicken, for example, began to show up in a marginally edible state, and I had to abandon the powdered milk when it reached the point at which the worms were too numerous to pick out and more than I wished to ingest.

Escape was always in the back—and occasionally in the front—of my mind. I was convinced on nothing more than blind faith that if I could get out, I would be able to find sanctuary with someone and eventually make it out of Iran, either through Kurdistan or via the Persian Gulf. During the first three months, with the situation extremely unsettled and armed guards everywhere, no opportunity presented itself. Now, after Christmas, I was alert for any chance that might come from complacency on the part of the guards. But there was an additional factor, too: it seemed that the worst was over. Our guards were no longer as hostile as they had been at first, and we no longer seemed to be in danger of execution or abuse. It also seemed that there were fewer guards, which might mean that overpowering a guard would provide an opening, or that laxity on the part of one guard might offer an opportunity to steal away.

I thought long and hard about these possibilities and then made a fundamental decision. If a guard's mistake or inattention allowed me to just sneak out, I'd go in a heartbeat. I thought so hard about that possibility, and looked for it so diligently, that I am convinced I would have done so without hesitation. But because of the changed, and improving, circumstances, I decided that I would take direct action against a guard only if there was reason to think that my life was in imminent jeopardy. Unlike a movie hero, I had no idea how hard you have to hit a person in the head to simply knock him unconscious; even less did I know how to do that and ensure that the object of my affection was not seriously harmed or killed. Any assault on the guards resulting in injury to them would have dire consequences for me if I were recaptured. And, frankly, by this time I knew that the kids guarding me were not ultimately responsible for my circumstances. It was not these teenagers I wanted to hurt. If my life were in imminent danger I would do anything, to anyone, to escape. Short of that, I would not harm the guards. But I never held the same reservation about the older ringleaders.

It required some months before I was able to come to terms psychologically with what was happening to us. It was a classical state of denial. I would go to bed each night firmly convinced—on no basis other than the inconceivability that the U.S. government could not stop a smelly bunch of idiot-acting kids from holding government officials captive—that it would all be over the next morning. And when the day passed and we were still prisoners of these students, I would have to deal with anger and frustration (which was much more difficult to control than the anger) until it was evening again. Then I would convince myself anew that the following day would bring release. It was months before I was able to live with the idea that the next day would just be another day of captivity.

I still could not believe that the president had allowed the shah to enter the United States when the potential damage to America's national security and the threat to our safety in Tehran had been so manifest. Not understanding the competing issues from the Washington perspective, I continued to think it was absolutely the dumbest decision I had ever heard. The unanswered humiliation of the United States and the loss of national prestige were more intensely frustrating to me than any other aspect of captivity. Nearly threescore U.S. diplomats were being held prisoner, and nothing our government did seemed able to end the situation, much less restore America's lost dignity.

What no doubt kept many of us from going nuts was a serendipitous supply of plentiful and excellent books. Just before the embassy take-over, the entire library of the Tehran American School had been delivered to the embassy warehouse for safekeeping. There was a large selection of novels, notably English mysteries, and thousands of nonfiction volumes. From the very first days in the Mushroom Inn, the Iranians were surprisingly good about keeping us supplied with books, although I suspect it had more to do with keeping us occupied (and hence less likely to cause trouble) than it was a matter of human kindness.

While in captivity, I read more than five hundred works from this bounty, covering a wide range of subjects. I plowed through dozens of volumes I enjoyed and learned from, many of which I would never otherwise have had the opportunity to read. I absorbed most of Dickens's works and lots of Agatha Christie and Ruth Rendell. I delighted in the adventures of Bertie Wooster and Jeeves. I devoured histories of Russia, Great Britain, World War I, early twentieth-century America, and all of Barbara Tuchman's works published up to that time. Some of the most enjoyable books I stumbled across were ones that I would never even have looked at in a normal life; I was, for example, fascinated by a biography of Blanche of Castile, the wife of Louis VIII of France and mother of Louis XI, Saint Louis.

There was another significant factor in staying sane throughout captivity: the ability to laugh, to find humor in the worst of times and the worst of circumstances. I am absolutely convinced that a strong sense of humor is second only to the desire to live in surviving hostile captivity. Sometimes it wasn't hard at all to laugh, as the guards would quite unintentionally do or say something that was indeed truly funny. Often they didn't understand what they had done or said, and more than once, trying to explain it to them would make me laugh even more. I used humor in my interrogations to break the intensity or mood, to relieve my stress, and to insult the interrogators when they said or did something that was either funny or that I could turn against them. I used humor with the guards after we began talking. And often, if there wasn't anything genuinely humorous to laugh at, I'd find something.

In looking back at my time in the Marines, the only thing that I took completely seriously was my work as an air traffic controller. In retrospect, there were too many times when I wasn't as serious about what I was doing as I should have been. But in prison, it is nearly impossible to use too much humor. Without that ability to laugh, to find humor in the most absurd or unpleasant situations, there is no way to dissipate stress, no way to keep the situation in perspective, no way to balance off the bad. Without humor, sanity, and even survival, are imperiled. Humor is an essential characteristic if a prisoner desires to end his captivity in the same psychological health as when he began.

But a sense of humor isn't the only quality a prisoner needs to possess. Even more important is the need to maintain faith: faith according to one's religious beliefs, faith in one's country and government, and faith in one's fellow prisoners. I never doubted my religious convictions, particularly faith in the concept that everything happens for a reason and that one must have a quiet confidence that all will turn out for the best. Faith in one's country and government was another issue that was never in question in my mind. Regardless of what the Iranians told me, I never doubted that the U.S. government, and my Agency specifically, was doing everything possible to bring us all home alive and well. I also knew, after the initial expectations of a quick resolution, that this would take time, probably a lot of time. I knew of CIA officers who had spent twenty years in Chinese prisons and, of course, of the POWs from Vietnam who spent as many as seven years in prison. By the first of the year I was psychologically prepared to spend a long time in Iranian prisons.

But I never, ever—not even for an instant—thought that my country or the CIA would finally give up and cease working for my return, much less that they would forget about us. I knew they would keep at it until we were all home again. And I believed with just as much conviction that the American people were behind us, no matter what the Iranians claimed. I am sure that my military officer colleagues, and most of the enlisted troops, held the same convictions.

Unfortunately, though, a few of the other hostages frequently expressed the belief—in letters to their families, to President Carter, and to the press (particularly one letter to a major daily)—that the American people had forgotten us or that the government was doing little or nothing to get us out. These statements were disappointing in that the authors, as diplomats, should have known from the beginning that two hostile countries negotiating issues on which there is no mutual understanding or common ground cannot resolve their differences within a few days, weeks, or even months. It was further regrettable in that several of these letters relied on the same verbiage that the Iranians themselves used while propagandizing us in their efforts to turn us against our own government and agencies.[1] And these assertions were surprising in light of the fact that these same hostages were recipients over the months of cards sent by American citizens expressing their support and love for us. I am at a loss to explain how anyone could have thought that we had been forgotten. Which also meant that my faith in some of my fellow captives was misplaced.

The Iranians with whom I had contact fit into two categories: the younger men, barely into their twenties (if that), who performed guard work; and the older men, in their thirties, who seemed to call the shots and conducted the interrogations. It was the younger Iranians who constituted my company for nearly fifteen months. Unlike the older Iranians, who had no illusions about why they had engineered the embassy takeover, the younger ones seemed to believe fervently that its only purpose was to coerce the United States into returning the shah. I never heard any of the young Iranians speak of ending the relationship between Iran and the United States, as did Hossein and his cohorts; nor, frankly, did the younger ones seem to want much of anything the older ones did. Virtually none of these youths, who were in fact real students at various universities, had ever traveled outside Iran. For many, the trip to Tehran to attend school was the first time they had ever left their villages. Their knowledge level seemed to be generally the equivalent of the average American eighth-grader. But they were just as fanatically devoted to Khomeini as were their older leaders.

Over the months we all came to know a number of the guards fairly well. Some were with us from Day 1 to Day 444. Others whom we saw frequently during the early days faded away after the first three or four months. Initially, the guards were apprehensive of all of us, the first Americans many had ever met, and uncertain what to think because their elders, including the clergy, had painted us as evil incarnate. As their contact with us increased, especially after we had been separated into smaller groups, they began to reevaluate their ideas of who and what Americans are. My embassy colleagues, possessing the same American characteristics that led many Japanese and Germans to like and respect Americans after World War II, soon managed to establish friendly relations with these young guards. But while it was fairly easy to like some or many of the younger ones, it was just as easy to despise the older Iranians, the ones who took our freedom, jeopardized our lives, and brought distress to our families.

I never came up with exact demographics for our captors, nor did I ever figure out precisely how they were organized, despite my unique vantage point.[2] But the CIA did. According to research by Agency analysts, the student leaders were, on average, around twenty-eight years old, and the guards about twenty-two—a bit older than I had estimated. I was right, though, about their academic pursuits, as the majority were studying science-related subjects, including the women, who made up about a quarter of the militants. As far as could be determined, none of the militants holding the embassy had ever had a career or held any sort of paid employment (limiting even more their already tenuous connection to anything remotely approaching a "real" world).

The leaders were more or less split between middle-class and lower-middle-class backgrounds, while the worker bees were mostly lower middle class. Thus, most were from socioeconomic backgrounds with strong ties to Islam and a resentment of Western values. Once in the embassy, they began calling themselves "Muslim Student Followers of the Line of the Imam" and studiously avoided (no pun intended) any identification with other established revolutionary groups.

U.S. intelligence reached the same conclusion about the takeover that we had come to in the embassy: our captors had organized the embassy takeover ahead of time and came prepared for at least a short siege. After the takeover there was little confusion because their duties had all been specified in advance and measures had been taken to ensure that members of rival militant groups would be excluded. This situation notwithstanding, I have always suspected that there were at least a few clandestine members of the Tudeh party in with the militants; if so, anything that happened within the compound would have eventually filtered back to the KGB. If this was not the case, then the KGB wasn't doing its job.

The leaders cooperated among themselves in a manner that was reasonably democratic, with a half-dozen or so senior leaders comprising a "Council of Cooperation" responsible for basic policy decisions. Below them were subordinate committees structured along functional lines. There were public relations people, translators, and others to handle logistics and security. Their spiritual leader was a cleric named Musavi-Khoeni who held the title Hojat-ol-Eslam. Khoeni was a wizened, kindly old man whom the students worshiped. As long as the council's decision-making process was chugging along, Khoeni remained in the background. When there was difficulty reaching a consensus, the cleric would provide guidance, "ostensibly," the CIA report notes, "by relaying Khomeini's comments but frequently adding his own, and usually backing the decisions of the Council against dissent from other militants." Each of the universities represented in the student group had a student representative on the council, although in practice there was often much dissent and occasional accusations of favoritism. The council's camaraderie was sometimes weakened by "consensus" decisions that were unanimous only in name.

One development of which we in the embassy were unaware until late into the crisis was the disillusionment of some of the students once they comprehended that the hostages and the embassy had become pawns in a larger power struggle between rival political factions. These disaffected students had taken the embassy on idealistic grounds—to rectify the injustices of the shah and end what they termed "imperialism" in the region—only to see their lofty goals degenerate into a down-and-dirty brawl for political power. They felt that they were being used. (Had I known this during my captivity, I could only have said, "Welcome to the real world.")

After my relocation into solitary, there were guards in my room(s) twenty-four hours a day. I never discovered the particular reason, if any, and at first I ignored them. I was angry at being held, angry at being in solitary, angry and frustrated at seeing them turn an American embassy into a graffiti-laden prison. I resented like hell having them in the same room with me, whether they spoke to me or not. I felt no impetus to make conversation, and so I didn't. The Iranians were quiet at first, too.

For almost their whole lives they had been told that the CIA was responsible for many (if not all) of the world's problems, and especially the problems in Iran. Their perspective of the shah's reign and their knowledge of the CIA-engineered coup in 1953 were naturally less than objective and by no means fully informed. Nor did they wish to hear a different point of view—the clerics told them all they needed to know. Understandably, they approached me warily, unsure whether I was a real human being or the monstrous bogeyman of their imaginations.

For the first several weeks in solitary, some young Iranian would be sitting at a small desk just inside my door while I walked, read, slept, or ate, completely ignoring my existence except when I needed to use the bathroom. The guard would then blindfold me, escort me down the hall and back, and resume his post. The guards changed at approximately two-hour intervals, and I neither bade them good-bye nor welcomed the next shift.

But human nature will have its way, and slowly and tentatively the young Iranians began to talk to me, as much out of curiosity as from a desire to make me understand the evil of my ways. Inevitably, the first words each of them spoke condemned various offenses, real or imagined, of the U.S. government and were laced with quotations from the Koran and Khomeini's sermons. I would grunt back a word or two and go on with whatever I was doing. The guards soon became more talkative, asking more questions and making fewer accusations, seemingly impelled by a desire to convince me that the country I served and the government I worked for were corrupt and immoral. I would toss out a contradictory comment and then, in Socratic fashion, ask a question intended to compel them to justify or expand on their comments or ideas. Before long all but two of my ten or so guards had become fairly garrulous. From then on, until I no longer had them in the room with me, almost every time the guard changed, the new watcher would come in ready to talk. And so we began to have conversations that ranged from amusing to amazing to surrealistic.

There were a number of common denominators among these young men. First and foremost, they were extremely religious, although none seemed to be truly fanatical. They were totally obedient to the wishes (or what they perceived to be the wishes) of the clergy, as personified in Khomeini. Literally hundreds of hours of talks with these kids distilled down to one basic tenet: Khomeini was infallible because he was the Imam, and he was the Imam because he was infallible. It was not necessary for any of them to have firsthand knowledge of any subject or to be independently convinced of the correctness of any position or action. If Khomeini said it was so, or if he ordered it done, then that was all they needed to know. Not once did I hear one discuss anything, whether the subject was religion, human rights, politics, or social responsibilities, in which he felt obliged or even willing to question Khomeini's judgments or to decide facts, opinions, and actions for himself.

My Iranian captors contended that America was responsible for all the evils and wrongs in the world. One of them declared to me that Iran had been America's main enemy for more than 400 years! Even after I informed him that America had actually been a nation for only 203 years, and populated only by Native Americans less than 300 years before that, he could not be swayed.

I "learned" from these Iranians that America had created plagues and national disasters in its efforts to control the world ("hegemony" was a favorite accusation); that all the West European countries and NATO as an organization were controlled by the United States; that America had decided—apparently just for the hell of it—to beat up on the peace-loving Vietnamese people, creating and then maliciously prolonging the war in Southeast Asia; and that America had never done anything positive or good for the world. When I pointed out the innumerable "non-political" things Americans had done that benefited the world (the Salk polio vaccine and other medical discoveries, to mention just one of the dozens of examples I gave), the Iranians would find ulterior motives underlying each accomplishment—world control (hegemony, again) was one of the all-time favorites, as were greed and profit. Or they would deny that the achievement was useful or say they had not heard of it, in which case it could not be really important or true. I asked one premedical student to compare the number of American Nobel Prize winners with the number of Iranian Nobelists, and the student replied that America always fixed the voting so that no Iranian could win; it was part of our "war" against Iran.

In attempting to counter these perceptions, I usually avoided the gratuitous insults that I so freely bestowed on Hossein and his pals, as these youngsters were in many ways very innocent of life and reality. But every discussion eventually reached a point at which further argument was fruitless, for their minds were absolutely closed. They had no wish, and probably no intellectual training, to objectively consider different points of view. Essentially, they had been programmed by the clerics to reject all ideas except those the clerics themselves offered.

Most of my captors stubbornly asserted that they were right—in every situation—and so, of course, everyone else was always wrong. If they broke any law, it was because they had a justification for doing so. One student told me that he had been in a car accident at 2:00 A.M. because a car had hit him broadside at an intersection. A bit of questioning revealed that he had run a red light and was creamed by the car that had the green light. With complete sincerity he proclaimed that the small amount of traffic at that hour made it perfectly OK for him to ignore traffic signals—no point in waiting at a red light when no one is coming from the other side. The other driver was totally at fault because he should have known that someone might be running red lights at that hour and therefore should have been stopping at intersections, even if the light was green. I asked the guard if he stopped at intersections even when he had the green, and he looked at me like I was nuts. Of course he wasn't going to stop, he said; he had the green light.

The corollary to never being wrong was that nothing was ever their fault. In the midst of our captivity, more than one of the guards complained to me that holding us hostage was ruining their lives: they could not go to school, they were not spending time with their families, they were not able to go home to their villages. In short, it was their lives that were on hold. And it was all our fault because we were there. The obvious solution—putting us on a plane and sending us home—made no impression.

I was frequently numbed by my captors' lack of knowledge about the world and about critical events that, they claimed, "proved" how right they were. I have never forgotten a conversation I overheard between a woman who I think was Tehran Mary and U.S. Air Force colonel Tom Schaefer, the embassy's defense attaché. For much of February and into March 1980, Tom and I were kept in small adjoining rooms in the basement of the embassy that shared a common air vent. By remaining still, I could often hear what was being said in Tom's little corner of paradise. One day an unknown (to me) female voice—I had no idea who Tehran Mary was until after I came home—started berating Tom for the U.S. decision to drop the atomic bomb on Japan, calling it barbaric, inhumane, and racist. Tom didn't debate her, but rather laid it out in simple terms: "The Japanese started the war, and we ended it."

That was obviously news to Mary, who asked in disbelief, "What do you mean, the Japanese started the war?"

And Tom replied, "The Japanese bombed Pearl Harbor, and so we bombed Hiroshima."

"Pearl Harbor? Where's Pearl Harbor?" asked Mary.

"Hawaii," said Tom.

There was a very long pause, and then, in a small voice pregnant with incredulity, Mary said, "The Japanese bombed Hawaii?"

"Yep," stated Tom. "They started it, and we ended it."

Mary's astonishment was easily discernible, even through the wall. After another long pause I heard her rush out of Tom's room. And she was one of the better-educated student leaders who had lived in America.

Even though conversations with the guards filled some of the solitary hours, I still was not happy to have them in the room; much better to be alone than to be with these people. And so I undertook my own covert action campaign to get them out. One lesson I learned from Doug Hegdahl's talks on survival in captivity was that it is vital to resist your captors in any way you can. By resisting in some fashion whenever the opportunity presents, the prisoner makes it more difficult or more uncomfortable for his captors to hold him; they are made to pay some price, however small, for denying the prisoner his freedom.

One small way I tried to make it harder on selected Iranian guards was to make their time in my room as unpleasant as I could. Doing things like breaking wind as I walked by their desk, belching after meals, and wearing only skivvies (that "public" state of undress being offensive in the Muslim religion) were steps toward this end. Once I had a cold, so I made sure to breathe hard and cough in the guard's direction as I passed by the desk on my lengthy strolls. And when a few days later I heard a guard complaining that he was doing double duty because a couple of his colleagues, who had previously stood watch in my room, had been taken ill with bad colds, I experienced one of those psychological boosts that helped keep me going. Soon afterward, around New Year's Day 1980, I was moved to a room on the ground floor in the back of the chancery, and from then on I lived without guards inside the room. It was a truly solitary existence, although the guards still dropped in to chat from time to time.

One threat Hossein made with sincerity in the early months, and later continued occasionally to toss out, was to place me on trial as a spy. It struck me that this was no idle threat. The Iranians, on the defensive from world criticism, felt a strong need to convince the rest of the world that they were justified in holding American diplomatic personnel captive and in demanding redress from the United States. I figured that the COS, myself, and any of a half-dozen military officers, particularly Tom Schaefer, Lee Holland, and Air Force lieutenant colonel Dave Roeder in the Defense Attaché's Office, were prime candidates for the dock, inasmuch as we were the ones who had been singled out for harsher treatment. Not to mention, of course, that the Iranians were convinced that we were all spies. I had memories of the *Life* magazine photos of Francis Gary Powers's show trial in Moscow, and it was not something I wanted to experience firsthand. As time passed and I learned more about the Iranians, their revolution, and their goals, I came to understand that if they did actually put us on trial, they would probably execute several of us and give the others long prison sentences. This would serve to justify their actions, "prove" the U.S. government had committed crimes against Iran, and also provide a unifying factor for their revolution.

The exceptionally supportive mood of much of the Iranian population toward the embassy takeover, together with the zealous desire of the militants to tighten their grip on the reins of government, elevated the possibility of trial (and execution). One disadvantage of having a room in the front of the embassy was that I could hear clearly the din of the huge crowds that would gather in front of the compound on Fridays. I learned later that some of these gatherings were attended by more than 500,000 Iranians, and I was always worried that some speaker would whip the crowd into a frenzy that would culminate in their storming the embassy bent on lynching the vile Americans.

There was also much talk of adding "war crimes" to the indictments for those of us who had fought in Vietnam. To bring this home, the Iranians taped to my wall a propaganda poster showing several American soldiers grinning and holding the severed heads of two Vietnamese. I used the poster as part of my own propaganda war: when a new guard came into my room I would walk to the poster, put my finger on one of the severed heads, and point out that when Americans went to war, they were serious about it—and one casus belli might be something like the capture and incarceration of American diplomats. The poster was soon removed.

But after the first of the year in 1980, talk of a trial receded. The last time it was mentioned to me was on George Washington's birthday. Hossein had come to my room for one of his increasingly infrequent visits and, in the midst of our chat, casually tossed out the threat of a trial. By that time even he seemed not to take it seriously. Iranian government spokesmen, however, continued occasionally in the world media to threaten to convoke public "spy" trials through at least May 1980, apparently as part of the propaganda war.

Roughly coincident with the apparent end of the threats to put us on trial was a welcome, albeit limited, improvement in our treatment. For me, this included a shower every week or ten days instead of the usual two weeks, several short periods actually outdoors just to enjoy the sun, and visits to the library—the economic counselor's office now served as a library for the books from the Tehran American School. I was given pen and paper for the first time, and I began to draw whenever I did not feel like reading.

I was also told I could write home, and from then on I wrote three letters a week to my mother. Midway through our captivity, however, I became certain that the Iranians had never mailed any of my letters. In fact, I later learned that I had not been heard of, or from, since Christmas 1979, when I was allowed to send a couple of cards. When the press irresponsibly reported that some hostages had been able to spirit out "secret messages" in such cards, the Iranians assumed that I was one of the culprits and my mail privileges were rescinded. I believe in freedom of the press, but in this case a little self-imposed restraint on the part of the media would have been helpful.

Nor was I ever filmed with visiting clergy like the others were, so my well-being and even my continued existence remained a mystery to my family and the Agency from December 1979 until the Algerian ambassador paid me a visit the night of 23 December 1980. Keeping me in solitary and putting my family through the agony of not knowing if I was alive was the Iranians' attempt to punish the CIA, as an organization, for all the "bad" things that had happened to and in Iran since the 1953 coup. Because these students could not get their hands on any of the CIA personnel who had served there earlier to punish them, my COS and I served as their surrogates. It was that simple.

There were, I believe, several factors that combined to ameliorate the harshness of our captivity, none of which I knew about until after we were released. One important factor was the Iranians' realization that the American people themselves, rather than merely those in the White House, posed a serious threat to them. The back-channel message from President Carter to the Iranians warning of dire consequences should we be put on trial was also a factor, as was the increasing and unwitting involvement of the fifty-two of us in Iranian domestic politics.

At first, amazingly, our captors fervently believed that all Americans would actually support their seizure of the embassy. Many of the younger and more naïve students believed that the American people might even begin a revolution in the United States to overthrow their own "evil" government. The older students merely expected that the support of the American populace would become sufficiently strong and influential to induce the Carter administration to give in to Iran's demands.

The reason for this bizarre belief that Americans would turn on their own government was simple: our captors had no concept of a "people's government" in the sense of the populace having any influence over or participation in their governance. To them, there was an unbridgeable chasm between government and the people, for under the shah's rule Iranian citizens had been completely alienated from political participation. Added to this was the Iranians' ethnocentricity, their belief that every other society in the world was just like theirs (although far less important)—a state of mind that was amplified by our captors' lack of life experiences and limited education. In this instance, the Iranians believed that the American people were as alienated from the U.S. government as the Iranian people had been from the shah's regime. As a corollary, the Iranians were certain that Americans were as angry with the U.S. government over its "injustices" to Iran as they were. (When I would point out that the vast majority of Americans probably had no idea where Iran even was before 1978 and couldn't have cared less, the Iranians couldn't comprehend it; their ethnocentricity placed them at the center of the world—everyone's world.) Thus our captors were at first perplexed and then greatly disappointed when the American public condemned their taking of the embassy. And this held true even for Hossein and his peers, who were older and better educated and had lived or traveled in the United States. They did not understand why the American people were showing so much antagonism and hatred over our captivity or why Americans were rallying behind President Carter. Our captors saw themselves as likable people who were acting appropriately, so of course they expected the American people to like them, too. This reflected a serious misunderstanding of the American character. One night in early December 1979, Hossein admitted to me that the reaction of the American on the street was the opposite of what the militants had expected. He added that it was clear to him and to the others that the U.S. government had instituted an enormous, improbably successful censorship program. Thus, government perfidy had once again prevented the "truth" from reaching the American populace. The solution to that problem was a public relations campaign by the militants.

After I returned home and read press accounts of our captivity, I saw that the Iranians had indeed tried such a campaign. The starting point was probably the distribution to the world press of "my" State Department special-channel message in early December 1979, followed by a series of appearances by Tehran Mary before the media. The culmination of this effort was the "Crimes of America" conference held in Tehran in June 1980. The Iranians induced several U.S. citizens, notably former attorney general Ramsey Clark, to come to Tehran and criticize American policies. This was the same Ramsey Clark whom the president had dispatched as his special envoy two days after the embassy capture.

By early February 1980 or so, it had finally sunk into the minds of our captors that nothing they could say to or produce for the media was going to generate a surge of sympathy (much less support) in the United States for their actions. And with that realization came a perception that they had much more to fear from the American public than they did from the White House. They had begun by assuming that Americans felt some affection for Iranians, and that it was this friendship that had kept the White House from responding militarily. It was truly a shock to their collective egos finally to accept the depth and intensity of the dislike with which most Americans viewed Iran. Along with this came the realization that the one thing that would almost certainly compel the White House to abandon its self-imposed restraint would be if any of us were harmed, for any reason. This realization at least partially translated into better treatment for us and, probably to a lesser degree, the end to threats of a trial.

The conditions and duration of our captivity were also products of our increasing utility to each side in the political power struggle between the moderates under Iranian president Abolhassan Bani-Sadr (elected with Khomeini's approval in February 1980) and the hardcore radical Islamic fundamentalists. In short, whoever controlled the hostages controlled the Iranian government. By the spring of 1980 the only Iranians who were still demanding the shah's return were the young guards, who kept hoping; the older Iranians, such as Hossein, now a rare visitor, had little interest in discussing the reasons for our continued incarceration.

One point all the Iranians repeatedly made was that they were going to make sure President Carter was not reelected, as "punishment" for his "crimes."

From February to almost the end of April 1980, life was the same, day in and day out. There were no more interrogations, no more guards in my room, fewer visits by any of the younger guards, and rare "drop-in" visits by Hossein and the other older students. The monotony was broken only by an occasional trip to a shower in some other building and, on a good day, maybe ten minutes outside in the sun. I was moved to five different rooms in the chancery during this period but was never told either that a move was coming or the reason why.

Easter Sunday, 6 April, passed quietly, but long after midnight that night I was awakened and taken upstairs to meet Orthodox Archbishop Hilarion Capucci, the former archbishop of Jerusalem, who had once been imprisoned by the Israelis for gunrunning. The meeting occurred in the ambassador's office, which was crammed full with our captors, some of whom I had not seen in months. It was a nonevent for me, however, and to this day I do not understand the purpose. My picture was not taken and I was not given anything. The archbishop said nothing memorable. After a few minutes I was taken back to my room, befuddled as to why my sleep had been interrupted for something that was apparently meaningless.

For the next three weeks, it was once again life as usual. As far as I knew, it was going to be like this until our release.

Washington, 15 January–24 April 1980

On 14 January, in something of a curious move, the Iranians expelled all foreign journalists from the country. The militants (and, by extension, the Khomeini regime) had been steadily losing the public relations campaign and were visibly frustrated that they had not gained more support for their attempt to humiliate the United States. Unable to convince the American public of the righteousness of their actions, perhaps they thought there was no longer any point in allowing foreigners to report. They may have thought that all Western reporters were spies. Or, as President Carter surmised, perhaps they were up to something that they wanted to conceal.[3]

While the safety of the fifty-three (at that point) remaining hostages was the president's foremost concern, the stress on their families back home also troubled him. In March 1980, President Carter received a report detailing the conditions of the families, who were said to be suffering profound physical and psychological stress. "At least eighteen families," the report noted, "are under stress that they cannot manage." A laundry list of physical ailments afflicting hostage family members included "depression, overpowering anxiety, sleeplessness, high blood pressure, exhaustion (resulting in hospitalization), vitamin deficiency." Wives, who had to be both mother and father to their children, found that "existing problems were exacerbated by the strain." The teenage sons and daughters of the captives required "extra support and therapy" to help them deal with the uncertainty of the situation. The picture was not entirely bleak, however. The report noted that "although every family member has been affected, many are holding well . . . and have found resources of strength and patience to carry on themselves and support others."[4]

The president also received a firsthand report on the status of the hostages from three clergymen who visited most (but not all) of the prisoners. The visits were not entirely humanitarian in nature, as almost all of the hostages who saw the clergy came away with the opinion that the visitors were much more interested in promoting themselves than in relieving the distress of the hostages or helping to end the crisis. Some hostages also believed that at least one of the clergymen was more supportive of the Iranian position than he was of American interests. Regardless, the clergymen returned with highly desired direct information on the health and mental state of the thirty-six hostages they had been able to see and talk with. The clergy were also allowed to bring back letters from thirty-seven hostages. A memo about their visit informed the president that prisoners Kalp, Barnes, Metrinko, Noyer, Ahern, Daugherty, and Moeller had been neither seen nor heard from.

According to the clergymen's report, the hostages were completely isolated from the outside world and displayed a wide range of "emotional postures," with some very strong and positive and others in varying degrees of depression. In what had to be double-edged news, the clergy also noted that some of the captives received "preferential treatment; some could receive letters and phone calls, others could not." And in news that without doubt was unwelcome, the clergy commented that the hostages had been divided into "segregated groups," a status that could also be inferred from the absence of information on seven of the captives.[5]

The prospect of American diplomatic officers standing trial in Iran was still very much a concern in Washington. The Iranians contended that the hostages were spies and not diplomats, and that the embassy was not a diplomatic facility but rather a cover for espionage, a "spy den." As such, the mission and the personnel assigned to it had forfeited any claim to diplomatic immunity. When informed of the Vienna Conventions on Diplomatic Immunity, the Iranians countered that (1) the new regime didn't recognize the treaty; (2) the treaty didn't apply to spies; and (3) international law had never helped the Iranians against the excesses of the shah's regime, and now international law wouldn't help those who had helped the oppressors. The Iranians' interpretations of the Vienna Conventions were, of course, completely erroneous with respect to its applicability to the PGOI and to trials of anyone, spies or otherwise, who possessed duly accredited diplomatic immunity. Treaty obligations disappear only when the signatory country completely disappears; treaty obligations continue in force when there is a change of government but the country itself remains a sovereign nation. Iran was still Iran, whether under the shah or under the new Islamic regime, and thus under the Vienna Conventions the PGOI was obligated to obey the treaties signed by the shah. The Khomeini regime was legally bound, that is, to accord the members of the U.S. embassy full diplomatic immunity, whether they were spies or not. Furthermore, neither the Koran nor Islamic law—which is, of course, founded on the Koran—permitted the mistreatment of diplomats. (When knowledgeable hostages pointed that out, the Iranians had a difficult time responding; but neither did they concede.)

The Iran militants had earlier allowed the press to make their case to the Iranian public and, coincidentally, to the rest of the world. An article published on 18 December 1979 in a principal Tehran newspaper presented the regime's plans and positions to its readership—and to the U.S. intelligence and foreign policy communities through the translation services of the FBIS. According to the article in the daily journal *Ettela'at*, the Ayatollah Mohammad Gilani-Sharia declared in a press conference at Evin Prison that the trial would take place "just as soon as Imam Khomeini gives permission." The tribunal's proceedings would follow the "precepts of Islam and the Koran," and the defendants would be "treated with justice." The article noted that "Islamic law prescribes the severest punishment for spies, who may be killed or turned into slaves." Although the spies would be allowed to defend themselves or engage lawyers, the writer was obviously concerned for the professional and personal reputations of any members of the bar who might undertake such a defense. And in any case, the article continued, "the crimes of these individuals are so evident that no informed human being will agree to defend such criminals." (Notably absent was any concept of innocent until proven guilty.) The punishment the "spies" received would be set by Imam Khomeini.[6] In anticipation of the hostages actually being hauled before a revolutionary tribunal, the Carter administration began seeking counsel from a range of legal experts to determine if the Iranians might have valid grounds for constituting an espionage tribunal. In late January 1980 the administration received a joint letter from John B. Jones, the dean of New York University Law School, and Norman Redlick of the prestigious Washington law firm Covington and Burling. The two attorneys noted that they had been unable to locate in international law, Iranian law, or Islamic law any basis for trying diplomatic personnel on any charge and suggested that the administration halt any preparations lest the Iranians think that such grounds existed.[7] But the administration was unwilling to face potential trials without being fully prepared ahead of time, and wisely so.

Attorney Jones followed up with another letter a week later in which he summarized a trip he had made to Egypt to consult with experts on Islamic law. Jones concluded, based on his discussions, that the Iranians' position was completely groundless. The argument went as follows: (1) until Iran became an Islamic state, Islamic law had no relevance in the Iranian legal system; (2) as explicitly stated in the Koran, Islamic law is not retroactive; (3) Iran officially became an Islamic state only in December 1979 with the adoption of a new constitution; (4) Islamic law grants immunity to diplomats as a matter of course; and (5) Islamic law respects all treaties that are in force. Hence, the Iranians were unquestionably in the wrong in their intent to try the hostages and completely without legitimate grounds for doing so. Regarding the militants' stated intent to try any hostages who had served in Vietnam for war crimes, Jones informed the president that the Iranians lacked any jurisdiction under Islamic law to try the hostages for any acts prior to February 1979.[8]

Of course, none of the above would have stopped the Iranians had they decided to pursue this threat, in that the entire legal experience of the Khomeini era was one of willful disregard for established laws and legal procedures. Certainly, any existing safeguards for the rights of defendants had been discarded by the militants and komitehs as soon as the shah's regime collapsed (not that legal proceedings under the shah had been the epitome of defendants' rights, to be sure). The Khomeini regime had violated the Koran, international law, and Islamic law in permitting the seizure of the embassy and holding the staff captive in the first place. At this stage in the Iranian revolutionary experience, "law" consisted of whatever measures the regime took to preserve itself, enforce order, and exact revenge for past wrongs. Probably more important to the Iranians, a tribunal would serve the ancillary purpose of allowing the Iranians to present to the world their "case" against the shah and his alleged "crimes" against the Iranian people. In this, the United States and a quarter-century of relations with Iran and the shah would have been on trial just as surely as the hostages.

It was clear to the Justice Department that the trials would be controlled by the Iranians and their outcome predetermined. In line with Jones and Redlick, who had established the illegitimacy of the trials, Justice raised the question of whether the United States should represent the hostages or send private lawyers to avoid conferring any legitimacy on the tribunal.[9] In the end, the determination was made to represent the hostages with private attorneys—who would have been among the very best legal talent and minds in America, working on a pro bono basis.

Throughout the winter and spring of 1979–80 the Carter administration tried mightily to resolve the crisis through negotiations. And if the substance of the crisis itself was not sufficiently difficult, there were other complications. One problem stemmed from the Iranians' propensity to treat any negotiation like a transaction among rug merchants in the bazaar, a trait further compounded by the addition of revolutionary fervor. A second obstacle was the Iranians' almost perfect ignorance of the U.S. government, the constitutional limitations on the president, and normal governmental (i.e., bureaucratic) processes.

Some of these difficulties were outlined in a memo to the president written during the summer of 1980. The document began by pointing out that the Iranians had "shown little sign of trying to devise a realistic solution" to the crisis. The Americans were thus immediately placed on the defensive, fearful that any accommodation would only generate more demands from the Iranians (just as when haggling over the price of a Kerman rug). Of fundamental concern was the fact that Iranian officials had refused to meet with U.S. officials to negotiate, discuss, or even just talk. Furthermore, the ongoing struggle between moderates and fundamentalists had created a power vacuum that prevented the negotiation of any agreement. Complicating the process even more, the Iranians refused to trust the United States and the United States could not rely on Iran's promises. And finally, each side, the memo said, "wants the other to perform first." The United States didn't want to appear to be paying blackmail, and Iran didn't want the world to think that it had backed down in the face of U.S. threats. And these were only some of the problems both sides faced in the negotiation process. It is little wonder that it took literally an act of war by Iraq threatening Iran's continued survival as a nation to coerce Iran to negotiate with any semblance of seriousness. And even then the good offices of a trusted third party, Algeria, were necessary to bring the process to a conclusion.[10]

A question that created much initial concern within the White House was whether the students had received any assistance from foreign countries—specifically the Soviet Union—in the takeover and subsequent occupation of the embassy. The Soviets officially approved of the embassy takeover and made this position known to the Iranians, no doubt delighting in the embarrassment to the United States. The Soviets also, of course, saw it as a positive development that might, a CIA report noted, "provide opportunities for the USSR to expand its influence" with Iran and in the region. Later, the Soviet government tried to delay the settlement by "encouraging the Iranians to insist on tough financial terms." The Soviets also worked to undermine U.S. sanctions by facilitating the flow of embargoed goods into Iran. The KGB's clandestine radio station, the National Voice of Iran, supported the students from the beginning as well. Less circumspect than official Soviet pronouncements, NVOI's tone was harsher and more biting.[11] But in terms of substantive support—the provision of matériel, funds, etc.—there was never any evidence that the Khomeini regime sought or received tangible support from any other government or political entity.

There was reason to rejoice, not only in the White House but throughout all of America, when, on 28 January, the six embassy staff members who had been hidden and safeguarded by the courageous Canadians were finally able to escape from Iran thanks to a skillful CIA deception operation and an inspiring display of fortitude on their part and that of the Canadians.[12] The Iranians were irate over the escapade, and in one of the numerous ironies that punctuated the crisis, condemned the Canadians for acting in an "illegal" manner. The same day, Abolhassan Bani-Sadr, the revolutionary government's first minister of finance, was elected president of Iran; soon thereafter, he was named head of the Revolutionary Council. He immediately sought to do what Khomeini had forbidden: negotiate with the United States. He also undertook to fulfill a campaign promise to gain control of the hostages from the radicals. The war between the moderates and the radicals was escalating.

By mid-March all attempts to negotiate with the Iranian government had collapsed, leaving President Carter with essentially two options: wait it out or attempt more forceful action. The American public was running out of patience, however, as were many in the administration, and waiting wasn't really an acceptable option. The Defense Department had been developing a series of rescue scenarios since almost the day of capture, and on 22 March, General Jones of the Joint Chiefs presented the latest iteration to the president at Camp David. President Carter approved a reconnaissance mission, and soon thereafter a CIA Twin Otter aircraft flew, at night and at very low altitude, more than six hundred miles into the Iranian interior. The aircraft was flown by a truly legendary CIA officer, a former Air America pilot who is probably the best pilot the CIA has ever had (and the organization hires only the best!); he was accompanied by a U.S. Air Force special operations officer. Landing in the midst of a salt desert known as the Dasht-e-Kavir, the air force officer procured soil samples to help ascertain whether the ground was hard enough to support the weight of a loaded C-130 transport aircraft. Before departing, the officer rode over the area on a small motorbike measuring out a landing zone in the hard terrain and placing remotely activated infrared beacons to guide in the C-130s at a future date.[13] The site, known as Desert One, was only three hundred miles from Tehran and was to be the first stop of a complex rescue mission (see map 4).

On 10 April, with negotiations with various contacts in the Iranian government at a standstill, Iraq threatened to invade Iran. The Iranians, who considered Iraq just another American stooge, quickly threatened to kill the hostages if the invasion took place. It was just one more unneeded complication for the president. The next day, the president decided that diplomatic efforts were no longer viable and convened a National Security Council meeting to review the latest version of the rescue plan; the NSC concurred with the president's intent to move toward a rescue attempt by military force.

Once again the administration reviewed conditions in Iran and the

Map 4. Iran

various options available. These included doing nothing and waiting an indefinite period until Khomeini had no further use for the hostages; searching for new channels of communications to Iran's ruling circle with the hope of stimulating negotiations; imposing new unilateral sanctions, although the effectiveness of the sanctions already in place was nil and new ones would be more symbolic than anything else; enlisting the support of allies and neutrals to impose their own sanctions (UN-ordered sanctions were moot so long as the Soviets could exercise a veto in the Security Council); mining or blockading Iranian harbors; punitive military strikes on Iran's oil refineries, railroads, power stations, and docks; and a rescue mission.[14] After all the options had been considered, the president and others found themselves leaning toward the rescue mission.

Secretary of State Cyrus Vance dissented from the NSC's conclusion, as he had done previously whenever the use of military force had been proposed. He had (or thought he had) the president's assurance that no military force would be applied until all diplomatic efforts, including sanctions, had been exhausted or proven ineffective. Since the first of the year Vance had been working to bring the European allies in line with America's unilaterally imposed sanctions. Reluctant at first, the Europeans finally agreed on 22 April to implement their own sanctions against Iran, effective 17 May, and Vance was hopeful that these measures would eventually lead to a resolution of the crisis. Vance also argued against using military force as long as there was no immediate danger to the hostages, which by mid-April seemed to be the case. The secretary was worried that military force might seriously disturb American interests in the Persian Gulf region and drive Iran into the arms of the Soviet Union. And, of course, the use of force would quite likely shore up Khomeini's position among Iranians and perhaps unite the Muslim world against America and the West.[15] These were imminently reasonable concerns, but Vance nevertheless stood alone.

National Security Adviser Zbigniew Brzezinski had debated the utility and odds of success of a rescue mission ever since the SCC meeting of 6 November, when he directed the secretary of defense to initiate contingency planning for one. The first draft of such a mission had been presented to Brzezinski at the Pentagon on 11 November. Brzezinski was also beginning to think in terms of a retaliatory mission tied to the rescue attempt in case of heavy American casualties (but, again, as a contingency only). Particularly appealing to him was the occupation of Kharg Island, Iran's oil export facility, and a blockade of Iran augmented by air strikes. Although this turned out to be a controversial proposal, it was precisely the sort of thing a national security adviser is paid to think of. The Soviet invasion of Afghanistan during the night of 25–26 December 1979 caused Brzezinski to back away from the retaliatory strike, but he continued to consider rescue a viable last-resort measure. A review of rescue planning in mid-March with Secretary Brown and General Jones gave Brzezinski some measure of optimism, leading him to conclude that the mission "had a reasonably good chance of success." But unlike the president, he was more realistic regarding what "success" might mean. Certainly it did not exclude the possibility of casualties among the hostages and the rescue force.[16]

At the NSC meeting of 11 April, President Carter gave his preliminary approval for the mission, now slated for 24–25 April; he reiterated the decision at a similar session on 15 April. Shortly thereafter, on the nineteenth, the president received a message from Bruce Laingen, who was still being held in the foreign ministry. The text commended the president for the additional (nonviolent) sanctions recently levied against the Iranians, including breaking off diplomatic relations and declaring the Iranian mission staff in Washington persona non grata, and noted that new measures "will succeed only if they hurt." Laingen ended the message by emphasizing that "the maximum support of our Allies and friends" was vital for the administration's efforts. But in yet another serious misinterpretation of a message from the field, the president somehow read the message as advocating "strong action against Iran" and moved closer to making the final decision to use military power.[17] It is not at all clear how the president came to read the message as an incitement for military force, but it is certain that Laingen had not meant to say that. On that same day, the president received a message from Ham Jordan informing him that the highly secret negotiations that he had been pursuing with a Frenchman and an Argentine had failed to bear fruit. Laingen's and Jordan's messages, considered in tandem by the president, convinced him that he had no other choice but to proceed with the rescue attempt.[18]

One other decision remained. On 23 April, the day before Operation Eagle Claw was set to begin, the president let it be known that he would not approve any collateral attacks against Iran. The president thought it best not to further complicate an already complicated and complex operation, and he also had no desire at this point to deal with the possible international repercussions of such attacks.[19] After receiving a final briefing and being informed that "there was little prospect of the hostages' release in the next five or six months and that everything was favorable for the rescue mission," the president gave the final authorization for the mission to proceed.[20]

CHAPTER 16

24 APRIL – 22 JUNE 1980

One evening near the end of April the routine went awry, and we were quick to notice. Late afternoon usually brought an increase in the sounds of life in the hall as the guards changed shifts, food carts were wheeled up and down the corridor, and prisoners were taken to and from the bathroom. There were also numerous ambient noises. I was once again in a room in the chancery facing the street, and noises reached me from the street as well as from the compound just beyond my window, where some guard would be working the action of whatever type of firearm he was carrying. Occasionally there would be a gunshot followed by the sound of feet running down the hallway as the Iranians rushed outside, only to find a shaken guard who had accidentally discharged his weapon while playing with it—a wonderful source of amusement for us captives.

But on the afternoon of 24 April 1980, none of the usual noises was heard, either within the embassy or from without. As dinnertime approached, the chancery grew eerily quiet. I pounded on the door for a restroom call, but no guard appeared. Listening closely, I could hear a radio down the hall emitting what sounded like a news broadcast, judging from the intonations of the speaker. Continuing to bang on the door, I finally roused a guard to escort me down the hall to the bathroom; he smiled neither when he came to the door nor when he hurried me back to my room. I could by now easily hear the radio, but nothing else.

Something big was happening. Long ago, I had learned that any unexpected shift in the routine was an almost sure sign that things were about to get worse. Dinner came late, and I was famished. In lieu of our usual weeknight fare of meat, vegetables, and bread, I was brought one bowl of thin, chili-like soup. Much later, in the middle of the night, I was handcuffed and a heavy canvas hood was placed over my head.

Then, in deathly quiet, I was taken from the chancery, seated in a van with perhaps five or six of my colleagues, and driven away. Not one word was said: we had no idea where we were going, or why.

The ride lasted thirty minutes or so, with most of it uphill. The van stopped and I was escorted through a large, possibly gymnasium-sized room, up several flights of metal stairs, and down a narrow corridor. Finally I was pushed into someplace small and told to remove my hood. When I saw my new quarters I became instantly enraged, my emotions intensified by the adrenaline that had been flooding my body since I had been taken from my room. My new "room" was a prison cell, about six feet long on one side and about eight feet across the back. The opposite-side wall ran only four feet before angling in for another three feet (a stainless-steel toilet was situated here) and then angling back to join the front "wall." This front wall was less than three feet in length and consisted almost entirely of a floor-to-ceiling steel door with a slot near the bottom for a food tray and a small, closed window at face height. The ceiling was perhaps fifteen feet above the floor, and one small transom-type window joined with a dim bulb to provide the only light. It was a scene out of Hollywood's worst B-grade movies. And I was furious.

I pounded on the door until my hands began to swell, but no one came. I paced angrily back and forth in the small area (three steps, turn; three steps, turn; three steps, turn) for what seemed like hours. Once, when the judas window opened and a strange face peered in, I rushed toward the door, whereupon the window was slammed shut. I let loose a string of the foulest obscenities I could think of, insulting the unknown peeper, our captors, Khomeini, and Iranians in general. No reaction; no response. I had heard other doors slam down the cellblock and at least enjoyed the small reassurance that I was not alone. After enough time had passed for the adrenaline to begin wearing off and I had calmed down slightly, I had two thoughts: first, whatever had been on the news broadcast probably had also caused our relocation; second, this never happened to James Bond.[1]

As dawn approached and I was running out of steam, one of the student "guard supervisors" came to see me. While he would not tell me what was going on, he was at ease and friendly. I told him that putting us in prison was not a good move for him and his colleagues, and noted that it would no doubt create more antipathy toward him, his fellow students, and Iran. For once, the student made no attempt to justify the embassy takeover or to condemn either the shah or President Carter. He replied that the move was carried out only for our own safety and that we really were not in prison, we were only in a "prison-like place." I gaped at him and waved my arm to encompass the medieval dungeon–like surroundings. He smiled and left.

We were in Evin for ten days. During that time I left the cell three times for showers, which were followed by short stints in a twelve-foot-by-twelve-foot exercise pen with fifteen-foot-high brick walls open only to the sky. For the rest of the time, it was pace, sleep, and try to read by the light of the bulb, which burned twenty-four hours a day. The food ranged from awful to abominable, and the only ingredient I ever recognized was the rice. At least I hoped it was rice.

The one exception to this routine occurred the morning of the second day, when a fellow hostage was put into my cell. While glad to see someone besides an Iranian, I was hoping the two of us were not going to have to live for a lengthy period of time in the matchbox-sized room. After an awkward greeting (for I had not known him well), this non-CIA "colleague" asked me what I knew about the recent events, whether I had been able to communicate with anyone, and if I had any thoughts or ideas about what might be happening. We talked awhile, but I had virtually nothing to tell him, having been in solitary for almost six months and not having talked in weeks with any Iranian who could or would tell me anything. He also professed to know virtually nothing, even though he had been kept with groups of others. I thought it a bit strange that after a short while this individual wanted to quit talking and just play cards. I also noticed that he had been able to keep his watch, which was odd. Everyone who had been with me in the dining room that first night had their watches and rings taken away and never saw them again, and I had assumed that all the others did, too. Nor were any of those who were with me in the Mushroom Inn or in the TDY bungalows permitted to keep their jewelry.

After we were all reunited at the air force hospital in Wiesbaden, Germany, I learned that this man was one of several who had been overly "cooperative" with the Iranians. He had been able to receive uncensored letters from home and had even been allowed to talk to his family on the telephone. In fact, I had heard him talking for a goodly period of time on the phone on Easter Sunday because the windows were open both in my six-by-ten-foot basement "room" and in the office he was using right above me. But he denied knowing anything of the outside world when he was in the cell with me just three weeks later. Nor, as it turned out, did he share any information with his cellmates during all that time. I later learned that he knew much about what had been happening that he did not share with me during our few hours together. I then understood why he had been put in my cell that day in Evin Prison.

I passed Day 180 in Evin. Then, in the middle of the tenth night, I was again attired in the season's fashion fad—the heavy canvas hood—seated in a van with several others, and driven for several hours to a new location. This time, it was an ostentatious villa that must have belonged to a very wealthy person. After crossing an elaborate marbled grand foyer (although still hooded, I could see well enough out the bottom to get a good sense of the surroundings) and ascending a wide, curving staircase carpeted with the deepest pile I have ever trod, I ended up in a room about twelve feet by fourteen feet that had once been the bedroom of a small girl. The bedspread, sheets, and wallpaper featured green and pink cartoon dinosaurs, the windows were framed with lace curtains, and there were Nancy Drew books in the bookcases. The bed was about two feet shorter than my six-foot, three-inch height. Although there was an adjoining bathroom, I was never permitted to use it; instead, I was blindfolded and walked down a corridor to an unbelievably sumptuous black-marbled bath with bright brass fixtures. Despite the luxury, I was still a prisoner, and there was always an armed guard outside the door of the little girl's room I called home. I was struck by the surrealistic sensations these surroundings evoked.

Along with the several colleagues who constituted our little tour group, I was moved four more times in a short period. The villa was home for only five days, followed by nine days in a ratty, filthy, rundown third-floor apartment in an urban area. Then I was moved to a ratty, filthy, rundown ground-floor room in the same building for another eight days. During this time I had only one shower and the food was no longer either American or adequate in quantity. By this time I had become so inured to moving that it no longer angered me to be awakened in mid-sleep and told to prepare to move out. Not that there was much to move out in the first place; my belongings consisted of a plastic shopping bag holding a change of clothes, a few toiletries, a towel, pencil and paper, and a couple of books.

My next move, along with U.S. Air Force captain Paul Needham and

Marine gunnery sergeant Don Moeller, was to a fairly modern Holiday Inn–type hotel situated several hours away. We were on about the fourth floor, me in solitary as usual, Paul and Don about three doors down. My room had two double beds, a bathroom, and a balcony fortified with steel plates about three inches thick and a foot wide. The plates were welded together to form a nearly solid wall from the floor to the ceiling of the balcony, making it impossible to see out. Until we were caught at it, Paul and I were able to communicate by whispering loudly across the separating balconies. In what seemed to be an indication that the Iranians weren't as hostile to us as they initially had been, our "punishment" for talking was that we couldn't sit on our respective balconies at the same time.

We spent six weeks in these comfortable surroundings. Spring had arrived, and it was very pleasant sitting in the fresh air, even if we weren't exactly "outside." They were not particularly bad weeks, except for our meals, which were so unpalatable even our Iranian guards had trouble choking them down. Most of the time I had no idea what it was we were being served, but I do know that there was never any meat. Beans I could distinguish, and rice was a no-brainer, but much too frequently neither taste nor appearance lent any clue to the origin or nature of the glop set before me. There seemed to be about eight different menus, but I could manage to swallow only two of them; one was just marginally satisfactory, and with the other I resorted to digging out the beans and tossed the rest. Otherwise, I ate only breakfast.

I lost a lot of weight here. When we arrived in Wiesbaden I tipped the scales at 133 pounds, down from about 180 on the day of capture. If it were not for the pistachio nuts and dates that appeared fairly frequently during our stay at the hotel, plus the barbari bread at breakfast, I would have weighed even less. On the positive side, the weather was superb, with cool evenings and warm days. I could sit out on the balcony in fresh air, even if I could not be in the sun. I had unlimited access to a real bathroom with a Western-type toilet rather than the usual porcelain holes in the floor—which I had—with utmost reverence, to be sure—dubbed "Khomeini holes." I was kept supplied with books, and I had a real bed with sheets I knew were clean because I washed them myself in the shower. In terms of captivity, it did not get much better than this. If it were not for the cuisine, this stay might even have been almost bearable. And then we were moved again.

Washington, 24–25 April 1980

"The longest day of my four years in the White House . . . the most bitter disappointment." —Zbigniew Brzezinski

"It was hard for me to accept that the careful plan had gone awry, that people had actually been killed . . . a tremendous wave of nausea gripped me." —Hamilton Jordan

"Bone tired, I returned home with a heavy heart." —Cyrus Vance

"That night I did not sleep at all . . . [for all involved] a crushing personal defeat. . . . What I was tasting, I said to myself again and again, was 'ashes in the mouth.'" —Gary Sick

"One of the worst [days] of my life. . . . I am still haunted by memories of that day. . . . I will always remember the people who gave me their support." —President Jimmy Carter

The details of the rescue mission, Operation Eagle Claw, are well known. Eight RH-53D Sea Stallion helicopters—belonging to the U.S. Navy but flown by Marine Corps pilots—attempted to fly from the aircraft carrier USS *Nimitz* (CVAN-68) off the southern coast of Iran to Desert One. Two helos dropped out with mechanical failure, and an unexpected dust storm (or *haboob*) skewed the helos' arrival time at Desert One. One helo pilot declared a still-controversial mission-ending mechanical problem at Desert One. An explosive collision between one helo and an EC-130 in the desert night left eight dead and numerous injured, including some severely burned. The result: a failed mission, fifty-one American officials and two American civilians still captive, and for all practical purposes the end of the Carter presidency.

Several cogent analytical works have been written about Eagle Claw, and most are generally critical. One volume, however, penned by the Desert One on-scene commander, U.S. Air Force colonel Jim Kyle, who was also deeply involved in planning the mission from the very first, places many of the criticisms in proper context and corrects others that are erroneous or unjustified. Although I intend neither to rehash the mission nor to offer a definitive response to any individual question, some observations are relevant.[2]

First, nothing about this mission was remotely close to being easy. The planning decisions, the distances and geographical obstacles involved, the logistics problems, the security nightmare, the training complications, and all of the other myriad problems to be overcome were in the aggregate nearly overwhelming. A highly dedicated, exceptionally professional group of men and women did their very best to accomplish an immensely forbidding objective. That so much was accomplished with so few casualties is truly remarkable. As Secretary of Defense Harold Brown later commented, "There is no other country in the world that could even have attempted such an operation."[3]

What did the hostages think of the rescue mission? While I will not attempt to speak for the others, I can say that I have heard only one hostage speak in favor of the mission, and that was expressed with strongly felt emphasis during our meeting with former secretary of state Cyrus Vance. Otherwise, opinions ranged from doubtful to firmly against. Had the rescue mission occurred much earlier in the crisis, it is possible, even probable, that more of the hostages would have supported it, even if there had been casualties. I have no doubt that I would have been one of the most supportive. But six months after the capture it seemed—from our perspective, to be sure—unnecessary in terms of risk and need. There was no longer any apparent immediate danger to the fifty-three hostages, and without that immediacy a rescue seemed—to us—to be a greater risk than simply waiting out the Iranians. When he ordered the mission President Carter believed that there was "little prospect" of release for at least five or six months.[4] It should be emphasized that the hostages had no idea of the full range of other pressures the administration was under at the time, nor did they have any knowledge of the success or failure of other, nonviolent, measures.

Most of the anxiety the hostages experienced over the long duration of our imprisonment was in response to potential dangers such as incurring a serious illness, illnesses or other problems of family members at home, and (for the older captives) simply dying of age-related causes. Living conditions had improved and stabilized for most, and they were at least marginally better even for those of us who were not in particularly good odor with the Iranians due to our former jobs in the embassy. We were in familiar and not too uncomfortable quarters in embassy buildings, modest medical care was available for treatment of colds and other minor problems, and our dietary needs were adequately met with American-style cooking. Most of us, I think, had concluded that the Iranians finally understood that harming us would not help them achieve their goals. More significant, perhaps, we were aware that our captors' issues with the United States were diminishing as the internal fight for control of their government against the moderates intensified. So, by April, a rescue mission arguably posed a much greater immediate risk to our lives than the Iranian militants did. Based solely on what we knew and suspected, most of us would have probably chosen not to see a rescue mission. But of course, most of us knew very little, and a few of us knew nothing.

There was another factor that almost certainly would have affected any preference for or against a military effort, had we known of it. Knowledge of the pending sanctions on the part of our European allies might well have imparted a sense of optimism to most of us, especially in the light of Iran's precarious economic and political situation. The alternative of waiting out a diplomatic resolution in relative safety would probably have appeared more attractive than the unknown but significant dangers of military action.

This (obviously one-sided) perspective seems to beg the question of whether the mission was, in fact, necessary—or at least necessary at that time. Certainly the president and all but one of his senior advisers believed that it was. They reached their decision when diplomacy no longer seemed viable and they were confronted with increasing public pressure for an end to the crisis. The president was facing a serious challenge in his run for a second term, not just from the Republicans but also from within his own political party, and that was a factor in his decision as well. The senior policymakers in the administration (Cy Vance excepted) believed the options had run out, leaving them no other choice.[5]

But there *was* another option: they could have waited. In October 1979, when the shah's entry into the United States was the dominant issue, Secretary Vance suggested having Bruce Laingen obtain what would have been the definitive Iranian reaction to the shah's admission. The president seemed to agree but shortly thereafter granted permission for the shah to come without that additional assessment. Now, once again, the president ignored Vance and chose not to wait for our European allies to apply sanctions against Iran, despite having directed Vance to work for just that goal and having just received a positive response regarding his labors. Without clear indications that the hostages' lives were in peril, was the risk indeed absolutely necessary? Had the options truly run out?

Zbigniew Brzezinski notes that although the Europeans had just promised to join the United States in sanctions, the president was frustrated by the lack of progress on any other front. Further, he was wary that the Europeans would first agree and then temporize, endlessly stringing out the implementation of sanctions. And there was always the possibility that the allies might back out of their commitments at the last minute, possibly in response to some Iranian ruse. Finally, any further delay would have run past the daylight limitations critical to the mission; if not now, then no rescue mission would have been possible until late fall. And there were too many unknowns for the president to accept that six-month wait.[6] The president weighed the options and made his decision. It is difficult to argue that he was wrong.

The daylight limitations were of utmost concern to the planners, second only to operational security. Clandestine operations are usually best accomplished in the shadows, and Eagle Claw's night phases demanded a finite amount of darkness. It is an immutable fact of nature that in springtime days grow longer and nights grow shorter. Eagle Claw had to go before the end of April or wait until late fall. And while the hostages seemed relatively secure that spring, no one could foretell what might happen during the summer.

Were there other military rescue alternatives to Eagle Claw, operations that might not require as much darkness and would therefore have been more amenable to summer conditions? The best special-operations personnel—the most experienced, most imaginative, most responsible, and most daring—in the military and in the CIA were assigned to planning Eagle Claw. All agreed on one fact: no "good" plan was possible given the geographical obstacles to overcome. Of all of the unsatisfactory options that were envisioned and subjected to scrutiny, Eagle Claw was simply the least awful. It has been criticized as a very complicated plan, but complex is probably a more apt description. And indeed it was; but so were all the others considered. Was it too complex? Even setting aside the issue of whether or not there were sufficient helicopters, the plan was still daunting. It also enjoyed, as is the nature of these things, little inherent flexibility and even less tolerance for error. It was a plan that held untold opportunities for Murphy's Law. And yet it was the "best" available.

None of the mission planners held any illusions that it was "anything but a high-risk venture," Gary Sick notes, although some of the non-military administration members were optimistic that Eagle Claw stood a reasonable chance of success.[7] But not one of the senior military commanders was confident of success. The mission's complexity, the operational security measures, and the inability to rehearse fully and intensively were not features that inspired optimism or confidence. The commanders were not, to be sure, certain that it would fail, but they recognized better than anyone else all that could go wrong and how much pure luck would be required for it to succeed.[8]

As for the actual troops on the ground—not the mission commanders but those who would land at Desert One, assault the embassy, fly with the hostages to a deserted airfield west of Tehran, and move the hostages from there to freedom—each Ranger, each Delta Force member, each airman, and each Marine believed deep in his heart of hearts that he could perform his part of the mission if he were given the opportunity. This belief was not founded in arrogance or blind optimism; rather it was a manifestation of the professionalism, confidence, and courage each soldier had developed in his career as a special-operations expert. And it was cemented in an intense desire to free Americans who were being deprived of their liberty by international outlaws. I thank God every day that America has men and women willing to take these risks and make the sacrifices.

Certainly one error was using Marines to fly the navy helos. Not that the Marines were not good pilots, because they were; they were very good. But they were very good at the missions they had been trained to fly, day in and day out. Here they were being asked to fly a specialized and demanding mission for which they had not trained. Special ops missions require more than outstanding flying skills; they require men and (now) women who also have certain psychological attributes and certain physical training and skills. They are volunteers who have been selected only after intensive physical and psychological testing. No special-operations mission should ever be undertaken by individuals who are not special-operations trained and qualified. But the Marine pilots were not special-operations evaluated, selected, or trained.

The navy's RH-53D helos had to be used because, of all the variants of this aircraft (the HH-53s flown by the U.S. Air Force and the CH-53s flown by the Marine Corps), only this version met the mission requirements. It had the range, carrier operability, electronics suites, payload, and spare parts availability (from stocks already onboard the carrier), and the navy's maintenance personnel were already familiar with it. There was one additional—and highly important—reason why the RH-53 was a good choice: the Soviets were accustomed to seeing these aircraft on carrier decks, while the appearance of the air force helos would raise immediate questions in the minds of Soviet naval intelligence.[9]

According to one researcher, the original plan was for each helo to have a Marine pilot as the aircraft commander and a navy pilot as copilot; as such, there would be one pilot experienced in over-the-beach assault operations and one pilot experienced in seaborne operations. But after a poorly executed training exercise, some pilots were replaced; the final contingent was all Marine save for one air force and two navy pilots. So why not air force special ops pilots? The air force had more than 100 special-operations-qualified and experienced HH-53 pilots on the roster, as well as nearly 100 former HH-53 special-operations pilots who could be requalified in short order. Of these 190 or so pilots, a large majority had combat experience flying HH-53s in Vietnam and were thus psychologically prepared for the pressures the mission would entail. Given that an earlier air force special-operations project had convincingly shown that it is easier and more effective for special-ops pilots to go from one variant of an aircraft to another variant of the same aircraft than it is to give special-operations training to non-special-ops pilots who are qualified on the desired aircraft, wisdom should have provided what the on-scene commander, Jim Kyle, had expected: special-ops-qualified air force HH-53 pilots flying the navy's RH-53.[10] It didn't happen.

Another question that remains unanswered is what would have constituted "success" in the mission? What level of American casualties could have been sustained and the mission still considered successful? There was always a chance that some of the rescuers might be captured and/or that not all of the hostages could be rescued (recall that three were still held in the foreign ministry, well away from the embassy grounds). How many Americans could remain captive in Iran and the mission still be labeled a success? By one account, President Carter was told that six or seven Delta Force members and two or three hostages might be wounded or injured; by another, the president was told that somewhere between three and eight casualties might occur.[11] But no one really knew what the casualties might be, which was also what General Vaught told the president. The president personally told Delta commander Col. Charlie Beckwith to use "whatever force is needed to save American lives," although he remained adamant that there be no "wanton killings." Beckwith informed the president that it was possible that his men might accidentally kill a hostage if any happened to pick up a weapon from a guard and run out into the open with it, a risk that could not be defused.

But anticipating a number of Americans killed and wounded is not the same as defining success. It may be that Delta or one of the other military organizations involved made more precise calculations of the odds of success and more closely defined what that success would encompass, but if so, they did not transmit those odds or supporting figures to the White House. Perhaps the heaviest criticism levied against the mission was that it was insufficiently trained and rehearsed and that at no time did all the elements of the mission, or even most of them, train together. That is a damning criticism, as far as it goes. The trouble is, it doesn't go quite far enough in explaining what happened or didn't happen and why. At all levels of the mission, from the Rangers on the ground up to the chairman of the Joint Chiefs, operational security was the most important concern. If any word of the mission leaked out, all would be jeopardized. Anyone involved in special operations or intelligence work understands the exquisite relationship between security and efficiency, between secrecy and success. Simply put, security and efficiency represent the perfect inverse relationship: as security measures increase, efficiency concomitantly decreases, and vice versa. In the case of Eagle Claw, operational security was the utmost concern because not only were the lives of the rescue forces in danger, the lives of the hostages and the prestige of the United States were also at risk. But it was not the Iranians that worried mission planners as much as it was the Soviet Union.[12]

Soviet spy satellites crossed over the United States several times a day. Soviet trawlers converted to intelligence collection shadowed every U.S. Navy carrier task force. Soviet submarines and Tupelov-95 Bison long-range reconnaissance aircraft likewise shadowed our fleets, and KGB signals intelligence collection sites in the Western Hemisphere (including from their embassy on Sixteenth Street N.W. in Washington, D.C., and at Lourdes, Cuba) vacuumed up as much telephonic and electronic communications as they could. KGB and Soviet military intelligence (GRU) in Washington, at the Soviet mission to the UN in New York, and in consulates in Chicago and San Francisco recruited and ran as many American agents as they could convince to spy against their county.

During the Iranian crisis of 1979–81, the Soviets were intensely interested in U.S. diplomatic and military plans, hoping to exploit the Amer-

ican-Iranian break for their own benefit. No one involved had the slightest doubt that the Soviets would not hesitate for a split second, if they
discovered the existence of an actual rescue mission, to inform the Iranians of what they had learned. The Soviets had nothing to lose and everything to gain by doing so. Keenly aware of all the Soviet eyes and ears
looking for any clues to a military operation, Eagle Claw planners made
the only decision they could: operation security was paramount, and the
effectiveness, efficiency, and confidence that would be gained from
repeated partial and full-scale rehearsals would be sacrificed. There was,
on this point, no compromising, no second-guessing, no cutting cor-
ners. There was, ultimately, no choice.

CHAPTER 17

22 JUNE – 23 DECEMBER 1980

Tehran

The good times at the "Holiday Inn" did not last, of course. On the night of 22–23 June 1980, Paul, Don, and I were moved to Komiteh Prison in Tehran, where we would reside for the next fifteen weeks. While my cell was bigger than the one in Evin, perhaps eight feet by ten feet, there was no toilet. I was back to sleeping on a foam pallet on the floor and had only a small desk, chair, and lamp for furniture; one small window high up on the back (outside) wall let in a little light during the day. It was the middle of summer, and to handle the heat I began sleeping during the day and staying up all night. There was an open ventilation grill over the solid steel door; by standing on my chair, I could look out into the cellblock.

Within a few days I had learned that my cell was at one end of the block and that five of my colleagues, including Tom Schaefer, were in the cell across from me and three of the Marine security guards were next door. I soon deduced from a number of clues in the toilet room and shower room (located at the opposite end of the cellblock) that there were about twenty of us in the cellblock, split among five or six cells. As usual, I was the only one in solitary.

Late in August and again in September, two memorable events occurred. One night in mid-August, at about 2:00 A.M., I was reading John Masters' enthralling wartime autobiography when I heard someone down the cellblock knock on the steel door, the usual sign that a visit to the toilet was in order. But I heard no sound of the door opening. A minute or two later the knocking came again, only louder. Again no response, and again a louder knock, followed by the crashing sound of a fist hammering the door. An amazed voice said, "Christ, he's sound asleep out there!" I pulled up the chair and looked out the ventilation grill (which someone else had also obviously done, too) and saw our guard, possibly the youngest—and smallest—of all the Iranians I had seen during my imprisonment, head down on his table and dead to the world only a few feet away from the pounding.

With that, colleagues started whispering back and forth across the cellblock. When I chipped in there was something of a startled hush. Everyone thought that I had been executed because I had been neither seen nor heard from for so long. Once beyond this revelation, the others piped down while Tom Schaefer brought me up-to-date on such things as the Desert One rescue attempt that had prompted our forced exodus from the embassy in April; the release of Rich Queen, who was sent home in July with multiple sclerosis (leaving now fifty-two hostages); and other information about who was where and what others had heard, seen, or suffered. This little over-the-garden-fence chat with Tom was wondrously rejuvenating.

The other momentous occasion was on the evening of 23 September, when all the lights suddenly went out, not just in my cell but throughout the prison. This was followed a few minutes later by a siren blasting away almost outside my cell window. Soon thereafter, mingling in with the siren, came the somewhat distant but unmistakable *whump, whump* of exploding ordnance—my first clue that the ruckus was an air raid. It took a minute for my bemusement to evaporate, and then my spirits soared at the thought that President Carter had finally unleashed the U.S. military against the Iranians in another rescue attempt or retaliation. But common sense and reasoning quickly returned, and I realized that this scenario was very unlikely.

I sat on the floor watching the flashing lights of shell bursts somewhere beyond the little window and tried to figure out the identity of the perpetrators. The only logical conclusion was that it was the Iraqis. In my general ignorance of the region I could not imagine why Iraq might be bombing Iran, but I did recall that the two neighbors had not always been the best of friends. Nor did I doubt that it was in the Iraqis' character to attack Iran on any pretext if they perceived the Iranians to be in a weakened position.

I was elated by the bombing, no matter who was behind it. I was reasonably sure that a prison would not be a prime target, and while a stray round could always drop in, I felt safe sitting in a room with walls that were at least three feet of reinforced concrete. So bomb away, I mentally encouraged whoever it was, and damn good luck to you. The muzzle blasts of several antiaircraft guns in close proximity to the prison kept the noise level high, but it was not greatly disconcerting. I was also intrigued, having flown dozens of missions in Vietnam whose primary purpose had been to drop bombs on people, by the novel sensation of being on the receiving end of an air assault.

Meanwhile, my Iranian guards popped in every five minutes or so, most of them in a state of goggle-eyed panic, apparently to see if I was sharing the same fear. Or perhaps to see if I was using some secret gizmo to guide the bombers; anything was possible to these kids, whose knowledge of the espionage business came from the fantasy world of Hollywood. One reason I had not been permitted to keep a wristwatch was that at least some of the Iranians believed I might be able to use it to talk to Washington. On the plane out of Tehran following our release, one colleague told of visiting the toilet room in Komiteh Prison, which was monitored by a video camera. While standing by the window, he continually looked back and forth between the sky and his watch, which he had been able to talk a sympathetic guard into returning to him, mimicking someone checking the expected time of arrival of some-thing—a satellite, for example. A minute or two later, he gave a nod of satisfaction and began alternately talking to his watch and holding the watch up to his ear. After a minute of that, the guards burst into the room and that was the end of the watch. Now, with bombs going off in the vicinity of the prison, the guards did not know what to think when they found me sitting serenely on the floor clapping at each explosion.

We were in Komiteh Prison only two more weeks before being moved back to Evin Prison, this time into a bungalow-sized house on the prison grounds that had been turned into a makeshift jail. From its hill-side perch I could sneak peeks through a less than perfectly blacked-out window at the night air raids on Tehran. Although my room was only about four feet wide, it was perhaps fifteen feet long, half of a larger room partitioned by a wall constructed of tile nailed to a framework of two-by-fours.

This divide was not very substantial, and soon I was having short, whispered conversations with the adjoining occupant, Dave Roeder, the air force lieutenant colonel who had arrived in Tehran just days before the takeover to serve as the air attaché. I had talked with him occasion-ally before we were captured, but now we began a short-distance rela-tionship that soon became a strong friendship. The dividing wall ended at the rear of the room and against a window, leaving about a quarter-inch gap between the wall and the windowpane. Dave and I soon began sliding notes back and forth between our respective cells; we communicated about many things, especially our prospects for release. (I always took great secret pleasure whenever the guards cautioned us not to write notes to the other hostages because, I was repeatedly assured, we would certainly be caught. I would nod sagely and within a few minutes would be drafting my latest correspondence with Dave.)

Dave had flown two tours in Vietnam, first in B-52s and later in F-105 fighters. Now, after nearly a year in captivity, he was thin, gray-haired, rather haggard looking, and possessed of a truly scraggly beard. He looked like a cross between somebody's benevolent uncle and a bum. We were again being tended to by some of our first guards, kids who had not accompanied us on our tour of the countryside and whom we had not seen since "the old days" back in the embassy. Some were actually happy to see us! There were also some new students (or perhaps just new to me) who did not seem to have the initial dread of us the first guards had exhibited right after the takeover. Most of the guards, old or new, soon came to consider Dave a pleasant and benign person, possibly something of a substitute father figure, and they would often stop to chat with him, sometimes being rather open in the news they would share. Dave passed along to me whatever he was told, and I reciprocated when I could, although the students were not nearly as forthcoming with me.

The news Dave passed on from the guards invariably generated more questions in my mind, and I would send a note back to him giving my thoughts and a list of questions. The next time he was visited by these guards, he would work the questions into the conversation and, when alone, would send the answers back to me. Thus, we had the classic intelligence cycle: a need for particular information was followed by tasking to a collector, who acquired information from sources and then reported it back to the requirements originator, where it was collated, analyzed, and disseminated, along with new requirements. By the time we were split up in late December, Dave and I had an efficient intelligence mechanism in place and working for us.

Other sources of "intelligence" were *Time, Newsweek,* and *Der Spiegel* magazines, which the Iranians began giving to us, albeit with information about our own situation carefully excised. Keenly interested in the coming U.S. elections because one of their goals was to unseat President Carter, the Iranians gleefully showed us stories of the political campaign and nominating conventions indicating that Ronald Reagan held a significant lead over the president in the polls.

Fortunately, the Iranians did not always catch all the items they wished to keep from us in these periodicals. In an issue of *Der Spiegel*, for example, our captors completely missed a story about the Desert One rescue attempt, complete with maps and diagrams of the mission plan as well as photos of the burned wreckage of the EC-130 in the desert. Although I did not read or speak German, the photos provided a clear picture of what the mission was to have been and, to a somewhat lesser degree, what had gone wrong. All this "open-source" information was factored into our "intelligence" system. Many conclusions Dave and I reached as a result of our "intelligence collection program" were either right on the mark or nearly so.

Other than my "conversations" with Dave, my most striking memory of this time is of the freezing showers. The shower room was unheated, the window was always partially open to the outside air thanks to a damaged frame, and for most of the time the water heater servicing the shower was inoperable. Tehran is about four thousand feet in altitude, and the prison was some hundreds of feet higher in the mountains north of the city. The temperature in the shower room was always near the outside air temperature, and in November and December that temperature is damn cold! I was permitted to shower only late in the evening, and I'd stand there staring out the window at the snow in the courtyard, shivering like a hairless dog sitting on an iceberg. And that was before undressing for the shower. Without hot water, the shower water was so cold I was always amazed that it didn't come out in ice chunks. It became a real art to shower myself clean, including washing my hair (which always seemed gritty), and finish before turning completely blue. Yet once dried, dressed, and back in my little room, I felt like a million bucks. Maybe it was because the shower was so energizing, or maybe it was like what happens when you drive copper nails into your forehead—it just feels so good when you quit. But I'll always remember those showers.

Our captors' hatred of President Carter was so deep and strong that they never focused on what his defeat might mean to Iran and to our situation. They believed Ronald Reagan would be their friend (but then, they always seemed to assume that everyone would be their friend) and would perceive all the injustices America had perpetrated on their innocent country for so many years. Our captors were certain that Reagan would understand their point of view and why they came to the embassy that November day.[1] There was no rational reason for them to believe this, of course; they just thought that anyone who was Carter's opponent would naturally be on the side of the Iranians. Dave and I told them otherwise, but our words did not resonate. Imagine, then, the Iranians' utter befuddlement when, several days after the election, President-elect Reagan called the Iranians "barbarians" and said that he did not bargain with such people. Being labeled barbarians was highly offensive to many Iranians, who saw in their history and culture a land of refinement and civilization—an attitude that provided me with an ever-present topic on which to insult them, even though they were essentially correct. When our young guards came to talk to Dave Roeder about this, Dave would ask, in effect, "What did you expect? You capture an American embassy, hold American citizens prisoner for over a year, claim that America is your number-one enemy, claim that you hate Americans, desecrate the American flag by burning it or hauling garbage in it, and you maintain that you are at war with America. And now you think that Ronald Reagan is going to be your friend? He will not be your friend; he will be your enemy. You have brought this on yourselves, and that is the way the world works." The overnight change in the Iranians' attitude was palpable. Their delight in Carter's defeat was replaced by a growing fear of the new administration.

Washington

For a lengthy period following the rescue attempt there was little the Carter administration could do but wait and watch. Politically, Iran was close to chaos as the battle for power between the moderates and radicals seesawed back and forth. The hostages were one of the keys to this struggle, for whichever faction exercised control over the hostages was also strong enough to exercise control over the government. The radicals under Khomeini were more intensely dedicated to winning and more willing to utilize nondemocratic means and violence to attain their goals (despite their condemnations of the "corruption" of America and European governments). No one was exempt: Foreign Minister Sadegh Ghotbzadeh, one of Khomeini's closest advisers, was executed for deviating too far from Khomeini's desired path; the popularly elected secular president, Bani-Sadr, eventually ended up fleeing the country in disguise to save his own life.

The Carter administration now recognized that the only solution to the crisis was through negotiation, and also that until the Iranians found it in their interests to engage in negotiations it was best to avoid doing or saying anything that might complicate the situation or increase the danger to the hostages.[2]

In early September, however, the Iranians surprised the administration by asking the U.S. government, through the good offices of the chancellor of West Germany, to meet with an emissary from Khomeini to discuss the release of the hostages. Deputy Secretary of State Warren Christopher was designated to head the negotiating team, thus beginning five months of mind-bending intellectual labor, uncountable frustrations, repeated emotional swings, thousands of miles of body-numbing travel, haggling over minute details substantial and otherwise, and ultimately success.[3] For the president, the Iranians' offer to negotiate was proof that economic sanctions and diplomatic efforts to isolate Iran were working.[4] For the Iranians, it meant that the rug bazaar was open.

The Iraqi invasion on 22 September and the concurrent aerial attacks were not immediately seen as decisive in Washington with respect to the hostage crisis. And the negotiations, which had just commenced, were not viewed with any great optimism by Brzezinski, who continued to think another rescue mission would be the only way to end the crisis.[5] But in fact the invasion generated tremendous pressure on the Iranians, both diplomatic and military. They desperately needed replacement parts for their now-dilapidated military equipment as well as stocks to replace those that had disappeared during the wild and wooly days of the early revolution. And they found out just how isolated they were diplomatically in October when Prime Minister Mohammed Ali Rajai traveled to New York to ask the United Nations for assistance against the Iraqis. To his dismay, few of the representatives from the member nations had any sympathy for Iran's plight.

The Iranians had carried out egregious violations of international law and conventions for nearly a year, during which they had arrogantly dismissed every attempt by the UN to bring about an end to the crisis. Moreover, the Khomeini regime had displayed the same contempt and disdain for law by ignoring the decision of the World Court when the United States sued Iran and won. The Khomeini regime not only didn't deign to respond to the court before the hearing, it didn't even send representatives to appear at the proceedings. Now these same Iranians came before the UN with demands that the organization censure the Iraqis for blatant aggression in contravention of the same body of international law they had so often ridiculed and criticized. It was a very "Iranian" thing to do.

Rajai's pleas fell on deaf ears. The response from the UN was clear: release the Americans or stand alone—we will not help you counter a violation of international law while you yourselves are perpetrating serious violations.

There was now hope in Washington that the hostages would be released soon. As September turned into October and the presidential race heated up, there began to appear in the media, particularly in partisan anti-Carter commentary, concern about or allegations of an "October surprise" being planned or hoped for by the administration. Succinctly put, the "surprise" would be the release of the hostages with little or no advance warning, thus handing Carter a much-needed boost in his reelection campaign against Reagan. Carter, who was aware that Khomeini had stated that there would be no release until after the U.S. elections in the fall, wasn't counting on it.[6]

Nevertheless, realizing that an October release would leave the administration open to allegations of manipulation for political gain, the president directed White House Chief of Staff Hamilton Jordan to mull over the possibilities and provide him with a summary. Jordan drafted a fourteen-page "Eyes Only" memo for the president in early October 1980, which he typed himself and did not copy, laying out suggestions for dealing with the possible allegations and partisan charges that would arise if the hostages should be released just prior to election day. Believing it sufficiently sensitive, Carter handwrote "Private" in the top margin and indicated that no copies were to be made. His marginalia also indicate that he gave the memo to Brzezinski, who was to pass it along to "Ed" and "Chris" (Secretary of State Muskie and Deputy Secretary Warren Christopher). Its return to the White House was noted elsewhere in the margins as "Seen and returned by Secy Muskie, 10/17/80" with the initials "sc" (for Susan Clough, the president's secretary).[7]

Jordan's first thought was that if the president could make the American people see the safe return of the hostages as "a vindication" of his "restraint, the American people's patience[,] and . . . the wisdom of quiet diplomacy," then any "partisan charges of 'October surprise'" would seem "petty and irrelevant." Jordan then elaborated step by step how to go about establishing "that appropriate and accurate atmosphere and perception." Most important would be the reactions of the hostages themselves. Jordan speculated that a number of the hostages would be "embittered about their captivity, psychologically affected and totally unaware of the great outpouring of love" from the public. The president must remember that the hostages would know virtually nothing about what had transpired during their captivity and particularly about the administration's "public and private efforts" to gain their freedom.

To enlighten the hostages about these measures (and collaterally, the memo insinuated, to garner their support in countering partisan accusations), Jordan recommended that the hostages be kept in Europe for a time before returning them to the United States. While the hostages were still in Europe, *"people who have credibility with the hostages"* (emphasis in the original) should be sent to meet with them "individually and in small groups and explain all that was done in and outside of government to win their release." Jordan thought that news clips, videos of presidential statements and congressional action, and other efforts to gain the hostages' release should be compiled into a one-hour film to help the hostages comprehend the administration's efforts. Jordan suggested that Henry Precht, "a professional who has worked with the families," and Hal Saunders, "who was involved from the outset," be among those relied on to help.

Evidently concerned that the hostages might develop harsh feelings toward the president over a "surprise" release with very real political undertones, Jordan advised the president to turn to the hostages' families for help. Specifically, he should solicit advice from one or two of the leaders of the hostage family group on how and when to bring the hostages home, the reunion with the families, and how to deal with the media. And, Jordan concluded, "You should possibly meet with [the families] privately yourself."

Jordan further suggested that Carter bring in former secretary of state Cyrus Vance as one with great credibility both inside and outside the government. He also recommended that the president publicly thank the foreign countries that helped bring about the release, including Switzerland, Panama, Canada, the Federal Republic of Germany, and nations friendly and otherwise. As for Congress, Jordan thought that the president might be able to rely on both Democrats and some of the less partisan Republicans to protect him from partisan attacks. Senators Robert Byrd, Howard Baker, Frank Church, Jacob Javits, John Stennis, Henry Jackson, and Sam Nunn, along with representatives Tip O'Neill, James

Wright, and John Rhodes, might be employed in this manner. The president, Jordan suggested, should brief these men personally.

In a section titled "Overall Posture," Jordan noted the importance of informing the public and the press of the release quickly. He should "nip in the bud any of this 'October Surprise' crap by having a press conference . . . to deny that this sort of thing was contrived, planned, etc." He cautioned the president to "avoid overreaching" and to "understate your own role and say that you simply did your duty as president and worked to get these people out." Realizing that the president could not reveal details about much of the story (especially the rescue mission), he suggested that Carter emphasize the point that the administration "worked endlessly . . . to obtain the safe release." Most important, it was essential that the administration "discredit the notion that we had any other option but to do what we did or any control at all as to when the hostages might be released."

Jordan also suggested that a white paper be written, perhaps by Christopher, detailing, to the extent permissible and practicable, the steps the White House took in attempting to gain the hostages' release. He envisioned a document divided into four sections, including "Initial Captivity," "Secret Negotiations," "Post Rescue Mission" (with Jordan's note that he was unable to draft that particular portion), and, finally, "Serious Negotiation." Jordan concluded by telling the president that "something similar to this should be attempted so that there will be a factual presentation of the history of these negotiations."

With the entry of the Algerian government as an intermediary, the last tile of the mosaic fell into place and negotiations were under way. The Iranian delegates approached the negotiations convinced that Iran was the aggrieved party, certain that their actions in taking the embassy were justified, and firm in their belief that the American people wanted the hostages returned so badly that the U.S. government would accede to all of their demands (which included the release of American military equipment purchased but not delivered to Iran prior to the fall of the shah). They were wrong on all counts.

CHAPTER 18

THE FINAL WEEKS

My positive attitude was smashed on 23 December, when we were moved again. After a short ride from Evin, I was led into a building and down several flights of stairs. Just before entering my new quarters, we walked across the marble floor of what seemed to be a large, unfurnished room. When I heard one of the guards plink at a piano somewhere in the room, I thought that we might be in a ballroom or some other similarly large gathering area. When the blindfold was removed and I looked around, I thought I had been magically transported to one of the men's restrooms at the Kennedy Center. I was standing in a room that resembled a small parlor; it was nicely carpeted and wallpapered, and furnished with an easy chair, table, lamp, and the ubiquitous foam sleeping pad on the floor. Wall sconces provided additional light. A short hallway on one side led (I soon learned) to the toilet. There was just one window in my "parlor," near the high ceiling on the wall opposite the double entry doors. Later, I learned that we were in the foreign ministry's guesthouse; my colleagues were ensconced in the luxurious guestrooms upstairs while I languished in the basement bathroom.

While my living situation was better than in most of my previous abodes, I was furious at being there, especially since the heat was off and it was damn cold. I was so angry that I lashed out verbally at the guards, even trying to pick a fight with them. In earlier days, an episode like this would have resulted in some form of punishment, probably either shackling or at least the loss of book privileges. Now the guards just shrugged, told me not to turn on the light, and left. As I shivered and stewed in the dark, a large-bore antiaircraft gun opened up just outside the room's only window, and I could again hear the *whump, whump* of exploding ordnance. The light from the muzzle flashes confirmed that I was in a basement (looking up and out the window, I could see that I was at least eight feet below ground level). I set about pacing across the room, full of anger and adrenaline, my path lighted by the flashes and a modest amount of ambient light. Finally, the gun went silent and I called it a day.

Still in a funk the next morning, I ignored the guards when they brought me breakfast and again when they returned to fix the heat and jerry-rig a shower in the toilet area. By day's end, after having taken long, hot showers following each of my two exercise periods, I was in a better frame of mind. But I continued to ignore the guards, just to be perverse and to remind them of my intense dislike of being treated like a commodity. I had again been made aware of my utter lack of control over my life. That never failed to anger and frustrate me, not only then but for years afterward as well.

Several hours after dinner on this Christmas Eve, the door opened to admit three Arab men in suits and ties, accompanied by a contingent of our guards, and I was introduced to the Algerian ambassador to Iran. He asked how I was faring and told me that if I wanted to write a letter home, he would personally carry it to U.S. government officials. I quickly accepted and then, speaking softly but quickly in fractured French, outlined my earlier treatment, including the four-hundred-plus days in solitary. When the guards started to react to this discussion, which they could not follow, I switched back to English and thanked the ambassador for his time.

I was in much better spirits following that visit, but I was still surprised when an Algerian returned to collect the letter. And I was even more surprised when I learned on release that the letter had made it to my mother. The Algerian ambassador's report to U.S. officials that he had personally seen and talked with me was the first news in a year that I was still alive, but they were glad to have the letter as confirmation. The letter was hand-delivered to my mother by an Agency officer, who sat down with her and went over it, asking her to confirm that it was my handwriting and that it reflected my personality. With that, my name was apparently checked off on the "still with us" list.

Along with Christmas breakfast I received a real present from home (the only package from home the Iranians ever let me have, out of many sent to me): a shoebox stuffed with goodies, including a crossword puzzle book, a deck of cards, and real Kleenex. (I had, while in Komiteh Prison, relied on a roll of toilet paper to handle a runny nose brought on by another cold; two guards were terribly upset that I would use toilet paper for my nose but they refused to bring me Kleenex. After that, I made it a point to reel off a wad whenever I was in the presence of these two guards and rub it all over my face.) It struck me that release was probably close, if not in the next day or two, then around 20 January (the symbolism of release on Inauguration Day was not lost on me).

I tried not to be too optimistic, reminding myself that it was possible I would not be freed then or anytime soon. If nothing happened during the week of the twentieth, then I should accept that I was in for a long term of incarceration and be grateful that things were not worse. (To put our situation in perspective, our treatment was worse than that received by American aviators in Germany's World War II stalags but unquestionably much better than Japan's treatment of POWs during that same conflict or that meted out by the North Vietnamese to the POWs in the Hanoi Hilton.)

During this time, one of the first guards I had had in the embassy during the eternity before our dispersal around the country reappeared. Mehdi was perhaps twenty or twenty-one, and he had consistently been kind to me while I was in his charge. We had spent hours talking on many topics, often with each trying to educate or explain things to the other. I was actually pleased to see him again, and he confessed to being pleased as well. It was interesting to note a change or two in him, particularly the improvement in his English, an ancillary benefit for many of our guards. None of Mehdi's occasional dourness was in evidence, and although not giving away any secrets, he spoke more openly and frankly than before. His optimistic attitude and those tidbits he did let drop (or I elicited) in our chats served as additional indexes of imminent release. Unlike any of the other guards with whom I spoke during those last few months, he had begun to engage in objective reflection on what it was that he and his cohorts had done and what their actions might mean in terms of his country's long-term stability. For example, Mehdi had concluded that Iran's loss of U.S. friendship and protection had encouraged the Soviets to invade Afghanistan and later encouraged the Iraqis to initiate hostilities with Iran. No other Iranian ever gave any sign of understanding this.

Now that something positive was finally in the offing, the days seemed to pass more slowly as we went from December 1980 into January 1981, with the only noticeable change being even less contact with the guards. By early January, the only Iranians who came to my room other than Mehdi, who still dropped by occasionally, were those who brought my meals. I did not mind this reduction in contact and was thus irritated when, several hours after dinner on 18 January, there was a knock on my door. I was startled by this unusual act of courtesy, and it did not occur to me to reply. The door opened, and I stood perplexed as a guard ushered in a young man dressed in a white jacket and carrying some sort of tray. On viewing the white jacket, I at first assumed that the guard had brought the cook down for a culinary review of that night's dinner. Then I took a good look at the tray and saw that it was a medic's blood kit. With sleeve rolled up and fist clenched, I watched with no small amount of trepidation as this youth approached my arm with a huge hypodermic syringe, fully intent on draining a gallon of my blood.

My fears notwithstanding, the experience left me unharmed and for the first time almost free of pessimism: I had been seen by the Algerian ambassador, I had been permitted to write a letter home that truly enjoyed some real prospect of being delivered, and my blood had been taken, almost certainly as part of a medical examination. Looking at this assembled evidence, I could not talk myself out of believing that the end was really coming.

January nineteenth lasted forever. I could not sleep, read, or close down my mind. I spent most of that day pacing the room and waiting for another knock. Dinner came and went while time dragged on and I grew more and more despondent. I had miscalculated, I thought; if I were not released now, then it would probably be a long time before I enjoyed any kind of freedom again.

But it did happen. Well after midnight I was blindfolded and walked outside to another building. When I could see again, I was in a large, institutional-type kitchen, and in the room beyond I could see some of my colleagues. I was taken to a smaller room where three medical examining tables had been set up, two occupied by colleagues I had not seen in more than a year. A smiling Algerian doctor gave me a rudimentary physical exam and told me I was fine. While pleased to hear that, what was really exciting to me was the thought that outsiders had verified that I was alive and in acceptable health, and the Iranians could not very well claim now that I had been shot trying to escape or had died in captivity. Moreover, knowing that the Algerians had been playing a significant role in the negotiations between Iran and the United States, I thought it highly unlikely that they would certify that we were alive and healthy and then walk away and leave us. I knew then for sure that we were going home.

Two other interesting events occurred that night. First, I had to appear before Tehran Mary and a film crew. Mary and her friends were smiling and acting as though this was the social event of the season. In front of the camera, I was asked how I was doing, and I replied, "Fine." Mary then asked if I had been treated well while I had been a guest of Iran. I burst out laughing and replied that I had been held against my will in solitary confinement for more than a year, had not been able to tell my family that I was even alive, had been interrogated, had been physically abused more than once, and had been threatened with trial and execution. And now I was being asked if I had been treated well. So the answer was, "No!" There were no follow-up questions. In 1998 Tehran Mary, whose real name is Massoumeh Ebtekar and who grew up in the Philadelphia area, was appointed vice president for the environment in the government of President Mohammad Khatami.

As for the second event, I had not been back in my basement bathroom long when, near daybreak, Hossein came to say good-bye. He sat on the floor and leaned back against the wall, looking tired and more than a bit haggard, but happy, too; almost gloating, in fact. He began by telling me that it was all over, that we were all going home and Iran was finally going to be free from outside interference so Iranians could have the kind of country they wanted. I responded that it sounded good but I was sure it was not going to happen because, in my view, Iranians lacked the necessary self-discipline to keep the past from repeating itself.

Hossein said that he did not understand. I noted that governing a nation and permitting at least some degree of freedom (which Hossein and his cohorts always maintained would be the case in Iran) required great tolerance on the part of the authorities. I said that the government of such a country could not lock people away or execute them just because someone with the power to do so did not like something those people said or did. I told him that rules and laws had to be applied to all citizens equally and that it took governmental and personal self-discipline to make this work. Looking him directly in the eyes, I told him that nothing I had seen, heard, or experienced in my time in Iran gave me any indication he and his fellow Iranians had any understanding of this. The revolutionary government was unwilling to grant its citizens any measurable degree of true freedom, and there was not, in my opinion, a snowball's chance in hell that it ever would. We talked about freedom of the press and freedom of speech, and he assured me that the Islamic regime believed very strongly in these rights, so long as they didn't insult the government or lie to the people. When that happened, however, the government (which, of course, would be deciding what was permissible or not) was correct in stopping the papers or arresting the people. As long as people didn't say something prohibited, however, they would be free to say or write whatever they wished. Even after spending fourteen months with this kind of thinking, I was still amazed at Hossein's remarks. I tried for a minute to explain what freedom of speech and press mean—that if you are free only to say things that others do not object to, then you have no freedom at all. It was fruitless.

Hossein rebutted my comments with the same idealistic revolutionary rhetoric that I had heard so many times, from him and from others, as well as the uniquely Iranian logic I had heard before. He ended by repeating that all Iran's problems had been caused by outsiders, most notably by America, and that now everything was going to be good in Iran. I did not carry the debate further. He tried to chitchat for a few minutes, but when he realized that I had no interest in a congenial farewell, he said he had many things to do. He then stood and wished me good luck. I shrugged and he left. In the years since, Hossein has served as a deputy foreign minister and during the early to mid-1980s played a major role in Iranian-sponsored terrorism, including events that caused the deaths of Americans. He is now ambassador to Syria.

The attitude that the hostages themselves were at fault for their captivity is still prevalent in Iran twenty years later. Former hostage taker Abbas Abdi, for example, one of the leaders in 1979 and now labeled a "reformer" by both the *New York Times* and *U.S. News and World Report*, was interviewed on the twentieth anniversary of the embassy takeover.[1] In neither article did Abdi apologize for the takeover, despite the fact that it brought to his country poverty, isolation, war with Iraq, and a regime far more oppressive than any of the shah's worst excesses. To the *Times* Abdi claimed that there was "nothing personal" involved in depriving men and women of their freedom and endangering their lives for nearly fifteen months. He is wrong: it was highly personal to me and probably to most of my colleagues as well; and certainly the distress and anguish our families experienced was highly personal. While acknowledging that the takeover "helped us deal with our internal problems," Abdi blamed the lengthy crisis on the Carter administration's "refusal to make any concessions." (This, too, was a prevalent view among our captors; since they were so clearly right, all of the concessions and admissions of errors had to come from America.) Abdi concluded his interview by stating: "Perhaps the Americans don't understand it, but it wasn't exactly an easy experience for us, either," as though they, too, had been captured and forced to endure the privations against their will. Certainly his quest for sympathy is wasted on this former hostage.

After sundown on 20 January, I was blindfolded for the last time and walked out of the building, minus the little bundle of possessions that I had managed to retain over the months. The Iranians had taken everything we had and sent us out of the country with only the clothes on our backs. I was helped onto a bus and pushed toward the back, able to see through the bottom of my blindfold that all the seats were filled with Americans. I was the last one on. Standing at the rear, I glimpsed my chief of station sitting in the seat in front of me. It was the first time I had seen him in nearly fifteen months.

As we slowed on the airport apron, we could hear a crowd yelling; the noise was almost deafening as the bus stopped and the door opened. Each of us was walked to the door of the bus, where the blindfold was removed. We were then more or less pushed off and propelled through a gauntlet of screaming Iranians toward the rear stairs of a Boeing 727. As I was moved along to the airplane, I recognized some of our former guards. The last thing I heard before tearing loose from the crowd at the bottom of the stairs and sprinting into the cabin was, "Hey, wait! Can you help get me a visa to America?"

CHAPTER 19

THE REST OF THE STORY

I want to record here some vignettes of our return that did not make the evening news and were not of any great import to what happened to the fifty-two of us as a group. But these brief moments hold indescribable meaning to me. Not coincidentally, whenever I have been privileged to speak before audiences, these have been the stories that seemed to touch individual listeners the most. Yet these anecdotes, which put a human face on events, are the least likely material to survive over time. And I do not want them to be lost. Too many Americans gave too much of themselves during that time to allow these memories to fade.

It may seem odd that the fourteen-plus months I spent as a captive of the Iranians endowed my life with memories actually worth safeguarding. Even some events that were not, and are not, things I like to dwell on had their uplifting and sometimes humorous aspects. My fondest memories, however, are those of our return to freedom. Confined in a solitary state for all but the first nineteen days of our captivity and generally deprived of news from the outside, I had no idea what awaited us outside Iran. Some of my colleagues who changed roommates more frequently than I had chances to shower had been able to glean a general idea of the public reception in the offing. I was clueless.

The above notwithstanding, I did have infrequent glimmers of the extent to which the American public supported us because the Iranians did, on rare occasions, give me one or two of the thousands of cards and letters sent to us by caring Americans throughout our captivity. These short missives without fail informed us that we were in their prayers, urged us to be strong, and ended with a hope for a speedy conclusion to our ordeal. Many thanked us for our sacrifice and for bringing the country together, even at such a cost to us and to our government.

The Iranians had waged a psychological war against all of the hostages, its intensity varying only with the degree to which they viewed each of us as an "enemy of the revolution." A measurable element in that war was the unrelenting effort to convince us that we had been abandoned by the American people, that Americans everywhere wanted to see us "justly" held in prison for "crimes" against the Iranian nation and people, and that on our return to the United States we would face only shame and humiliation. Permitting us to read those wonderful cards, which spoke just the opposite to our hearts, undermined their efforts to reduce our will to resist. I am still amazed that the Iranians ever let us read them. Nonetheless, even with the joy and strength those cards brought to me, I never envisioned anything like what awaited us in Germany and back home.

It was only by happenstance that I even knew we would be heading to Germany. Tom Schaefer had shared this tidbit with me through an air vent one February day when we were next door to each other in makeshift cells in the chancery basement. Beyond that one specific piece of intelligence, I was left with only my imagination when it came to dreaming about and planning for my return home. And I must humbly note right now that I was dead wrong about every image, idea, and dream I had about our return.

We left Tehran on the Air Algerie 727. At the time it seemed surrealistic; it still does. But it was the best plane ride I have ever had. We hoisted small glasses of champagne when we left Iranian airspace, and when dinner was served drank bottles of Algerian wine to celebrate our release. There were not many of these, and when they were emptied no more appeared. (Some years later, I remarked that I thought the wine was excellent, only to have a skeptical friend point out that my taste buds might not have been in top working order at that particular moment.) Moreover, the feast of delicacies that I had assured myself would certainly be presented to us did not appear either. Our first meal in freedom was hard rolls and butter. Four or five of us were milling around in the aisle, somewhat perplexed at what was passing for our "welcome to freedom" dinner, when the plane's captain stopped by.

A remarkable man, the Algerian captain had a marvelous sense of humor and loads of charisma. The disappointment that must have filled our faces as we contemplated the rolls and butter drew his concern. He inquired if everything was OK, and one of us managed to stammer out with some embarrassment that, while we did not mean to appear ungrateful, we had been looking forward to a more substantial meal.

The captain made a small joke, but then turned serious and apologized for the meager fare.

The reason, he explained, was that the plane had left for Tehran several days ago, unsure of exactly when, or even whether, our release would take place. He described landing in Ankara to top off the fuel tanks and stock the larder, and told us that the only food that would keep on the plane more than a day or so without spoiling was rolls and butter. "So you see," he said softly, "we did not know how long we would be in Tehran, and we would not allow the Iranians to cater your food."

The Air Algerie 727 was configured in three sections, with first-class seating at the front and two economy seating areas behind. The VIPs onboard were up front, and my colleagues and I were in the middle section. At Mehrabad Airport, we had boarded in such a rush that I hardly noticed the occupants in the rear of the plane. When I later visited the restroom in the back, though, I noticed a number of large, tough-looking chaps sitting in seats too small to contain their bulk. Later, I learned that they were Algerian commandos. On landing in Tehran, the commandos had set up a protective perimeter around the plane so that no one could get within several hundred feet of the aircraft.

Actually, two Air Algerie aircraft had come for us. Identical 727s were used, not only to carry everyone connected with our release (negotiators, the Algerian doctors who examined us, Red Cross personnel, commandos, and so forth), but also for an added layer of protection. At departure time, the two planes taxied away from the lighted apron together; by the time they had reached the runway, no one watching could be certain which plane held the former hostages. The two planes took off within a minute of each other and, once airborne, changed positions a time or two. If the Iranians had been of a mind to attempt to bring down our aircraft, they would have been confused as to which plane was ours. We have many reasons to be grateful to the Algerians.

After we landed in Algiers for the formal turnover from Algerian custody to the U.S. government (under the terms negotiated by the Algerians with the Iranians and our government), we were ushered into the VIP suite at the terminal. Some months later, I was watching a video of TV coverage of the event and, when the 727 came to a stop, I eagerly awaited my appearance. The opportunity to see myself on worldwide television was more than just a novelty. So, I waited. And waited. A half-hour passed before the aircraft's door opened, and then more time elapsed before Bruce Laingen walked down the stairs toward the terminal. Watching the video, I was astonished at the time lapse. I still am. To this day I have no idea where the time went or what we did in the plane while we were waiting to disembark.

The walk to the terminal served as a modest introduction to the welcomes we were to experience in the days and weeks to come. The first thing I noticed was a Boeing 707 from the U.S. Air Force Special Missions unit at Andrews Air Force Base parked about fifty yards away from our 727. A crew member was hanging halfway out the copilot's window, his face one huge grin, wildly waving a small but very visible American flag. The first of what could be called our "cheering crowds," several hundred smiling members of the American business community and embassy in Algiers, were ecstatically waving more American flags.

Oddly, the scene inside the VIP lounge could easily have been mistaken for a routine diplomatic cocktail party, except that fifty-two of us were a bit underdressed. We strolled in, accepted a small tumbler of tea or fruit juice, and then stood around making polite conversation with people we had never seen before and, at least in my case, have not seen since. It was clear, though, that these strangers were delighted to see us.

I do remember Foreign Minister Benyahia of Algeria officially transferring custody of us to the State Department representatives. Other than shaking his hand before we left, we had no chance to meet him or talk with him; but I know that we were all saddened when he died in a plane crash in 1982. He devoted the better part of a year's energy and patience to gaining our freedom.

By 3:00 A.M. we were aboard two U.S. Air Force C-9 Nightingale medevac aircraft heading for Rhein-Main Airbase in Frankfurt, Germany. I was sitting in the jump seat on the flight deck, between the pilots, having something of a normal conversation in abnormal circumstances. The two pilots seemed as pleased to have been chosen to fly us as we were pleased to be in their charge. In the midst of this conversation, the Italian air traffic control service handed off our flight to French controllers as we entered France's airspace.

After the check-in calls, the French controller departed from established radio procedure in his signoff message to the pilot. "I am sure all of your special passengers must be asleep in the back," he said (which was decidedly not true: all the interior lights were on, and my colleagues were acting as though they were at an airborne New Year's Eve bash).

"But when they awake before landing, please tell them that all France is happy their ordeal has ended and that French citizens everywhere wish them the best as they return to freedom." The pilot rogered his thanks and we flew on. Only much later did I realize that I should have asked the pilot for the microphone to thank the controller personally for his wishes. I have always regretted not thinking faster.

It seemed as though most of the American population of Europe watched us leave the aircraft at Frankfurt, walk across the ramp, and disappear into blue air force buses for the short trip over to the USAF hospital at Wiesbaden. A good number of my colleagues had the presence of mind to wave to the crowd that met us; I did not. I felt overwhelmed and indescribably awkward and out of place. Later, I realized I was experiencing a species of culture shock; I did not know what to do or what was expected of me.

I soon learned that these wonderful Americans were from the Rhein-Main Airbase and surrounding area, and that they had been waiting for hours during the coldest part of that January night to welcome us. A huge American flag was hanging from the control tower, and almost everyone present was waving a small American flag and cheering without restraint. It was the warmest welcome anyone could ever dream of receiving. There was also a sea of yellow ribbons, bows, and garlands fluttering in the breeze. No other colors, just yellow. There was even a huge yellow bow tied around the control tower. I mentally chalked up these displays of yellow to some quaint local German custom and headed for the bus.

Once at the hospital, we followed the short walk from the buses up to the hospital's main entrance through a corridor full of beaming faces and more flags and yellow ribbons. As I went to my room, it was impossible not to notice the wall decorations. Lots of artwork by youngsters in grammar and middle schools led me to conclude that the air force had cleared out a pediatrics ward for us. And once again we were afloat on a sea of yellow ribbons. Later, when I had the time to look at each one, I saw that the drawings were letters of welcome from children of American military personnel. At the time, however, my only sensation was of color and smiling faces.

I was looking forward to the medical exam, certain I had come through captivity in fine shape save for the loss of a couple of pounds and a slight decrease in my cardiovascular endurance. The examination went well, and the doctor was wonderful, as was everyone connected with the hospital. But when I learned the outcome, I thought at first I had gotten someone else's results. I was flabbergasted to discover that I had lost forty-seven pounds. My surprise was even greater when I saw my physical state described as "general wastage." I certainly didn't feel "wasted." Fortunately, it was a temporary condition remedied by a lot of eating.

When we arrived back home, many people—family, friends, neighbors, the groups we spoke to, as well as the folks who stopped us on the subway, in airports, and at neighborhood taverns—were curious about our first days in freedom, especially at Wiesbaden and, later, at West Point. That was because the State Department took great care to isolate us and our immediate families, and media reporters were not allowed near us. I will try to satisfy some of that curiosity.

I confess that I cannot remember what my first real meal was after we were released. I was especially looking forward to pizza and Heineken beer, and, as a good Oklahoma boy, a thick T-bone, but the first meals we were served in Wiesbaden were not at all memorable. The doctors were doing a seemingly endless series of laboratory tests that required donations of about half the blood supply in our bodies, and for accurate test results our diets had to be restricted to bland foods. On our last night in Wiesbaden, however, we enjoyed Maine lobsters sent to us by a generous (and imaginative) American. What certainly had to be the best cooks in the air force prepared the lobsters and served them with an incredible array of side dishes. This feast was a most memorable event.

It is impossible for me to express my gratitude adequately to the staff of the Wiesbaden Air Force Hospital. The people working at the hospital, including U.S. military personnel and American and German civilians, were as happy to have us there as we were to be there. I cannot begin to describe the genuine kindness and expert care we received from these folks.

In the middle of the second day, Tom Schaefer and I were talking with the ward's head nurse, Maj. Toni Carner, trying to tell her how much we appreciated everything her staff was doing for us and how grateful we were to be in their care. Recognizing what we were trying to say, Major Carner stopped us by taking our hands, looking up at us, and softly saying, "We've been waiting for you for four hundred and forty-four days."

After the lobster feast we were invited to a party in the enlisted barracks. A bar had been set up and music was playing, and many of the medics we had seen during our three days were there in casual clothes. I think about nine of the Tehran bunch showed up, to be welcomed with a large traditional German stein and beverages of our choice. With no dietary restrictions now, we could enjoy the world's greatest beer. I took special care to make sure the stein made it back home with me, and it now sits in my home office where I see it every day.

We were given a lot of things while we were in Germany, among them collector plates from several German cities depicting a local landmark, usually a cathedral or the city hall; coffee-table books with photos of these cities; a yearbook of the Wiesbaden Air Force Hospital; a crystal Christmas tree ornament; and a porcelain bell compliments of Chancellor Schmidt. We received flowers by the truckload. On the day of our departure, about eight of us loaded up shopping carts and rolled through the hospital wards giving the still-beautiful flowers to real patients. But when it comes to gifts, what I remember most of all is the "klepto table."

Our ward was L-shaped, with the long side running along the center front of the hospital and the shorter side heading off to who knew where. (Well, I knew where, actually, and so did several of the others—it led to a small men's restroom and lounge in which several of us shared some contraband beers on our second day, smuggled in by a kind soul who shall remain nameless.) At the angle of the L was a large open area where a long, wide table had been set up before our arrival. And on that table were stacked many of the gifts, along with the myriad floral arrangements, that had been sent to us from people all over the world.

Two items on the table stood out: an amazing number of T-shirts (once back home, it was years before I had to buy another one) with mostly patriotic designs, and an enormous Hershey's chocolate bar. This slab of chocolate was probably close to four feet in length and an inch or two thick. Someone had tossed a wicked-looking knife on the table next to it so that we could hack off whatever amount we wanted. We ate so much chocolate that it is a wonder we did not all get off the plane at Newburgh resembling a bunch of ambulatory pimples.

It soon became second nature, whenever passing the gift table, to look it over for the latest arrivals, take one each of whatever there was, and then hew off a chunk of chocolate before walking away. It amuses me now to recall how quickly we became accustomed to getting unsolicited gifts. (Several months after we returned, seven of us were guests of Radio City Music Hall in New York City at opening night of a special production with a patriotic theme. We were staying in the exclusive Towers section of the Sheraton, and I had already entered an elevator when, just as the doors started to close, one of my Tehran colleagues jumped in. As we began the ride up, he looked at me and said, "Nice tie. Did you have to pay for it?") By the time we left Wiesbaden, I felt like a latent kleptomaniac and fervently hoped this instinct would not manifest itself the next time I was in Sears.

A German orderly at the hospital was assigned to us, and he was always there when we needed anything. Herr Gottfried Pfeiffer had been at the hospital since at least World War II days, when the hospital served the German army, and we all became indebted to him for his many kindnesses. Herr Pfeiffer even serenaded us on his accordion at the lobster feast, beaming with pride as he played.

Two years later, almost to the day, I was in Wiesbaden as a tourist and I made it a point to go to the hospital to look up old friends. Many of those who had waited for 444 days to care for us were gone; I saw no one I recognized as I walked up the main staircase. There were no yellow ribbons on the walls and no crayon drawings by schoolchildren. I walked past the room Don Cook and I had shared and into the central part of the ward. There was no klepto table, no wall of flowers. And then Herr Pfeiffer came around the corner. He recognized me immediately, and we greeted each other with joy. He then took my arm and led me to a wooden plaque on the wall. This lovely tribute informed all readers that they were standing in "Freedom Hall" and encased a group photo of the fifty-two of us taken minutes before we left the hospital for Rhein Main Air Base and the flight home. If there had been a "before" photo to go with the "after" photo, the viewer would have no trouble noticing the difference. And much of that difference was due to the wonderful people at the hospital who cared so much for and about us.

We had two special visitors at the hospital: Jimmy Carter and Cyrus Vance. Their receptions could not have been more different. We all gathered in our ward's lounge area to meet Mr. Carter, who arrived with former vice president Mondale, former secretaries of state and the treasury Edmund Muskie and G. William Miller, and several former key members of the White House staff. No one I talked with beforehand had much interest in seeing Mr. Carter. In fact, the atmosphere in the room as we were waiting for him to arrive was so chilly that Tom Schaefer felt obliged to remind everyone that Mr. Carter had been our president and commander in chief, and as such deserved respect, regardless of our personal feelings. When he entered, the former president appeared to me to be ill at ease, uncertain of his reception.

Mr. Carter was introduced to us one by one and gave each of us a hug. Few embraces were returned with any enthusiasm. He spoke to us for about ten minutes, relating some background on why he had made the decision to admit the shah, the rescue mission, the agreement for our release, and what had been done to obtain our release. He then asked if there were any questions. There were several soft questions, posed mostly out of politeness, and then a State Department officer stepped forward. He stated that he did not have a question but wanted to remind the former president that the embassy had provided plenty of advance warning of what would happen if the shah were admitted to the United States.[1] Mr. Carter looked down at the floor for a moment, then raised his head, smiled, and said he wanted his picture taken with each of us. End of meeting. (I still have the photo stashed away somewhere; the former president looks awkward and I look like an unsmiling cadaver.)

I do not deny that President Carter's handling of the crisis after the Iranians took over the embassy was the primary reason we all returned alive from Iran. Although hindsight shows that some missteps occurred, Mr. Carter's efforts were for the great part well thought out and ultimately successful. But I believe that he has to bear the responsibility for creating the circumstances that brought about the crisis in the first place. The embassy, in my view, probably would have been left alone had the shah gone directly to the United States from Tehran in January 1979; it was a mistake to allow him into the United States after he had roamed the world for ten months.

The above said, I will be the first to acknowledge with pride that Mr. Carter has distinguished himself and honored our country with his service to humankind after leaving the White House. God bless you, Mr. President.

Cyrus Vance, on the other hand, we met with admiration and respect. He had opposed the rescue attempt and had resigned his office in protest, but only after the attempt had taken place, so as not to jeopardize the security of the operation or undermine the president's authority as commander in chief to conduct it. He related honestly and forthrightly how and why various decisions were made and what was done after the embassy was taken.

The fifty-two of us had mixed opinions as to whether it had been wise to try a military rescue operation, but that diversity did not lessen the esteem we felt for Vance. He answered our many questions frankly, and when he had finished we gave him a standing ovation. I doubt that any of us left his presence without feeling that we had been well served by an American of great dignity and honor.

On the flight home, we stopped to refuel in Shannon, Ireland, and were turned loose in the terminal for about an hour. Because I have an Irish name, I was selected, along with one other, to receive on behalf of the group a gift of one bottle of Irish Mist from the company that makes it. There was a nice little ceremony, after which I ended up talking to one of the company's managers. We were soon joined by a friendly guy who, when I mentioned in passing that I occasionally enjoyed a Guinness stout, suggested we repair to the bar for a glass or two.

The Irish Mist representative, this other chap, and I spent thirty minutes or so at the bar, where we each had several glasses of Guinness. Midway through a glass, this nice man asked to see the Waterford crystal Christmas bell that had also been given to each of us at Shannon. While he was appreciating it, I mentioned the Waterford beer mug I had been given as a gift before I left Washington a lifetime ago and lamented its loss to the Iranians. A minute later, when the Irish Mist representative was talking, I almost did not notice when the other gent turned and whispered something to a couple of big fellows who seemed to be just hanging around in the background.

A few minutes later, the hangers-on returned and handed him a box, which he in turn handed to me. It held a lovely Galway crystal beer mug. It was not Waterford, the man said, but he hoped that I would enjoy it and think of Shannon and true Irish hospitality whenever I drank from it. And I do. Because that is how Prime Minister Charles Haughey of Ireland came to present me with a Galway beer mug over a few glasses of Guinness stout at the Shannon Airport bar.

The reception in America is still difficult for me to describe. It could not have been any warmer or more memorable. We landed at Stewart Airport near Newburgh, New York, and, after cheerful and tearful reunions with our families, boarded buses for the ride to West Point, where we were to have a sheltered two days with our loved ones before going to Washington for our official welcome home. It took more than two hours for our buses to cover the eighteen miles from the airport to West Point; the way was lined with well-wishers who carried all types of signs expressing their happiness to see us back and their feelings toward the Iranians who had held us captive.

One of the more common signs we saw featured different cartoon characters or caricatures of famous people condemning Iranians in general or Khomeini in particular. One frequent expression of disapproval was the blatant presentation of a hand with the middle digit extended in the universal symbol that decidedly does not mean "We're number one." We loved every one of those posters. And around every turn there were still more people waiting, with more signs and posters. There were masses of American flags and yellow ribbons everywhere. We all waved at the crowds until our arms grew tired, and then we waved some more. All of us were deeply touched by this parade.

The U.S. Army and the entire staff at West Point were as caring, giving, and gracious as the U.S. Air Force personnel had been at the hospital in Wiesbaden. I was amazed at the number of people in both institutions who thanked us for coming to be with them. But we were the ones who were really grateful, and we were extremely proud to have met all those who were involved in some way with our care.

About an hour before dinner that first night at West Point's historic Thayer Hotel, I made the rounds of the hotel lobby and meeting room looking at more pictures and letters sent by local grade-school children, surrounded as always by yards of yellow ribbon. Like those in the hospital at Wiesbaden, these missives all expressed happiness at our return. I wish I had thought to have these collected on our departure and displayed somewhere where the public could see them. To me, these works by hundreds of young Americans were priceless.

If the West Point faculty and staff were unbelievably kind and generous to us, their welcome almost paled in comparison to the one we received from the Corps of Cadets. During the second day, we and our families were invited by the Corps to dine that night in the cadets' dining hall. Although I found out later that many cadets expected a low turnout (anticipating that we would want to spend time alone with our families), almost all of us accepted. And of all the heartwarming and exciting events we experienced, this dinner with the Corps ranks at the top. As our buses neared the front of the dining hall we could hear a distant roar, almost like thunder, intruding into the quiet of the evening. The closer we got, the louder the roar became. By the time we stepped out of the buses it was deafening.

The din, which was coming from inside the dining hall, was our greeting from the Corps. As we walked into the building we witnessed an extraordinary spectacle: cadets of all ranks and classes were cheering and yelling at the top of their lungs, many standing on their chairs while creating this mind-numbing noise. This welcome home was the most touching of all to me, and it was all I could do to hold back the tears. I do remember being seated at a large table with perhaps ten cadets, including several of the first women to enter the academy, and being enormously pleased to be with these future leaders of America. I do not think I have ever met a more impressive, motivated, and intelligent group. Today, I cannot adequately relate the pride I felt in being an American while in the company of these outstanding men and women.

On the morning of our third day we retraced our route back to Stewart and boarded planes for the flight to Andrews Air Force Base, where we were greeted by more family and by close friends and colleagues. We were then driven in another bus caravan past thousands of people through the Maryland suburbs and the streets of Washington, D.C., to 1600 Pennsylvania Avenue. We were separated from our families there and escorted to the Blue Room, where we were introduced to President and Mrs. Reagan and Vice President Bush. President Reagan welcomed us home in a short speech and gave each of us a silk American flag in a personalized rosewood presentation box.

I embarrassed myself somewhat in this simple ceremony. A presidential aide would call a name, and that person would walk up to President and Mrs. Reagan, shake the president's hand, and receive his flag. I was busy chatting with two colleagues as the others were called, however, so I did not quite follow everything. When my name was called I went up to the president, shook his hand, shook Vice President Bush's hand, and walked directly back to where I had been standing. Only then did I notice that I was receiving a strange look from Mrs. Reagan, as well as a few pointed comments from my friends.

What I had not noticed before was that each person, after shaking hands with the men, had received a kiss and a hug from Mrs. Reagan. I was chagrined when I realized I had walked right by the First Lady. So, after the last name was called, I went quickly up to her and, apologizing profusely, asked if it was too late for me to get a kiss. The First Lady laughed and gave me a warm hug and a kiss on the cheek. Holding my hands in hers, she smiled and welcomed me home. After that we followed the president out through the diplomatic reception entrance onto the south lawn.

When the ceremony was over, we went back inside for a reception and reunion in the East Room, where the atmosphere was like New Year's

Day and the Fourth of July rolled into one. In the midst of this, Anita Schaefer, Tom's wife, pulled me aside and said there were some very special people she wanted me to meet. As we walked down the wide corridor leading from the East Room into the mansion, Anita told me that she was going to introduce me to the families of the eight servicemen killed during Desert One. I almost stopped dead in my tracks, all coherent thought evaporated from my mind. What, I asked myself, do you say—what can you say—to total strangers whose husbands and fathers died trying to save your life and regain your freedom? How can you tell them you understand and share their sorrow? How can you tell them you are more grateful than you could ever possibly express? And how can you ever thank them enough for what their men tried to do for you?

While all this was running through my mind, Anita had been moving us down the hall and into another room, and suddenly I was in the middle of this group. It was the most moving and emotional experience of my life, before or since. The wives and children of these heroes were elated by our release and very happy that we were all safely reunited with our families. Their smiles were as big as those worn by our own family members, if not more so. If they had any regret or sorrow, there was absolutely no sign of it. They missed their men, I am sure, but on that day they were proud that their husbands and fathers had participated in such a noble cause, even though at terrible cost. I was immensely thankful to Anita for making it possible for me to spend this brief time with those magnificent women and children. I wouldn't trade those ten minutes for anything.

The day of celebration ended, and we soon went our separate ways, back to our careers and families and to a normal life. We went from being "hostages" to "former hostages," until, with the passage of years, we were not even that. That much has changed over the years is clear to me through at least one marker. For many years, when I spoke to groups about my experience, I was often speaking to people who had been teenagers or young adults during the time of the hostage crisis. They had a clear memory of the events, and many had participated in letter-writing campaigns or school projects related to the crisis, or simply followed national and international affairs, often for the first time.

As an audience, these folks were greatly interested in all aspects of the event. They wanted to learn and understand more about something that had directly influenced their lives. But by the early 1990s there were few people in the audiences who were much over five or six years old when

Iran and the United States were involved in this struggle of national wills. Now I teach college students who weren't even born when Iran decided it would commit an international crime. It is history to them, an academic event remote from, or even unrelated to, their own lives. And, now, it often seems that way to me, too.

NOTES

Sources and Abbreviations

Jimmy Carter Presidential Library Sources

HDF Files of Presidential Special Assistant Hedley Donavon
JCPF Files used by President Carter at his Plains, Georgia, residence to write his postadministration memoirs
JPF Files of Presidential Press Secretary Jody Powell
LCF Files of Counselor to the President Lloyd Cutler
ZBF Files of National Security Adviser Zbigniew Brzezinski

Collections

Iran: The Making of U.S. Policy 1977–1980, collated by the National Security Archives, Washington, D.C. Cited as NSA/Iran.
Documents from the Den of Espionage, published in Tehran, Iran, and constituting nearly seventy volumes of documents that were in the U.S. embassy in Tehran on 4 November 1979 and were captured by Iranian militants. Cited as Spy Den.
Clandestine Service History, "Overthrow of Premier Mossadeq of Iran: November 1952–August 1953." Central Intelligence Agency Historical Paper no. 208, dated March 1954, by Donald N. Wilbur, classified Secret. Published in the *New York Times,* 16 April 2000. Cited as Wilbur.

Interviewees

CWN Charles W. Naas
DDN David D. Newsom
GP Eugene Poteat
GS Gary Sick
HMP Henry M. Precht
LBL L. Bruce Laingen
MJG Mark J. Gasiorowski
RMH Richard M. Helms
ZB Zbigniew Brzezinski

Chapter 1. The Assignment

1. This first embassy takeover was not, as is widely believed, perpetrated by "students." See Sullivan, *Mission*, 257–68, for a description of what he termed "guerrillas," many of whom "wore the familiar checkered scarf of the Fedayeen, indicating that they had been trained in the PLO camps by George Habash [a leading PLO terrorist]" (*Mission*, 262).

2. Saunders memo to White House Press Secretary Jody Powell, November 1979, JPF, box 62, "Hostages in U.S. Embassy 11/79–1980," folder 3.

3. Brzezinski, *Power*, 470.

4. DDN, 17 May 2000. Gary Sick also notes this in *All Fall Down*, 190.

5. CWN, 23 April 2000.

6. Ibid.

7. Gates, *Shadows*, 130; NSC Weekly Report no. 149, 7 August 1980, in ZBF, box 42, WR 136–50, folder 4/80–8/80.

8. Memo, Donavon to Saunders, "Meeting with James Bill," 25 January 1980, Secret/Sensitive, HDF, box 2, Memos to President 8/21/79–8/14/80.

9. Hal Saunders in Christopher, *Hostages*, 54.

10. Laingen, *Yellow Ribbon*, 54.

11. For the sake of clarity, a note on terminology is necessary. Too frequently authors use the word *agent* to mean both the CIA employee and the spy. The truly clueless use *agent* for both interchangeably in the same paragraph, and confusion as to who is what usually results. In correct usage, it is a CIA "officer" (or "case officer") who deals with an "agent," the foreigner who is recruited by the CIA officer to provide secret information (i.e., to spy). The reader who sees the phrase "CIA agent" meaning the staff employee and not the spy (or meaning both) should be wary of the knowledge of the author and the accuracy of the story.

12. At the time, Gregg was creating a new relationship with Congress following the establishment of the House and Senate intelligence oversight committees. He later served as national security adviser to Vice President George Bush and then as ambassador to South Korea.

13. Sick, *All Fall Down*, 33.

14. Charlie Naas relates a similar story about a talk he had with an Iranian woman in 1979; she was convinced the United States had deliberately undercut the shah and maneuvered Khomeini into power in order to weaken the Soviet Union's control of its southern republics (CWN, 23 April 2000). And Gary Sick relates nearly identical incidents, with Iranians asking, "Why did the United States want to bring Khomeini to power?" (*All Fall Down*, 34). Indeed, almost everyone who dealt with Iranians at that time can tell similar stories.

15. Phil Gast returned to Washington as a lieutenant general and director of operations for the Joint Chiefs, a position he held during the Desert One/Eagle Claw rescue mission.

Chapter 2. Retrospective: A History Lesson

1. Bill, *Eagle,* 4. For a complete treatment of Persian/Iranian history, see Gasiorowski, *Policy;* Bill, *Eagle,* 4–51; Cottam, *Iran,* 3–55; and Ledeen and Lewis, *Debacle,* 3–13.

2. Bill, *Eagle,* 5, 16; Cottam, *Iran,* 5.

3. Not until the 1970s did large numbers of Iranians and some Americans—including human rights activists, liberal politicians, and several of the more eminent scholars at American universities—begin asserting that the coup was the turning point.

4. Kissinger, *White House Years,* 1258.

5. Treverton, *Covert Action,* 49. Ledeen asserts that "Iran's destiny is her geography" (*Statecraft,* 91).

6. Gavin, "Politics," 65.

7. Ledeen, *Statecraft,* 91; Moens, "President Carter's Advisors," 214.

8. Iran's 1,600-mile border with the USSR, when joined with about 650 miles of border with Iraq, constituted a "grave threat" to Iran itself, regardless of the interests of the West (Kissinger, *Upheaval,* 668).

9. Nixon, *The Real War,* 90.

10. Gavin, "Politics," 66; Ball, *Past,* 461.

11. Gavin, "Politics," 66.

12. See Holt, *Secret Intelligence,* 98.

13. Ledeen and Lewis, *Debacle,* 54

14. Kissinger, *Upheaval,* 667.

15. Richelson, *American Espionage,* 90. Richelson notes that one site was probably equipped with seismic gear to monitor Soviet nuclear tests.

16. Space Development Agency, located on the World Wide Web at spaceboy.nasda.gov.

17. Bamford, *Puzzle Palace,* 198–99; H. Smith, "Loss of Post"; Torgerson, "U.S. Spy Devices"; Richelson, *American Espionage,* 89–93; Klass, "Monitoring Capability."

18. Bamford, *Puzzle Palace,* 198–99.

19. Richelson, *American Espionage,* 90.

20. Moens, "President Carter's Advisors," 214. Charlie Naas states that the sites were "essential" to the ratification of SALT II by the Senate (CWN, 23 April 2000).

21. Department of State, Inspector General's memo for the Secretary, dated October 1974, in response to "Follow-up in President Talks with Shah of Iran," NSC memo dated 25 July 1974, drafted by Henry Kissinger for the secretaries of state and defense. Both memos were originally classified Secret. The IG's memo is found in Spy Den 8:76–98.

22. For details on this period of Iranian history, see Cottam, *Iran,* 55–66. For

some reason, Bill, in *Eagle,* manages to overlook entirely this crucial period in Iranian history. Instead, he concentrates on the oil connection.

23. Cottam, *Iran,* 55.

24. Gasiorowski, *Policy,* 43.

25. Goode, *U.S. and Iran,* 4.

26. Sullivan, *Mission,* 53.

27. Acheson, *Present,* 500; Gosnell, *Truman's Crises,* 301. Iran itself became eligible for Lend-Lease, which was also administered by the U.S. forces. See Stempel, *Inside,* 61.

28. Gosnell, *Truman's Crises,* 301.

29. Ibid.

Chapter 3. The Soviet Calculus

1. Acheson, *Present,* 349.

2. Rossitzke, *Secret Operations,* 14–15.

3. Kimball, *Nixon's Vietnam War,* 18.

4. Gavin, "Politics," 62. Gavin also notes (p. 64) that the U.S. embassy in Moscow was speculating in January 1951 that Iran might be the next target of Soviet aggression.

5. Ambrose, *Ike's Spies,* 200.

6. CIA Intelligence Assessment, *Soviet Involvement in the Iranian Crisis,* National Foreign Assessment Center, March 1979, 1; all portions declassified on 23 January 1986 (hereinafter cited as *Soviet Involvement*).

7. Cottam, *Iran,* 66. Cottam (p. 67) points out that the "pathetically weak" Iranian forces were no match for the Soviet forces in Azerbaijan.

8. Feis, *Trust,* 81.

9. Cottam, *Iran,* 66, 68.

10. Acheson, *Present,* 197.

11. State Department diplomatic efforts are partially detailed in more than twenty official documents from the period 2 February–31 December 1947, NSA/Iran.

12. Feis, *Trust,* 83.

13. Gosnell, *Truman's Crises,* 303.

14. "The Azerbaijan Settlement," reproduced in Kuhns, *Assessing,* 51.

15. Central Intelligence Group, "Developments in the Azerbaijan Situation," 4 June 1947, classified Secret (declassified 21 July 1992).

16. "Present Soviet Intentions in Iran," in Kuhns, *Assessing,* 296.

17. Kuhns, *Assessing,* 422–23.

18. "A Report to the President by the National Security Council on the position of the United States with Respect to Iran," 27 June 1951, NSC-107/2, 1–2. The quotations are cited in and borrowed from Richelson, *Spies,* 249.

19. Gavin, "Politics," 59.

Chapter 4. The 1953 Coup

1. CWN, 23 April 2000.

2. Remarks of Secretary of State Madeleine K. Albright before the American-Iranian Council, 17 March 2000, Washington, D.C.

3. Kissinger, *Upheaval*, 670–74, and *White House Years*, 1258–65; also, Kissinger, "Kissinger on the Controversy."

4. Treverton, *Covert Action*, 77.

5. Holt, *Secret Intelligence*, 161; Gasiorowski, "Coup," 279.

6. Data provided by Eugene Poteat, a former senior scientific intelligence office engineer in the CIA's Directorate of Science and Technology, from his unclassified article "Stealth, Countermeasures, and ELINT."

7. DDN, 17 May 2000.

8. Goode, *U.S. and Iran*, 36.

9. Ibid., 104.

10. Ibid., 105.

11. Ibid.

12. Gavin, "Politics," 62 et seq.; see also Gasiorowski, "The 1953 Coup," 261.

13. Gavin, "Politics," 72.

14. Ibid., 80.

15. Defense spending increased fourfold in 1949–53; see ibid., 75–76.

16. Thomas, *Very Best Men*, 107. The details of the events leading up to the coup are complex and at times confusing, and this work is not the place to treat that history. See Gasiorowski, "The 1953 Coup," 261–86; Bill, *Eagle*, 51–98; Acheson, *Present*, 499–511, 679–85; and Cottam, *Iran*, 85–109. While Kermit (Kim) Roosevelt's memoir, *Countercoup*, should be the definitive version, it is not, being unfortunately rife with errors and misstatements. In correspondence with the author, Gasiorowski advised that Roosevelt had written the memoir as rehabilitation therapy following a stroke and his memory was not what one would have hoped. Gasiorowski was able to interview Roosevelt prior to his death and clarified a number of errors. Reporter James Risen further contributed to the available knowledge about the coup with his story on the CIA's official history of the coup. See Risen, "Plot." Risen obtained a copy of the still classified document, which totaled close to two hundred pages.

17. Stempel, *Inside*, 63. Stempel also quotes two Iranians "intimately involved" in Iranian security issues at the time as proclaiming that the CIA's role was less than perceived: "the fact that the Americans were interested in establishing a stable government gave psychological support to those key Iranians who were ready to act anyway."

18. Risen, "Secrets."

19. Stempel, *Inside*, 64; Roosevelt, *Countercoup*, 210.

20. Gasiorowski, "The 1953 Coup," 270, 276. That middle- and lower-level

CIA officers were opposed to this covert action program is not an extraordinary circumstance. Throughout the Agency's history the intelligence professionals in the trenches have opposed such covert action programs as Guatemala in 1954, the Bay of Pigs in 1960, and Chile in 1969 and 1970. Directed by various presidents to execute these programs, the CIA obeyed—often reluctantly—only to be pilloried in the press and by a large segment of the public afterward.

21. Treverton, *Covert Action*, 56.

22. Gavin, "Politics," 81.

23. Ambrose, *Ike's Spies*, 196; Eisenhower, *Mandate*, 161.

24. Gasiorowski, "The 1953 Coup," 270.

25. Wilbur, 2:18–19.

26. By some accounts Mossadegh was "allied" with the Tudeh and thus, by extension, the Soviets (Roosevelt, *Countercoup*, 117). See also Cottam, *Iran*, 105.

27. Eisenhower, *Mandate*, 130.

28. Ambrose, *Eisenhower*, 109.

29. Gasiorowski, "The 1953 Coup," 271.

30. Thomas, *Very Best Men*, 108.

31. Eisenhower, *Mandate*, 160.

32. Ibid., 163.

33. Ibid.

34. Ibid.

35. Wilbur, 5:31–32.

36. Eisenhower, *Mandate*, 163, fn. 5.

37. Ibid., 163.

38. Gasiorowski, "The 1953 Coup," 273–75; Roosevelt, *Countercoup*, 179–97; and Wilbur.

39. Eisenhower's State Department was well aware that "social, economic, and political problems" would remain after the coup and continue to undermine stability and progress in Iran unless they were at least partially resolved (Gavin, "Politics," 85n.).

40. Ambrose, *Eisenhower*, 130.

41. Roosevelt, *Countercoup*, 8. But with respect to this opinion as well as the others, it is, Gregory Treverton says, "impossible to determine the immediate consequences fifty years later" (*Covert Action*, 77).

42. Gasiorowski, "The 1953 Coup," 261, 279.

43. Ibid., 261.

44. Bill, *Eagle*, 86.

45. Ibid., 97.

46. Stempel, *Inside*, 64.

47. Treverton, *Covert Action*, 176. Bill postulates that the coup succeeded because of the "deep fragmentation" of Iranian society, the weak economy, the organizational skills of the Iranian leaders, the naiveté of Mossadegh and his fol-

lowers, the "conscious decision" of the Soviets to remain aloof, and "good luck" (*Eagle*, 93).

48. Any number of authors writing about intelligence or Iran have asserted that the Iran coup provided proof to U.S. presidents that the CIA could overthrow governments antagonistic to the United States. And certainly it influenced Eisenhower's decision to try a similar coup in Guatemala in 1954, Kennedy's decision to invade Cuba at the Bay of Pigs in 1961, and Nixon's actions regarding Chile in 1970. But that was misreading the Iranian coup. As a former DDCI writes, the 1953 coup in Iran "did not prove that the CIA could topple governments and place rulers in power; it was a unique case of supplying just the right bit of marginal assistance in the right way at the right time" (Cline, *CIA*, 154). Kim Roosevelt believed the same and therefore declined to lead the Guatemalan operation and left the Agency before the Bay of Pigs "disaster" proved the "validity" of his opinion (Roosevelt, *Countercoup*, 210).

Chapter 5. America and Iran, 1953–1977

1. Bill, *Eagle*, 98, 131–82; Eisenhower, *Mandate*, 165; Stempel, *Inside*, 64–78.

2. Gasiorowski, *Policy*, 101.

3. Ambrose, *Eisenhower*, 129–30; Bill, *Eagle*, 111.

4. The "critical" designation is from NSC-175 of 21 December 1953; "anti-communist" is from NSC-5504 of 15 January 1955 (Gasiorowski, *Policy*, 95, n.19).

5. Gasiorowski, *Policy*, 117. A detailed account of SAVAK and its relationship with the CIA and Israeli's intelligence service, Mossad, is found in this same work on pp. 114–21.

6. Ibid., 116–17.

7. Gasiorowski among others makes the case for Mossad personnel instructing SAVAK in the methodology of torture. See *Policy*, 124.

8. *Soviet Involvement*, 2.

9. Bittman, *KGB*, 113.

10. Meyer, *Reality*, 361.

11. Gasiorowski, "Qarani," 627.

12. Bill, *Eagle*, 114. Stempel gives figures totaling $486.5 million from 1953 through 1966 (*Inside*, 65). Stempel's numbers are broken down for each year, while Bill merely gives one overall figure. The reason for the sizable discrepancy between the two is not readily apparent.

13. DDN, 17 May 2000.

14. Stempel, *Inside*, 64.

15. Ibid., 67.

16. Ledeen and Lewis, *Debacle*, 17.

17. Bill, *Eagle*, 130; Gasiorowski, "Qarani," 628.

18. CWN, 23 April 2000.

19. See Gasiorowski, "Qarani," 628–29, for additional insights.

20. Stempel, *Inside*, 67; Bill, *Eagle*, 131.

21. Bill, *Eagle*, 139–40; Stempel, *Inside*, 67.

22. Cottam, *Iran*, 129.

23. DDN, 17 May 2000; Gasiorowski, *Policy*, 186–87.

24. Bill, *Eagle*, 147–48.

25. Lyndon Johnson, his administration consumed by the battle for the Great Society at home and the tragic war in Vietnam overseas, devoted very little time and attention to Iran. In the half-dozen most recent biographies of LBJ there is nary a reference to Iran, and LBJ's own autobiography likewise refers to neither Iran nor the shah.

26. Department of State/NEA to the Secretary, briefing paper: "Visit of Shah of Iran, August 22–24 1967, dated 15 August 1967 and originally classified Secret, NSA/Iran.

27. Stempel, *Inside*, 68.

28. Ledeen and Lewis, *Debacle*, 41–42.

29. Ball, *Past*, 454.

30. This is the so-called Nixon Doctrine. See Kimball, *Nixon's War*, 154–55.

31. Stempel, *Inside*, 72.

32. Garthoff, "American," 552; Ledeen and Lewis, *Debacle*, 43, 53; Gasiorowski, *Policy*, 207. Garthoff also points out that Nixon intended to signal to China, which he had visited just a few months earlier, that he would keep his promise to the Chinese to build "regional positions of strength" around the USSR ("American," 552).

33. Ledeen and Lewis, *Debacle*, 43.

34. Prados, *Presidents' Secret Wars*, 97; Bill, *Eagle*, 97; Treverton, *Covert Action*, 77.

35. Teicher and Teicher, *Twin*, 18.

36. Ibid., 23.

37. Kissinger, *White House Years*, 1265.

38. See Bill, *Eagle*, 200–202.

39. Sick, *All Fall Down*, 13. See particularly Rubin, *Paved*, 158–89, for the effects of the arms sales on the Iranian people.

40. Bill, *Eagle*, 210–11.

41. National Intelligence Survey, "Iran: Country Profile," dated May 1973 and originally classified Secret, NSA/Iran; Spy Den 60:78–99.

42. Sick, *All Fall Down*, 14.

43. Rubin, *Paved*, 137–38.

44. Ibid., 197.

45. Ibid., 134.

46. Jentleson, "Commitments," 678.

47. Bill, *Eagle*, 201.

48. Memorandum to the Secretaries of State and Defense from Henry Kissinger, dated 25 July 1972, "Follow-up on the President's Talk with the Shah of Iran," classified Secret, NSA/Iran.

49. Report of the Senate Committee on Foreign Relations, Subcommittee on Foreign Assistance, Staff Report, *U.S. Military Sales to Iran*, viii–ix, cited in Bill, *Eagle*, 200. See also Sick, *All Fall Down*, 14–15 and 344, n.15; Ledeen and Lewis, *Debacle*, 59; Jentlesen, "American," 678; Kissinger, *White House Years*, 1264.

50. Sick, *All Fall Down*, 354, n. 4.

51. Kissinger, *White House Years*, 1264.

52. The only items absolutely ruled out by the president were nuclear weapons.

53. Rubin, *Paved*, 261.

54. Kissinger, *Upheaval*, 620; Sick, *All Fall Down*, 19, 21.

55. Figures are from data presented in Gasiorowski, *Policy*, 112.

56. The 1971 order for matériel is found in Rubin, *Paved*, 133.

57. Moens, "President Carter's Advisors," 214.

58. Bill, *Eagle*, 202; Rubin, *Paved*, 171.

59. Jentleson, "Commitments," 678.

60. This situation was not uncommon and was not found just in the IIAF. These traits were also hallmarks of Imperial Iranian Army commanders, who, rather than make a decision or initiate action that might result in displeasing the shah, would instead make no decision at all. Ledeen and Lewis claim that the military was "unable to act as a coherent unit," lacked combined-arms training or capability, and had no "history of independent leadership or small unit initiative" (*Debacle*, 40). In short, an army and air force equipped with the finest weapons available would have been nearly useless in the regional policeman role envisioned by Nixon, Kissinger, and (later) Brzezinski due to inept leadership, poor and limited training, and mechanics and technicians who were incapable of properly maintaining the sophisticated systems.

61. Rubin, *Paved*, 260–61; Sick, *All Fall Down*, 56–57.

62. Tehran document A170 to State Department, dated 8 April 1975, originally classified Confidential, NSA/Iran; Spy Den 61:31–42.

63. RMH, 2000; Kissinger, *Upheaval*, 670.

64. Bill, *Eagle*, 387; Rubin, *Paved*, 137.

65. Stempel, *Inside*, 74.

66. Bill, *Eagle*, 380–82, 388; Ledeen and Lewis, *Debacle*, 33; Sullivan, *Mission*, 208.

67. Results found in twenty-four cables sent from U.S. diplomatic facilities in Iran to the State Department in the period 18 February 1976–20 April 1976, NSA/Iran and Spy Den.

68. Ledeen and Lewis, *Debacle*, 31; Bill, *Eagle*, 387–88. After the fall of the shah, the PGOI canceled more than $34 billion worth of domestic infrastructure

projects ordered by the shah, from nuclear plants to six-lane highways to a new Tehran airport to multiple steel mills—all of which was on top of the billions of dollars of arms sales from the United States and other countries (Branigin, "Iran Set to Scrap").

69. Gasiorowski, *Policy,* 209.

70. Ibid., 208.

71. Kissinger, *Upheaval,* 668, 670.

72. Author's personal discussions with numerous Iranians. See also Rubin, *Paved,* 136; Ledeen and Lewis, *Debacle,* 62–63; and Bill, *Eagle,* 217.

73. Cottam, *Iran,* 147.

74. Cottam notes that Kissinger had no "awareness of the history of American-Iranian relations or any understanding of the basis of the shah's vulnerability" (*Iran,* 147).

75. Moens, "President Carter's Advisors," 214.

Chapter 6. Revolution

1. Carter, *Faith,* 534.

2. Sick, *All Fall Down,* 22.

3. Vance, *Choices,* 317.

4. Executive Order 12036, *United States Foreign Intelligence Activities,* January 24, 1978, 42 FR 4311. The SCC was the president's highest-level policy group responsible for general policy management and review, crisis management, approval and oversight of covert action programs, and development and review of policies for critical issues. Its members were the secretaries of state and defense, the chairman of the Joint Chiefs, and the DCI. The national security adviser chaired the meetings.

5. Forsythe, "Human Rights," 440.

6. Moens, "President Carter's Advisors," 215; Cottam, *Iran,* 156.

7. Cottam, *Iran,* 157.

8. Presidential Directive/NSC-13, 13 May 1977, originally Secret/Sensitive, declassified 27 August 1981.

9. Jentlesen, "American," 679; Rubin, *Paved,* 196.

10. Sick, *All Fall Down,* 22–24; Moens, "President Carter's Advisors," 215.

11. McLellan, *Vance,* 126.

12. Cited in ibid., 126–27.

13. An INR assessment from January 1977 stated that the shah and Iran were "free from serious domestic threat" and predicted the continued stable rule of the shah during the next few years, at least. The report is cited in Cottam, *Iran,* 172.

14. *Soviet Involvement,* 2.

15. Kuzichkin, *Life,* 201.

16. Sullivan, *Obbligato,* 263.

17. Kupchan, "Globalism," 602.

18. Stempel, *Inside,* 78.

19. Ibid., 80.

20. Brzezinski, *Power,* 360.

21. Vance, *Choices,* 317.

22. *Soviet Involvement,* 5.

23. "Active measures" is KGB terminology for covert action operations.

24. Kuzichkin, *Life,* 191.

25. Bittman, *KGB,* 113; *Soviet Involvement,* 7.

26. Carter, *Faith,* 443.

27. It would have been impossible to stop the graft, but then, in the Iranian culture (as in many lesser-developed countries) the population just accepted that the elite would steal; the problem here was that the corruption was egregious and openly flaunted. That the shah was not corrupt himself is the judgment of Ambassador Richard Helms, who knew him better than any other American and states that there is no evidence that the shah ever sent billions of dollars out of Iran for his personal use. To Helms, this is reasonably credible evidence that the shah never intended to leave Iran (RMH, 14 April 2000, telephone interview). Regarding the shah's alleged billions, see Scherer, "Shah's Fabled Riches"; and Pincus, "Iranian Investigation."

28. Ball, *Past,* 455–56.

29. CWN, 23 April 2000.

30. Sick, *All Fall Down,* 31.

31. Sullivan, *Mission,* 134; Carter, *Faith,* 437; Vance, *Choices,* 323.

32. Carter, *Faith,* 437; Vance, *Choices,* 323. Ambassador Sullivan is said to have described Carter's remarks as "far out" (Armstrong, "Fall").

33. Bill, *Eagle,* 235; Rubin, *Paved,* 365; Armstrong, "Fall."

34. Rubin, *Paved,* 214. Charlie Naas, who was in Tehran at the time, believes the number of dead at Jaleh to have been fewer than 200 (CWN, 23 April 2000). Sick cites official Iranian figures as 122 killed and 2,000–3,000 wounded (*All Fall Down,* 51). Iranian doctors who treated the wounded believed that 300–400 were killed and about ten times that many wounded. One undated chronology of Iranian events located in the Carter Presidential Library gives figures of 121 killed and 200-plus wounded (ZBF, box 11, Iran File, 10/78–12/13/78). The Iranians holding the embassy spoke of "thousands" dead.

35. Gasiorowski, *Policy,* 219.

36. Bill, *Eagle,* 236. Bill's calculations are based on estimates that are probably high. One measure he used to estimate the number killed was to count the number of new graves at the "martyrs' plot" of Beheshti Zarah cemetery in Tehran. But Charlie Naas was told by an Iranian clergyman in 1979 that any Muslim who died in that period, from whatever cause, was interred in martyrs' field to build up the numbers. The cleric related that he had personally witnessed this (CWN, 23 April 2000).

Chapter 7. Intelligence Failure

1. Sick, *All Fall Down*, 92.

2. Ibid., 91.

3. U.S. House of Representatives, Subcommittee on Evaluation, Permanent Select Committee on Intelligence, Staff Report, "Iran: Evaluation of U.S. Intelligence Performance Prior to November 1978," cited in Donovan, "National Intelligence," 160.

4. Ibid. Donovan makes a prima facie case that the intelligence obtained from the field was useful and timely, and that while some finished products were erroneous, other assessments were correct. He is very much in the minority, however.

5. CWN, 13 January and 23 April 2000.

6. Ibid.; HMP, 23 April 2000.

7. CWN, 23 April 2000.

8. Ibid.

9. HMP, 23 April 2000.

10. HMP, 16 January and 23 April 2000.

11. Helms is cited in Bill, *Eagle*, 402.

12. CWN, 13 January and 23 April 2000.

13. In fact, Nixon and Kissinger apparently preferred it that way.

14. ZB, 5 June 2000. It should be noted that many of the positions cut were in the covert action components rather than among the intelligence collection branches. And, too, not all of the positions cut were actually encumbered by an officer. Nevertheless, several hundred DO case officers were cut loose either to find jobs in other directorates or to retire or resign.

15. DCI report, "Focus on Iran–Part II: Action Review," dated 27 December 1976 and originally classified Secret, NSA/Iran; Spy Den 8:148–51.

16. RMH, 14 April 2000 (telephone interview).

17. HMP, 16 January 2000.

18. HMP, 23 April 2000.

19. Donovan, "National Intelligence," 148.

20. Ibid., 149; Bill, *Eagle*, 249. This is not to imply that Sick was unqualified or lacked any knowledge of the region at all; quite the contrary. But he had not specialized in Iranian affairs, culture, and history. His memos and analyses from that time are proof that his analytical assessments and understanding of the Iranian internal situation and regional dynamics were outstanding.

21. HMP, 23 April 2000. The expectation was that a civilian regime composed mostly of National Front types or a military government would surface, but nothing like the Khomeini regime was foreseen by anyone inside or outside the government. One Iran scholar admitted to Dick Helms that the U.S. academic community had expected the NF or similarly inclined political figures ultimately to gain control in a democratically oriented Iran. The accession of Khomeini and

the radicals was as surprising to that Iran expert as it was to the Carter administration (RMH, 14 April 2000, telephone interview).

22. Former DCI Turner has noted Brzezinski's lack of understanding regarding the intelligence discipline of covert action, but Brzezinski's actions concerning Iran between the spring of 1978 and January 1981 may also lead knowledgeable observers to question his comprehension of the subtleties of positive intelligence collection and analysis. See Turner, *Secrecy,* 88 and 113–29. Interestingly, Turner (in *Secrecy,* at 120 and 144) commends Brzezinski for his continuing efforts throughout the Carter administration to protect intelligence products, sources, and methods from exposure by the White House's political operatives who wanted to help the president's standing with the public on various issues.

23. Tenet, "CIA," 137.

24. Donovan, "National Intelligence," 145; Sick, *All Fall Down,* 69; Bill, *Eagle,* 245–46; Hal Saunders in Christopher, *Hostages,* 43.

25. Saunders in Christopher, *Hostages,* 43.

26. NSA/Iran; Rubin, *Paved,* 209.

27. Carter, *Faith,* 446.

28. The report, INR Document III E[2]-14 of 1 September 1978, is in NSA/Iran and is cited in Cottam, *Iran,* 173.

29. Much of the following is gleaned from Donovan, "National Intelligence," 143 and passim. The State and DIA reports can be found in their entirety in NSA/Iran. Intelligence reports found in other sources will be so identified.

30. Donovan, "National Intelligence," 148.

31. Sick, *All Fall Down,* 31.

32. Ibid., 32.

33. Ibid., 40.

34. DDN, 23 May 2000.

35. Turner interview in *Washington Post,* 5 February 1979, cited in Rubin, *Paved,* 203.

36. Brzezinski, *Power,* 355, 396.

37. DDN, 17 May 2000.

38. ZB, 27 April 2000; Brzezinski, *Power,* 369–70.

39. Brzezinski, *Power,* 360, 383. Vance and Ball had for some reason come to believe that the Brzezinski-Zahedi communications were more extensive than was the case and that the relationship was carried on without the knowledge of the president, but Brzezinski's rebuttal is clear and firm. See Vance, *Choices,* 328, for his (erroneous) explication of the contretemps.

40. Brzezinski, *Power,* 397.

41. RMH, 14 April 2000 (telephone). This was the unanimous opinion of all involved in the Iranian crisis, regardless of their positions.

42. The analysis, "The Shah's Illness and the Fall of Iran," appeared in the summer 1980 edition of *Studies in Intelligence,* 61–63. The author's name did not

survive the declassification process, being blacked out. Likewise the original classification level has been obliterated as well as two inserts (photos or, possibly, charts). Otherwise, save for a redacted portion of one sentence, the entire document text is available. I am grateful to Jeff Richelson for providing the declassified version of this document.

Chapter 8. End of a Regime

1. DDN, 17 May 2000.
2. Brzezinski, *Power*, 354.
3. ZB, 5 June 2000.
4. Ibid.
5. Ibid.
6. Brzezinski, *Power*, 355; Cottam, *Iran*, 175; Bill, *Eagle*, 249; Rubin, *Paved*, 222–23; Sick, *All Fall Down*, 70.
7. Stempel, *Inside*, 126–27.
8. Bill, *Eagle*, 251.
9. CWN, 23 April 2000.
10. Tehran Embassy cable 10816 of 6 November 1978, in ZBF, box 38, file "Sensitive," 11/78–12/78.
11. Brzezinski, *Power*, 359.
12. Sick, *All Fall Down*, 72.
13. Ibid., viii.
14. Ibid., 4, 74.
15. Carter, *Faith*, 447; Moens, "President Carter's Advisors," 219; Ledeen and Lewis, *Debacle*, 159; Brzezinski, *Power*, 364.
16. ZB, 27 April 2000; Brzezinski, *Power*, 365.
17. Sullivan, *Obbligato*, 269–70.
18. Carter, *Faith*, 359.
19. Brzezinski, *Power*, 365.
20. ZB, 5 June 2000.
21. Brzezinski, *Power*, 364; McLellan, *Vance*, 129; Sick saw no problem with Brzezinski's call (*All Fall Down*, 72). Also CWN, 2 April 2000.
22. ZB, 27 April 2000.
23. Arjomand, "Revolution," 386.
24. Ibid.; Sullivan, *Mission*, 212, n. 7.
25. Brzezinski, *Power*, 395, 397.
26. Moens, "President Carter's Advisors," 221.
27. Ibid., 222. Brzezinski omits any details of this meeting from his memoirs but does note that DCI Turner reported that the CIA didn't have much intelligence on the events at that time (*Power*, 367).
28. CWN, 23 April 2000.
29. Sullivan, *Mission*, 201.

30. Quoted in Brzezinski, *Power*, 394.

31. Moens, "President Carter's Advisors," 218, 220; Sick, *All Fall Down*, 43.

32. Sullivan, *Mission*, 201–3.

33. Vance, *Choices*, 329; Moens, "President Carter's Advisors," 222. Moens writes that in a 12 September 1989 interview, former undersecretary of state David Newsom commented that Sullivan had voiced similar opinions but Brzezinski "didn't want to hear them." For his side, Brzezinski made little comment about this significant missive save to say that it muddled the situation further (*Power*, 368).

34. Charlie Naas readily acknowledges that his and Sullivan's enlightenment came "late in the day" (CNW, 23 April 2000).

35. Sullivan, *Mission*, 204; Moens, "President Carter's Advisors," 224.

36. HMP, 23 April 2000; CNW, 23 April 2000.

37. Brzezinski, *Power*, 394–95.

38. Carter, *Faith*, 452–54.

39. CWN, 23 April 2000.

40. Brzezinski, *Power*, 371.

41. Ibid., 375; see p. 371 for Brzezinski's confirmation of the shah's need for the United States to make decisions and take responsibility, including for the use of force.

42. Ibid., 376.

43. Stempel, *Inside*, 145.

44. CNW, 23 April 2000.

45. Sullivan, *Mission*, 236.

46. Sick, *All Fall Down*, 131.

47. Carter, *Faith*, 451.

48. Brzezinski, *Power*, 376.

49. Sullivan, *Mission*, 228; Huyser, *Mission to Tehran*, 14–15.

50. Carter, *Faith*, 453.

51. Brzezinski, *Power*, 378, 382–83.

52. Ibid., 383.

53. Sick, *All Fall Down*, 133.

54. Ibid., 131–34; GS, 8 August 2000. Sick also presents, on pp. 134–37, a detailed examination of each element of the plan and discusses the possibilities of success and the difficulties therein.

55. Tehran Embassy cable 10816 to Washington, 061025Z, February 1979.

56. Sick, *All Fall Down*, 156.

57. Vance, *Choices*, 602.

Chapter 9. The Shah Comes to the United States

1. Before leaving Washington I had been told that the consequences resulting from the admission of the shah were so obvious that "no one would be

dumb enough to let him in," and that an embassy takeover was unlikely because the Iranians had already proven they could do that. I didn't respond, but thought to myself that no president was immune from doing dumb things, and that if the Iranians had taken the embassy once, the only thing it proved was that they could do it again if they wished.

2. Sick, *All Fall Down*, 177.

3. Ibid., 177.

4. Vance, *Choices*, 343–44.

5. Brzezinski, *Power*, 472–73.

6. Kissinger, "Kissinger on the Controversy."

7. It is possible that Kissinger had actually made these arrangements three months earlier during a trip to Mexico. See Simons, "Shah, Entourage in Mexico."

8. Carter, *Faith*, 453–55; Brzezinski, *Power*, 474.

9. Tehran Embassy cable 07930 to State Department, "Shah's Desire to Reside in United States," originally classified Secret/Cherokee/NoDis, dated 28 July 1978, NSA/Iran; Sick, *All Fall Down*, 180–81.

10. In addition to the memoirs of Carter, Vance, Hamilton, Brzezinski, Sick, and others, see also Altman, "Shah's Health"; T. Smith, "Why Carter Admitted the Shah"; Nossiter, "Shah Welcome"; Gwertzman, "Carter Emissary" and "U.S. Decision"; State Department Chief Medical Officer memorandum, addressee deleted in the FOIA/declassification process, dated 20 October 1979, and Chief Medical Officer to the Secretary of State, "Summary of Medical Findings," dated 25 October 1978 and originally classified Secret, both in NSA/Iran; Cohen, "Rockefeller Keys"; Crittenden, "David Rockefeller Says"; Kissinger, "Kissinger on the Controversy"; Morgan, "Chase Manhattan's Ties"; Oberdorfer, "The Making of a Crisis"; Pincus and Morgan, "Pahlavi Fortune"; Richards, "Ball Asserts Kissinger's 'Obnoxious' Pressure"; Schwartz, "No Comment"; Simons, "Shah, Entourage in Mexico."

11. Carter, *Faith*, 463.

12. Brzezinski, *Power*, 474; T. Smith, "Why Carter Admitted the Shah."

13. Peter Jennings of ABC-TV News, in the lead-in to an ABC documentary series of the same name, April and May 1999.

14. See, inter alia, Carter, *Faith*, 464; Vance, *Choices*, 371; and Jordan, *Crisis*, 31.

15. Vance, *Choices*, 344; Tehran Embassy cable 07930 to State, NSA/Iran.

16. Vance, *Choices*, 370–71.

17. Ibid., 371; Carter, *Faith*, 464; Sick, *All Fall Down*, 184.

18. State Department cable 275001 to Tehran Embassy, 21 October 1979, originally classified Secret; Laingen, *Yellow Ribbon*, 9 (Laingen mistakes the date as 22 October).

19. DDN, 17 May 2000.

20. Related to the author in confidence by a senior Carter administration official.

21. Carter, *Faith*, 463–64; Vance, *Choices*, 372; Jordan, *Crisis*, 32; Gates, *Shadows*, 128; Brzezinski states only that Bruce asked for protection and that the "official response was positive" (*Power*, 475).

22. Tehran Embassy cable 11133, 21 October 1979, originally classified Secret, NSA/Iran; LBL, 17 January 2000; HMP, 16 January 2000. Both Laingen and Precht read the text of the Washington cable as clearly indicating that the decision to admit the shah had already been firmly made and that he was already in New York or else on the way there. Precht checked the issue later with several State officers who were in a position to know for certain, and they unanimously confirmed that the final decision had already been made.

23. LBL, 7 January 2000; HMP, 16 January 2000.

24. Sick, *All Fall Down*, 186–94.

Chapter 10. 4 November 1979

1. CIA, *Iran: The Seizure of the Embassy in Retrospect*, NESA Paper 81-10022, November 1981, 1, 3; declassified 17 May 1993 (hereinafter cited as *Seizure*).

2. Ibid., 6; Omestad, "Savvy," 63; Burns, "Iranian's Career."

3. This scenario was related to me numerous times by my captors, both the leaders and the guards who interacted with us every day. The only real difference between the leaders and the guards (at least in my discussions with them) was that the latter, who were much younger than the former, seemed to be much more interested, even unrealistically so, in the shah's return and much less aware of the underlying issues.

4. HMP, 23 April 2000; Sick, *All Fall Down*, 189; Gates, *Shadows*, 128–30.

5. Brzezinski, *Power*, 475–76; Gates, *Shadows*, 129–30; Sick, *All Fall Down*, 189.

6. *Seizure*, 7.

7. Ibid.

8. Laingen, *Yellow Ribbon*, 12.

9. Saunders in Christopher, *Hostages*, 42.

10. Laingen, *Yellow Ribbon*, 14.

11. Carter, *Faith*, 503.

12. Sick, *All Fall Down*, 206.

13. DDN, 17 May 2000.

Chapter 11. 5 November 1979

1. Saunders in Christopher, *Hostages*, 73.

2. Sick, *All Fall Down*, 207; Brzezinski, *Power*, 477–78.

Chapter 12. 6 November 1979

1. *Seizure*, 8.

2. Sick, *All Fall Down*, 209.

3. Saunders in Christopher, *Hostages,* 74.
4. Sick, *All Fall Down,* 210.
5. Ibid., 212.
6. Brzezinski, *Power,* 482; Sick in Christopher, *Hostages,* 144.
7. Sick in Christopher, *Hostages,* 145.
8. Vance, *Choices,* 377; Carter, *Faith,* 468; Sick in Christopher, *Hostages,* 145.
9. Kyle, *Guts,* 18.
10. Sick in Christopher, *Hostages,* 145.
11. Ibid.
12. Ibid., 146.
13. Carter, *Faith,* 470.
14. Sick in Christopher, *Hostages,* 146–47.
15. Saunders in Christopher, *Hostages,* 72–83; Vance, *Choices,* 377.
16. *Seizure,* 9.

Chapter 13. 7–22 November 1979

1. Carter, *Faith,* 474. The PLO apparently played a notable role in convincing Khomeini to release the women and minorities. See Vance, *Choices,* 378.
2. *Seizure,* 10.
3. Bittman, *KGB,* 116.
4. Sick in Christopher, *Hostages,* 148.
5. Bittman, *KGB,* 116.
6. Saunders in Christopher, *Hostages,* 48.
7. Ibid., 51–52.
8. Carter, *Faith,* 474.
9. Saunders in Christopher, *Hostages,* 81.
10. Ibid., 81–83.
11. Ibid., 147.

Chapter 14. 23 November–31 December 1979

1. As of 1999, Doug Hegdahl was still serving his country and potential POWs by continuing his work with the Defense Department joint services organization that is responsible for researching and teaching survival in captivity.
2. ZB, 5 June 2000; Sick in Christopher, *Hostages,* 148.
3. Carter, *Faith,* 475–76; Sick, *All Fall Down,* 234; Sick in Christopher, *Hostages,* 148.
4. The effect of the threat is unknown because there was no credible information from the Iranians in that regard. Some, such as Hal Saunders, were skeptical that it had much effect (in Christopher, *Hostages,* 90). But, coincidentally or not, after January our treatment began to improve and talk of trials had evaporated by late February.
5. DDN, 17 May 2000.

6. Memo, Brzezinski to the President: "NSC Weekly Report no. 122," 22 December 1979; ZBF, box 42, Weekly Reports to the President 102–20 (7/79–12/79).

7. ZB, 24 July 2000.

8. Ibid.

9. Ibid.

10. Carter, *Faith*, 476.

Chapter 15. 1 January–24 April 1980

1. One letter in particular, sent to and printed by a major daily newspaper, represented the Iranian positions on the key issues and was highly critical of the U.S. government. A second letter, by another individual to the president, was of the same ilk. Both letters are found in the "Plains Files" in the Carter library; a copy of the former missive is in the author's files.

2. The data in the following paragraphs are extracted from *Seizure*, 12–16.

3. Carter, *Faith*, 490.

4. Unsigned memo to the president, numbered 14A and dated only March 1980, entitled "Effects of the Hostage Crisis on the Families of the Hostages," JCPF, box 26, Iran Update, 3/80.

5. Unsigned memo to the president, 11 April 1980, JCPF, box 26, Iran Update, 4/80.

6. FBIS translation of *Ettela'at* article of 18 December 1979, located in LCF, box 95, Iran Special 12/80, Iran Trials, 11–12/79.

7. Letter to State legal adviser Roberts B. Owen from John B. Jones, the dean of New York University Law School, and Norman Redlick of the prestigious Washington law firm of Covington and Burling, dated 25 January 1980, LCF, box 95, Iran Trials 1–6/80.

8. Letter to State legal adviser Roberts B. Owen from John B. Jones, dated 31 January 1980, LCF, box 95, Iran Trials, 1–6/80.

9. Blind memorandum, Office of the Attorney General, dated only December 1980, LCF, box 95, Iran Special 12/80, Iran Trials, 11–12/79.

10. Undated blind memo titled "The Concept," JCPF, box 26, Iran Update, 7/80. Even a casual reading of the detailed history of the policies and discussions involved in negotiating an end to the crisis by Christopher, *American Hostages in Iran*, limns a nearly stupefying process as the two distrustful governments and cultures jousted with each other. Clearly, until Saddam Hussein's invasion of Iran on 23 September 1980 the Iranians had little interest in negotiating; and even afterward there were more than a few times when the Iranians could not be counted on to deal in good faith. Indeed, even with just a day to go and the negotiations seemingly concluded, the Iranians still tried to initiate changes.

11. *Seizure*, 16.

12. This absolutely fascinating tale is told by the CIA officer who led the

operation. See Antonio J. Mendez, *The Master of Disguise: My Secret Life in the CIA* (New York: William Morrow, 1999), 267–305. See also Jean Pelletier and Claude Adams, *The Canadian Caper* (New York: William Morrow, 1981, first U.S. edition).

13. The rescue mission would use three MC-130s and three EC-130s, as well as (it was planned) eight RH-53D helicopters.

14. Sick in Christopher, *Hostages*, 152.

15. Carter, *Faith*, 510–20; Vance, *Choices*, 408.

16. Brzezinski, *Power*, 489–90.

17. Carter, *Faith*, 522.

18. Laingen, *Yellow Ribbon*, 115.

19. Brzezinski, *Power*, 496.

20. Carter, *Faith*, 524.

Chapter 16. 24 April–22 June 1980

1. Actually, the fine intelligence historian Jeff Richelson later reminded me that it did happen to James Bond, citing *Goldfinger*, in which Bond is not only captured once, but is recaptured after an escape. At any rate, unlike Bond, I lacked a secret gizmo in my watch or fountain pen to help me escape, and I was never locked up with a beautiful woman.

2. Some of the information in this section was related to me by a very senior Department of Defense official who had direct and full access to Operation Eagle Claw participants and planning from the first day to the last. This official discussed the mission in a not-for-attribution setting and so must remain anonymous (he imparted no classified information, nor was any requested).

3. Brown press conference, cited by Sick in Christopher, *Hostages*, 154.

4. Carter, *Faith*, 524.

5. There has always been a suspicion in some minds that the rescue mission was primarily a political move by the president, who was falling in the polls and had been defeated by the Massachusetts Democrat in the Pennsylvania presidential primary two days prior to the mission. In researching this work, however, I found absolutely no evidence to support this allegation, and the people I interviewed denied it both on and off the record. The most anyone would say is that the president's political staff were concerned, but that was their job. Neither the presidential election nor any other political element was ever discussed, much less given any weight, in policy deliberations over the rescue mission or any other military contingency.

6. ZB, 5 June 2000.

7. Sick in Christopher, *Hostages*, 154.

8. Confidential discussion with a high-level official in the Carter Department of Defense who was intimately involved in the mission planning.

9. Ryan, *Mission*, 36–38.

10. Ryan, *Mission*, 41–43; Kyle, *Guts*, 82–86, 119–23; Beckwith, *Delta Force*, 224–29.

11. Beckwith, *Delta Force*, 7; Kyle, *Guts*, 199.

12. Jim Kyle relates the Russian problem in *Guts*, 47. At least as probative, in my discussion with the senior Defense official the latter was very emphatic about the threat posed by Soviet intelligence assets to the mission and the consequences if the Soviets had discovered its existence.

Chapter 17. 22 June–23 December 1980

1. Of course, back in 1976, many of these same Iranians had assumed, from an equally uninformed basis, that Carter would "be their friend."

2. Carter, *Faith*, 542.

3. Christopher details these negotiations, Iranian demands and actions, Algerian mediation, and other related issues in *Hostages.*`

4. Carter, *Faith*, 567.

5. ZB, 5 June 2000.

6. Carter, *Faith*, 582.

7. Memorandum from Jordan to the president, undated, but late September or early October 1980 (Carter's handwritten note shows clearly that it had been read by him; circulated to Brzezinski, Muskie, and Christopher; and returned to him on 17 October). The memo is labeled "EYES ONLY," with "Private" added in the president's hand. It is in JCPF, Iran 10/80, Iran 10/80–1/21/81 [1].

Chapter 18. The Final Weeks

1. Burns, "Iranian's Career"; Omestad, "Savvy."

Chapter 19. The Rest of the Story

1. Ham Jordan identifies this individual as Tom Ahern, but that is incorrect; Jordan also misquotes the individual and says his voice was "trembling, angry." The statement as I have given it is the correct version, and neither the individual who spoke nor Tom Ahern, for that matter, was "trembling" or "angry." Jordan's account differs considerably from my own recollections in other ways as well. See Jordan, *Crisis*, 412.

BIBLIOGRAPHY

Acheson, Dean. *Present at the Creation.* New York: W. W. Norton, 1969.

Altman, Lawrence. "The Shah's Health: A Political Gamble." *New York Times,* 17 May 1981, A48.

Ambrose, Stephen E. *Eisenhower: The President.* New York: Simon and Schuster, 1989.

———. *Ike's Spies.* New York: Doubleday, 1981.

———. *Nixon.* Vol. 2: *The Triumph of a Politician, 1962–1972.* New York: Simon and Schuster, 1989.

Andrew, Christopher. *For the President's Eyes Only.* New York: HarperCollins, 1995.

Armstrong, Scott. "The Fall of the Shah." *Washington Post,* 26 October 1980.

Ball, George. *The Past Has Another Pattern.* New York: W. W. Norton, 1982.

Bamford, James. *The Puzzle Palace.* Boston: Houghton Mifflin, 1982.

Beckwith, Charlie A., and Donald Knox. *Delta Force.* New York: Harcourt Brace Jovanovich, 1983.

Bill, James. *The Eagle and the Lion.* New Haven: Yale University Press, 1988.

Bittman, Ladislav. *The KGB and Soviet Disinformation: An Insider's View.* McLean, Va.: Pergamon-Brassey's, 1985.

Branigin, William. "Iran Set to Scrap $34 Billion Worth of Civilian Projects." *Washington Post,* 30 May 1979, A22.

Brzezinski, Zbigniew. "Being There." *Foreign Affairs* 78, no. 6 (November–December 1999): 165–66.

———. *Power and Principle: Memoirs of the National Security Adviser, 1977–1981.* Rev. ed. New York: Farrar, Straus and Giroux, 1985.

Burns, John F. "Iranian's Career: From Hostage-Taker to Reformer." *New York Times,* International, 13 October 1999.

Carter, James Earl. "Being There." *Foreign Affairs* 78, no. 6 (November–December 1999): 164–65.

———. *Keeping Faith: Memoirs of a President.* 3d ed. Fayetteville: University of Arkansas Press, 1995.

Christopher, Warren, et al. *American Hostages in Iran: The Conduct of a Crisis.* New Haven: Yale University Press, 1985.

Clifford, Lawrence X. "An Examination of the Carter Administration's Selection of Secretary of State and National Security Advisor." In *Jimmy Carter: Foreign Policy and Post-presidential Years,* ed. Herbert D. Rosenbaum and Alexej Ugrinsky. Westport, Conn.: Greenwood Press, 1994.

Cline, Ray S. *The CIA under Reagan, Bush, and Casey.* Washington, D.C.: Acropolis Books, 1981.

Cochran, Burt. *Harry Truman and the Crisis Presidency.* New York: Funk and Wagnalls, 1973.

Cohen, Richard. "Rockefeller Keys Open Door for Sick Shah." *Washington Post,* 20 November 1979.

Cook, Blanche Wiesen. *The Declassified Eisenhower.* New York: Penguin, 1984.

Cottam, Richard W. *Iran and the United States: A Cold War Case Study.* Pittsburgh: University of Pittsburgh Press, 1988.

Crittenden, Ann. "David Rockefeller Says Aim in Aid to Shah Was Solely Humanitarian." *New York Times,* 17 November 1979, A7.

Donovan, Michael. "National Intelligence and the Iranian Revolution." In *Eternal Vigilance? Fifty Years of the CIA,* ed. Rhodri Jeffreys-Jones and Christopher Andrew. London: Frank Cass, 1997.

Earl, Robert L. "A Matter of Principle." *U.S. Naval Institute Proceedings,* February 1983, 30–36.

Eisenhower, Dwight D. *Mandate for Change.* Garden City, N.Y.: Doubleday, 1963.

Emerson, Steven. *The Secret Warriors: Inside the Covert Military Operations of the Reagan Era.* New York: G. P. Putnam's Sons, 1988.

Feis, Herbert. *From Trust to Terror: The Onset of the Cold War, 1945–1950.* New York: W. W. Norton, 1970.

Ferrell, Robert H. *The Eisenhower Diaries.* New York: W. W. Norton, 1981.

Forsythe, Daniel P. "Human Rights in U.S. Foreign Policy: Retrospect and Prospect." *Political Science Quarterly* 105 (fall 1990): 435–54.

Garthoff, Raymond L. "American-Soviet Relations in Perspective." *Political Science Quarterly* 100 (winter 1985–86): 541–60.

Gasiorowski, Mark J. "The 1953 Coup d'Etat in Iran." *International Journal of Middle East Studies* 19 (1987): 261–86.

———. "The Qarani Affair and Iranian Politics." *International Journal of Middle East Studies* 25 (1993): 626–44.

———. *U.S. Foreign Policy and the Shah: Building a Client State in Iran.* Ithaca: Cornell University Press, 1991.

Gates, Robert M. *From the Shadows.* New York: Simon and Schuster, 1996.

Gavin, Francis J. "Politics, Power, and U.S. Policy in Iran, 1950–1953." *Journal of Cold War Studies* 1 (winter 1999): 56–89.

Goode, James F. *The United States and Iran, 1946–1951: The Diplomacy of Neglect.* New York: St. Martin's Press, 1989.

Gosnell, Harold F. *Truman's Crises.* Westport, Conn.: Greenwood Press, 1980.

Grose, Peter. *Operation Rollback.* New York: Houghton Mifflin, 2000.

Gwertzman, Bernard. "Carter Emissary Dissuaded Shah from U.S. Exile." *Washington Post,* 20 April 1979, A1.

———. "U.S. Decision to Admit the Shah; Key Events in 8 Months of Debate." *Washington Post,* 18 November 1979, A1.

Hersh, Seymour M. *The Price of Power.* New York: Summit Books, 1983.

Holt, Pat M. *Secret Intelligence and Public Policy.* Washington, D.C.: Congressional Quarterly Press, 1995.

Huyser, Robert E. *Mission to Tehran.* New York: Harper and Row, 1986.

Jeffreys-Jones, Rhodri, and Christopher Andrew, eds. *Eternal Vigilance? Fifty Years of the CIA.* London: Frank Cass, 1997.

Jentlesen, Bruce W. "American Commitments in the Third World: Theory and Practice." *International Organizations* 41 (autumn 1987): 667–704.

Jordan, Hamilton. *Crisis: The Last Year of the Carter Presidency.* New York: G. P. Putnam's Sons, 1982.

Kimball, Jeffery. *Nixon's Vietnam War.* Lawrence: University Press of Kansas, 1988.

Kissinger, Henry. "Kissinger on the Controversy over the Shah." *New York Times,* 29 November 1979, A19.

———. "No Ground Forces for Kosovo." *Washington Post,* 22 February 1999, A20.

———. *The White House Years.* Boston: Little Brown, 1979.

———. *Years of Upheaval.* Boston: Little Brown, 1982.

Klass, Philip J. "U.S. Monitoring Capability Impaired." *Aviation Week and Space Technology,* 14 May 1979.

Kuhns, Woodrow J., ed. *Assessing the Soviet Threat.* Washington, D.C.: Center for the Study of Intelligence, Central Intelligence Agency, 1997.

Kupchan, Charles A. "American Globalism in the Middle East: The Roots of Regional Policy." *Political Science Quarterly* 103 (winter 1988–89): 585–616.

Kuzichkin, Vladimir. *My Life in Soviet Espionage.* New York: Ivy Books, 1995.

Kyle, James H. *The Guts to Try.* New York: Orion Books, 1990.

Laingen, L. Bruce. *Yellow Ribbon.* New York: Brassey's, 1992.

Ledeen, Michael A. *Perilous Statecraft.* New York: Scribner's, 1988.

Ledeen, Michael A., and William Lewis. *Debacle: The American Failure in Iran.* New York: Alfred A. Knopf, 1981.

McLellan, David S. *Cyrus Vance.* Totowa, N.J.: Roman and Allanheld, 1985.

Martin, David C., and John Walcott. *Best Laid Plans: The Inside Story of America's War against Terrorism.* New York: Harper and Row, 1988.

Meyer, Cord. *Facing Reality: From World Federalism to the CIA.* New York: Harper and Row, 1980.

Moens, Alexander. "President Carter's Advisors and the Fall of the Shah." *Political Science Quarterly* 106 (summer 1991): 211–38.

Morgan, Dan. "Chase Manhattan's Ties to the Shah: Rockefeller and His Bank Have Been Active in Iran for Years." *Washington Post,* 16 November 1979, A4.

Nixon, Richard M. *RN: The Memoirs of Richard Nixon.* New York, Grossett and Dunlap, 1978.

Nossiter, Bernard D. "Shah of Iran Welcome in U.S. but He's Told Later Would Be Better." *Washington Post,* 21 April 1979, A16.

Oberdorfer, Dan. "The Making of a Crisis: U.S. Agonizes over an Exile's Entry." *Washington Post,* 11 November 1979, A1.

Omestad, Thomas. "Savvy, but Not Sorry." *U.S. News and World Report,* 8 November 1999, 63.

Pincus, Walter. "Amateur Iranian Investigation Team Sifts Documents to Find Royal Crime." *Washington Post,* 7 December 1979, A22.

Pincus, Walter, and John M. Goshko. "U.S. Officials Had 'Understandings' with Shah." *Washington Post,* 26 March 1980, A1.

Pincus, Walter, and Dan Morgan. "Pahlavi Fortune: Many-Branched Tree, Rooted in Iran." *Washington Post,* 23 December 1979, A1.

Pisani, Sallie. *The CIA and the Marshall Plan.* Lawrence: University Press of Kansas, 1991.

Poteat, Eugene. "Stealth, Countermeasures, and ELINT, 1960–1975: Some Beginnings of Information Warfare 1960–1967." *Studies in Intelligence* 42, no. 1 (1998).

Prados, John. *Presidents' Secret Wars.* Rev. ed. Chicago: Ivan R. Dees, 1996.

Ranelagh, John. *The Agency: The Rise and Decline of the CIA.* New York: Simon and Schuster, 1986.

Richards, Bill. "Ball Asserts Kissinger's 'Obnoxious' Pressure Preceded Entry of Shah." *Washington Post,* 26 November 1979, A8.

Richelson, Jeffery T. *American Espionage and the Soviet Target.* New York: William Morrow, 1987.

———. *A Century of Spies: Intelligence in the Twentieth Century.* New York: Oxford University Press, 1995.

Risen, James. "How a Plot Convulsed Iran in '53 (and '79)." *New York Times,* 16 April 2000, A1.

———. "Secrets of History: The CIA in Iran." *New York Times,* 16 April 2000, A15.

Roosevelt, Kermit. *Countercoup: The Struggle for the Control of Iran.* New York: McGraw-Hill, 1977.

Rossitzke, Harry. *The CIA's Secret Operations.* New York: Reader's Digest, 1977.

Rubin, Barry. *Paved with Good Intentions: The American Experience and Iran.* New York: Penguin Books, 1981.

Ryan, Paul B. *The Iranian Rescue Mission: Why It Failed.* Reprint. Annapolis: Naval Institute Press, 1984.

"Scapegoating" [editorial]. *Washington Post,* 2 December 1979, D6.

Scherer, Ron. "Shah's Fabled Riches: Millions? Billions?" *Christian Science Monitor,* 23 April 1980, Financial Section, 1.

Schwartz, Tony. "No Comment on Iran Statement." *New York Times,* 15 November 1979, A19.

"Shah's Admission to the U.S. Linked to Misinformation on His Sickness." *New York Times,* 13 May 1981, A1.

Sick, Gary. *All Fall Down: America's Tragic Encounter with Iran.* New York: Random House, 1985.

Simons, Marlise. "Shah, Entourage in Mexico with Aid of Kissinger; Kissinger Aids in Shift by Shah." *Washington Post,* 11 June 1979, A1.

Smith, Hedrick. "U.S. Aides Say Loss of Post in Iran Impairs Missile-Monitoring Ability." *New York Times,* 2 March 1979, A1.

Smith, Terrence. "Why Carter Admitted the Shah." *New York Times,* 17 May 1981, A36.

Stafford, Thomas T. "Hidden in Plain Sight: Searching for the CIA's 'New Missions.'" *International Journal of Intelligence and Counterintelligence* 13, no. 2 (2000): 144–59.

Stempel, John D. *Inside the Iranian Revolution.* Bloomington: Indiana University Press, 1981.

Sullivan, William H. "Dateline Iran: The Road Not Taken." *Foreign Policy* 40 (fall 1980): 175–96.

———. *Mission to Iran.* New York: W. W. Norton, 1981.

———. *Obbligato: 1939–79. Notes on a Foreign Service Career.* New York: W. W. Norton, 1983.

Teicher, Howard, and Gayle Radley Teicher. *Twin Pillars to Desert Storm: America's Flawed Vision in the Middle East from Nixon to Bush.* New York: William Morrow, 1993.

Tenet, George J. "The CIA and the Security Challenges of the New Century." *International Journal of Intelligence and Counterintelligence* 13, no. 2 (summer 2000): 133–44.

Thomas, Evan. *The Very Best Men. Four Who Dared: The Early Years of the CIA.* New York: Simon and Schuster, 1995.

Torgerson, Dial. "U.S. Spy Devices Still Running at Iran Post." *International Herald Tribune,* 7 March 1979, A1.

Treverton, Gregory F. *Covert Action: The CIA and American Intervention in the Postwar World.* London: I. B. Tauris, 1987.

Turner, Stansfield. *Secrecy and Democracy.* Boston: Houghton Mifflin, 1985.
————. *Terrorism and Democracy.* Boston: Houghton Mifflin, 1991.
Weigley, Russell F. *The American Way of War.* New York: Macmillan, 1973.
Wicker, Tom. *One of Us: Richard Nixon and the American Dream.* New York: Random House, 1991.
Yergin, Daniel. *Shattered Peace.* Boston: Houghton Mifflin, 1977.

INDEX

Abdi, Abbas, 207–8
Acheson, Dean, 35
Afghanistan, 18, 83, 177, 204
Ahern, Tom, 170
air raids, Tehran, 193–94, 202–3
Albright, Madeleine, 30
Algeria: Brzezinski meeting
  Bazargan/Yazdi in, 114–16, 122; hos-
  tages and, 174, 201, 210–12
Algerian ambassador, 166, 203
Algerian doctors, 205
America, USS (CVA-66), 137–38
American public, 157–58, 208–9, 214
Americans in Iran, 52–53, 61, 69
Anglo-Iranian Oil Company, 26, 33
apartment building, hostages moved to,
  182
Arab-Israeli talks, 83, 85–86
arms sales to Iran, 58; "blank check,"
  46–47, 49–50; Defense Dept.'s scaled-
  back proposals, 48; Iranians on,
  51–52
atomic bomb, Soviet, 23, 24
Azerbaijan Socialist Republic, 18, 25

Baghdad Pact, 42
Baikonur missile testing complex, USSR,
  19–20
Baker, Howard, 200
Bakhtiar, Shahpour, 89–90, 92, 93
Ball, George, 63
Bani-Sadr, Abolhassan, 133–34, 168,
  175, 197

Barnes, Clair, 170
bazaaris, 68–69
Bazargan, Mehdi, 11, 93, 98, 103, 121;
  Brzezinski meeting in Algiers, 114–15,
  122; resignation, 125
Beckwith, Charlie, 189–90
Beneš, Edvard, 23
Berlin blockade, 23
Beyahia (Algerian Foreign Minister), 212
Bill, James, 11, 38
Black American hostages, 130–31
British embassy takeover, 123
British Secret Intelligence Service (SIS),
  34–35, 36
Brown, Harold "Hal," 90, 127, 132–33,
  177
Brzezinski, Zbigniew, 10, 83, 90–91, 133,
  198; Bazargan meeting in Algiers,
  114–15; covert operation plans,
  152–53; on Iran, 85, 151–52, 177;
  Iranian understanding, 54; isolation
  from State and CIA, 76–77; military
  option memo, 150–53; Nov. 6, 1979,
  126; on Operation Eagle Claw, 184,
  186–87; on the shah, 61, 62, 95–96;
  shah and, 59, 84–85; on Soviet intentions in Iran, 11; on Sullivan and Khomeini camp, 92; "Thinking the
  Unthinkable" cable and, 87, 88; on
  U.S. shah policy, 80–81, 82
Bush, George, 220
Byrd, Robert, 200

Camp David Accords, 83
Canadian diplomats, Tehran, 119,
    174–75
Capucci, Hilarion, 169
Carlucci, Frank, 98, 184
Carner, Toni, 214
Carter, Jimmy: admits shah to U.S., 94,
    97–98; Arab-Israeli talks and, 85–86;
    on Brzezinski's military option
    memo, 150, 153; cables shah, 84, 85;
    freezes Iranian assets, 132; hostage
    concerns, 97, 99; hostage families
    concerns, 169–70; human rights
    agenda, 56, 57–58; Iran understand-
    ing, 54, 68, 74, 90–91; Nov. 4, 1979,
    121; Nov. 5, 1979, 125–26; Operation
    Eagle Claw, 185, 186, 189–90; rescue
    mission considerations, 177–78; retal-
    iation warning, 148–49; on retaliatory
    strikes planning, 128; sends aircraft
    carriers to Arabian Sea, 134; on the
    shah, 62, 82, 90, 97; shah and, 59, 64;
    on Sullivan and Khomeini camp, 92;
    on Sullivan's hedging and question-
    ing, 88–89; surprise release proce-
    dures memo and, 199; visits released
    hostages, 216–17
Carter administration: after rescue
    attempt, 197–98; embassy staff reduc-
    tions, 11–12; hostage escapes Jan.
    1980 and, 174–75; intelligence con-
    tradictory to policy preferences and,
    66–67; on Kissinger's arms sales to
    Iran directive, 50; negotiating hostage
    settlement, 173–74; shah policy,
    81–82; spy trials concerns, 171,
    172–73. *See also* intelligence failure,
    U.S.; National Security Council; Oper-
    ation Eagle Claw; Special Coordinat-
    ing Committee on Iran
Central Intelligence Agency (CIA), 27,
    47, 69–71; acknowledges Khomeini's
    consolidation of power, 129; on hos-
    tage guards, 159, 160; *Iran after the
    Shah* (report), 74; Iranian intelligence
    gathering 1960s–70s, 67–68; 1953

coup and, 29, 34; reconnaissance mis-
    sion into Iran, 175; SAVAK and, 41
chancery, U.S. Embassy, 104, 105–7
Christopher, Warren, 97, 198, 199
Church, Frank, 200
Churchill, Winston, 35
Civiletti, Benjamin: Nov. 6, 1979, 126
Clark, Ramsey, 168
clergy, Iranian, 68–69, 82–83, 105. *See
    also* Khomeini, Ruhollah
clergy visiting hostages, 166, 169, 170
Clough, Susan, 199
Cold War, 23–26
"cooperative" hostage, 181–82
Council of Cooperation, 160
"Crimes of America" conference, 168

Daugherty, William J., 193; Algerian
    ambassador visits, 166; on Carter,
    217; CIA recruitment, 5–7; CIA train-
    ing, 6–9; "cooperative" hostage and,
    181–82; cover-blowing cable and,
    143–45; daily hostage routine, 154,
    169, 179–81, 182, 183; education and
    intellectual capacity, 139; escape
    plans, 155; faith, 157–58; "Foreign
    Service" role, 140; harassing interroga-
    tors, 142–43; Hegdahl's captivity
    training and, 138–39, 140; humor,
    156–57; interrogations, 130, 135–36;
    Komiteh Prison, 192–93; last talk
    with Hossein, 206–7; letters home,
    166, 203; Marine Corps training,
    136–37, 139–40; medical exam, 205,
    213–14; moved to chancery, 131;
    Needham and, 183; as "new guy,"
    146–47; Nov. 4, 1979 early morning,
    103, 105; Nov. 4, 1979 questioning, 1,
    110–13; office location, 107; present
    from home, 203–4; psychological
    denial, 155–56; reading in captivity,
    156, 166, 192; release, 208, 210–14;
    Roeder and, 194–95; shredding doc-
    uments, 107–9; solitary confinement,
    160–61; spy trial threats and, 164–66;
    starts at U.S. embassy, 15–16; sur-

render on Nov. 4, 1979, 110; Tehran assignment, 12–14; vault opening and, 116–17; Vietnam service, 137–38; West Point Corps of Cadets dinner, 219–20

Defense, U.S. Department of, 48, 175

Defense Attaché's Office (DAO), 10

Defense Intelligence Agency (DIA), 74

Desert One, 175, 184, 221. *See also* Operation Eagle Claw

"Developments in the Azerbaijan Situation" (1947), 26

documents, U.S. Embassy: destruction, 107–9; reconstruction, 147–48

Donovan, Hedley, 11

Dulles, Allen, 36

Dulles, John Foster, 36, 42

Duncan, Charles, 126

Eastern Europe, Soviet moves into, 23

Ebtekar, Massoumeh. *See* "Tehran Mary"

Egypt, U.S. and, 45

Eisenhower, Dwight, 24, 35, 36–37, 38

Entezam, Abbas Amir, 98

European allies, sanctions by, 176–77, 186

Evin Prison, 179–81; bungalow, 194–96

families, hostages', 169–70

Federal Bureau of Investigation, 41

F-14 Tomcats, 48, 50–51

food for hostages, 179, 185; inadequacy of, 182, 183

Foreign Broadcast Information Service (FBIS), CIA, 129

France, SAVAK and, 41

French flight controller, 212–13

French Resistance, WWII, 141

Gasiorowski, Mark, 38, 53–54

Gast, Phillip, 16

Gates, Bob, 115

Ghotbzadeh, Sadegh, 197

Gilani-Sharia, Mohammad, 171

Golovanov, Valdimir, 59

Great Britain: Iran and, 17, 18, 21–22, 40; oil boycott, 34; SAVAK and, 41; Suez withdrawal by, 45. *See also* Anglo-Iranian Oil Company

Gregg, Don, 14

GRU, Soviet intelligence service, 41–42, 190

guards, hostage, 158–60, 204; American soldiers propaganda poster, 165; conversations with, 161–63; Council of Cooperation, 160; on denying Carter's reelection, 169, 195–97; Evin Prison, 180–81, 195; on hostages' watches, 194; reduced contacts with, 204–5; spy trial threats, 164–66; world events knowledge of, 163–64. *See also* students, Iranian

Haig, Alexander, 90

Harriman, Averell, 25

Hass II, King (Morocco), 94–95

Haughey, Charles, 218

Hegdahl, Douglas, 138–39, 140, 142, 164

Helms, Richard M., 29, 52, 69–70

Henderson, Loy, 35

Hiss, Alger, 24

Holiday Inn-type (hostage) hotel, 182–83

Holland, Lee, 165

Hossein Sheik-ol-Eslam, 135, 142–43, 144, 167–68, 206–7; patriotic fervor, 146; spy trial threats by, 164–66

House of Representatives, U.S., 66

Hussein, Saddam, 125

Huyser, Robert E. "Dutch," 90, 91

Intelligence and Research (INR), State Dept.'s Bureau of, 72, 74

intelligence failure, U.S., 66–79; accurate reports' lack of impact, 74–76; CIA Iranian intelligence gathering 1960s–70s, 67–68; CIA political reporting during 1960s–70s, 69–71; erroneous reports and, 72; intelligence collection and analysis limits, 73; NSC isolation, 76–77; predicting

intelligence failure (*continued*)
future events and, 74; presidential
policies and, 68; shah's illness, 77–79
interrogators, 111, 112–13, 136; emotional buttons, 142–43; WJD-cover-
blowing cable and, 143–45; on WJD
ignorance of culture/language,
145–46. *See also* Hossein Sheik-ol-
Eslam
Iran: Americans in, 52–53; Carter fore-
goes policy review of, 56; on Carter
warning, 148–49; collapse, 92–93;
communication lines severed, 133;
demonstrations and violence, 64–65;
deterioration, 89; foreign journalists
expelled, 169; geographical importance, 18–19; hostage release terms,
153; Islamic Revolutionary Council,
125; Khomeini's return, 92–93; modernization under shah, 19; negotiating
hostage settlement, 173–74; political
prisoner releases, 82; post-coup
period (1953–77), 40–55; SAVAK
and, 40–41; Soviet Cold War aggression, 24–25; technical shortcomings,
47–48; U.S. aid to, 40, 42; U.S. arms
sales to, 32, 44–45, 46–47; U.S. history with, 17–22; U.S. mutual assistance treaty, 42; White Revolution,
43–44; WWII and U.S. alliance,
21–22. *See also* Bakhtiar, Shahpour;
Iranians; 1953 coup; Provisional
Government of Iran; shah of Iran
Iran after the Shah (CIA/INR report), 74
Iran Branch Chief, Directorate of Operations, CIA Headquarters, 3, 5
Iranian Affairs, State Dept.'s Office of, 72
Iranian foreign ministry's guest house,
202
Iranian Ministry of Court, 69
Iranians: on Americans in Iran, 53;
Carter toast to shah and, 64; on denying Carter's reelection, 169; ethnocen-
tricity, 167; on hostage escapes Jan.
1980, 174–75; look to Khomeini, 65;
negotiating hostages' release, 198;

negotiations hopes, 201; psychological warfare against hostages, 208–9;
public relations campaign by militant,
168; shah's modernizations and,
60–61; on U.S. arms sales to shah,
51–52; world view of, 15–16. *See also*
guards, hostage; students, Iranian
Iran Working Group, U.S. State Department, 73–74
Iraq, 11, 45, 174, 175, 198; consulates in
Iran seized, 125
Islamic law, 172
Islamic Revolutionary Council, 125,
130–31
Israel, shah's support for, 54, 57

Jackson, Henry, 200
Jaleh Square demonstration/shootings
(Jan. 1978), 71
Javits, Jacob, 200
Johnson administration, 43, 44–45, 68
Jones, David C., 126–27, 133, 175, 177
Jones, John B., 172
Jordan, Hamilton, 178, 184, 199–201

Kalp, Malcolm, 170
Kennedy, John F., 43, 68
KGB, 41–42; in Iran, 59–60, 61–62; U.S.
and, 144, 190–91
Khatami, Mohammad, 206
Khoeni. *See* Musavi-Khoeni
Khomeini, Ahmad, 161–62, 172–73,
198, 199; U.S. embassy takeover justification by, 120, 121–22
Khomeini, Ruhollah, 10, 44, 68, 87, 89;
assumes control, 125; contradictory
pronouncements, 133; embassy takeover and, 120, 131; influence in exile,
63; Iranians look to for leadership,
65; releases Black Americans and
women, 130–31; returns, 92–93; on
spy trials, 130–31
Khomeini holes, 183
Kimball, Jeffrey, 24
Kissinger, Henry, 17, 31–32, 46, 54; arms
sales memorandum, 48–49, 50; on

"blank check" arms sales, 49–50; on shah in U.S., 96, 99

Kittyhawk, USS (CVA-63), 134

"klepto table," 215–16

Komiteh Prison, 192–94

komitehs, 92; Iranian students and, 103

Korean conflict, Iran and, 33

Kostromin, Lev Petrovich, 59

Krys, Sheldon, 120

Kyle, Jim, 184, 189

Laingen, L. Bruce, 16, 106, 111–12, 150, 186; message to Carter, 177–78; release, 212; on shah in U.S., 96, 97, 98; on surrender, 109–10; Washington contact, Nov. 4, 1979, 120

letters, hostages', 158, 166, 170

Luce, Clare Booth, 62

Malenkov, Georgy, 36–37

Mao Zedong, 24

Marine Corps, 11–12, 136–37, 188

Marxist guerillas Feb. 1979 takeover, 10

McCloy, John J., 96

media: on Iranian intelligence deficit, 67

Mehdi (hostage guard), 204

Melody program, 31–32

Metrinko, Michael, 170

Midway, USS (CV-41), 134

military, U.S., 188

Military Assistance Advisory Group (MAAG), 10, 71

military Code of Conduct limitations, 140

Miller, G. William, 132, 216

Ministry of National Guidance, Iran, 131

Moeller, Don, 170, 183, 192

Mondale, Walter, 85, 96, 126, 216

Moore, Bert, 110

Mossadegh, Mohammed, 26; 1953 overthrow of, 29, 34–35; regime disintegrates, 35–36; seeks external assistance, 35, 36–37; U.S. concerns over, 32–33

Mossad (Israel's foreign intelligence service), 41

Musavi-Khoeni, 160

Muskie, Edmund, 199, 216

Muslim Student Followers of the Line of the Imam, 159

Naas, Charles W., 10–11, 29–30, 63, 89–90; on shah, 72, 85; on State Dept. staff reductions, 68; "Thinking the Unthinkable" cable and, 86, 87, 88; on U.S. embassy, 67

National Front, 63

National Security Council, 72, 76–77, 126–27, 128–29, 175–76

National Voice of Iran, 42, 62, 131–32, 174

Nazi-Soviet Nonaggression Pact, 21

Needham, Paul, 182–83, 192

Newsom, David D., 10, 75, 114, 122; on shah, 80, 98

Newsweek, 195–96

Ngo Diem Dinh, 81

Nimitz, USS (CVAN-68), 184

1953 coup, 23, 29–39; British oil boycott and, 34; criticism, 30–31; 1979 hostage crisis and, 38–39, 114–15; Operation Boot, 34–35; strategic importance, 37–38; Tacksman sites and, 31–32; Truman policy, 33–34; violence/instability and, 35–36

Nixon, Richard M., 45–46, 47, 48, 54, 68

North Korea, 24

November 4, 1979, 103–22, 105; ambassador's dining room, 118–19; anticipated duration of takeover, 113–14; Brzezinski meeting Bazargan/Yazdi in Algiers, 114–16, 122; clerics and fundamentalists, 105; embassy description, 105–7; four-drawer safe, 118; helicopter lands on second day, 119; interrogators, 111, 112–13; invasion begins, 107; Islamic significance of, 103; student justification of, 120; students, 103; U.S. document shredding, 107–9; vault focus, 112–13; vault opening, 116–17; Washington

November 4, 1979 (*continued*)
reaction to, 120–22; WJD interrogation, 1, 110–13
November 5, 1979, 123–24
November 6, 1979, 125–29
November 7–22, 1979, 130–34; U.S. sets sanctions, 132–34
November 23–December 31, 1979, 135–53
Noyer (hostage), 170
NSC-68, 33–34
NSC-107/2, on loss of Iran to communists, 28
NSC-136, 28
NSC-136/1, 28
Nunn, Sam, 200

O'Neill, Thomas P. "Tip," 200
Operation Eagle Claw, 178, 184–91; alternative options, 186–87; enormity of, 184–85; hostages' opinions of, 185–86; pilots, 188, 189; RH-53Ds, 188–89; risks, 187–88; Soviet surveillance of U.S. and, 190–91; success parameters, 189–90; training/rehearsal, 190, 191

Pahlavi, Mohammad Reza, 22, 46. See also shah of Iran
People's Republic of China, 83
Pfeiffer, Gottfried, 216
Political-Military Affairs, State Dept.'s Bureau of, 72
political prisoners, 82
Powers, Francis Gary, 165
Precht, Henry, 68, 69, 88, 114, 200; on CIA self-censorship, 71; on shah, 73, 98; Swift's call and, 120
Presidential Directive 13 (PD-13), "Conventional Arms Transfer," 58
prisoner "breaking" process, 141–42
prisoner resistance, 140–41, 164; by WJD, 164, 180–81, 202–3
Provisional Government of Iran (PGOI), 10, 52, 98; Vienna Conventions and, 171

Queen, Rich, 193

Radio Moscow, 129
Radio Tehran, 115–16
Rajai, Mohammed Ali, 198, 199
Reagan, Nancy, 220
Reagan, Ronald, 196–97, 220
Redlick, Norman, 172
release, 208; Air Algerie 727s, 210–12; from Algeria to Germany, 212; Carter and Vance visit hostages, 217–18; first party, 214–15; gifts, 215–16; medical exams, 213–14; meeting families of servicemen killed during Desert One, 221; parade to West Point, 218–19; Rhein-Main Airbase, 213; Shannon, Ireland, stop, 218; West Point Corps of Cadets dinner, 219–20; White House reception, 220–21; yellow ribbons, 213, 219
Revolutionary Guards, 131
Reza Shah, 21–22
RH-53D Sea Stallion helicopters, 184, 188–89
Rhodes, John, 200–201
Rockefeller, David, 96, 99
Roeder, Dave, 165, 194–95, 196, 197
Roosevelt, Kermit "Kim," 36, 38
Rubin, Barry, 47, 48
Rundstedt, Gerd von, 21
Rusk, Dean, 44

Sadat, Anwar, 94
SALT II negotiations, 83
Saunders, Harold, 10, 120, 200
SAVAK (Iranian security organization), 40–41, 55, 63, 69, 136
Schaefer, Anita, 221
Schaefer, Tom, 163–64, 165, 214, 216–17; Komiteh Prison, 192, 193, 210
Scott, Chuck, 109–10
Senate Select Committee on Intelligence, 66
shah of Iran, 9, 36, 53, 62–63, 64; arms sales to, 32, 44–45, 46–47; in Baha-

mas, 95–96; Brzezinski calls to, 84–85, 89; Carter allows entry to U.S., 94, 96–97; on Carter's policies, 58–59; CIA inquiries, 70; demonstrations policy, 82; dictatorship, 54–55; dissolved government, 85; Johnson administration and, 43, 44–45; Kennedy administration and, 43; leaves Iran, 89, 92; medical condition, 77– 79, 97, 115; in Mexico, 96; military arms orders by, 50; Nixon administra-tion and, 45–46; ruling style, 61; SAVAK, 40–41; White Revolution, 43–44
Shi'ism, 69
Sick, Gary, 15, 57, 66, 99, 122; cable to shah, 89; as NSC Iran action officer, 72; on NSC policy objectives and guidelines, 128; on Operation Eagle Claw, 184, 187; on shah's-invincibil-ity attitude, 75; on U.S. and shah, 47, 59
Soviet Strategic Missile Forces, 20
Special Coordinating Committee on Iran (SCC), 57, 83, 84, 132, 133–34; Camp David strategic proposals, 149–52; Nov. 5, 1979, 123–24; Nov. 6, 1979, 126; retaliatory strikes plan-ning, 127–28
"Special Evaluation No. 39, Possibility of Soviet Aggression against Iran," 27–28
Der Spiegel, 195–96
spy trials, 130–31, 164–66, 171–73
Stalin, Joseph, 23, 24–25
State Department, U.S., 27, 67–68, 73–74, 76–77, 85
Stempel, John, 15, 34, 38
Stennis, John, 200
Stratton, Richard, 139
students, Iranian, 103, 114, 158–59, 160, 167. *See also* guards, hostage
St. Valentine's Day Open House (1979), 10, 95, 114
Sullivan, William H., 60, 72, 83–84, 85, 95; on Bakhtiar, 89, 90; Khomeini camp and, 91–92; "Thinking the Unthinkable" cable, 86–88

Swift, Ann, 109, 120

Tacksman listening posts, 19–21, 31–32, 57, 95
Taft, Robert, 36
Taiwan, 83
Taylor, Kenneth, 119
Tehran American School, 166
Tehran Conference (1943), 25
"Tehran Mary," 144, 163–64, 168, 206
Teicher, Howard, 46
Tenent, George I., 73
"Thinking the Unthinkable" cable, 86–88
Thomas, Evan, 34
Time, 195–96
Tomseth, Vic, 109, 120
Treverton, Gregory, 38
Tripartite Treaty of Albania (1942), 22, 25
Truman, Harry, 23, 24, 25, 28, 33–34
Tudeh party, 25, 26, 42. *See also* Mossa-degh, Mohammed
Turner, Stansfield, 70, 76, 133
"Twin Pillars" policy, 46

United Nations, 25–26, 198–99
United States, 127; aid to Iran, 40; arms sales to Iran, 32, 44–45, 46–47; intel-ligence failure, 66–79; intelligence lis-tening posts, Elbourz Mountains, 19–20; Iran mutual assistance treaty with, 42; Iran policy disagreements, 75; official attempts at meeting with Iranian dissidents, 69; religious-coalition's-incapability attitude, 75–76; sets sanctions, 132–34; and shah of Iran, 44, 59–60; shah's-invin-cibility attitude, 75; "Twin Pillars" policy, 46. *See also* Central Intelligence Agency (CIA); Federal Bureau of Investigation
U.S. embassy: on Brzezinski calls to shah and Zahedi, 89; CIA station staff, 94; document destruction, 107–9; evacu-ation potential, 99; intelligence

U.S. embassy (*continued*)
    gathering 1960s–70s, 67–68; Marxist
    guerillas takeover, 10; Revolutionary
    Guards protect, 131; security drill,
    107; shah's entry to U.S. and, 94,
    96–99; staff and security after Feb.
    1979 takeover, 11–12; staff growth
    during 1979, 114; surrender, 1,
    109–10; WJD assignment to, 12–14.
    See also Naas, Charles W.; November
    4, 1979; Sullivan, William H.
U.S.-Iran Status of Forces Agreement, 44
USSR, 19–20, 23–24, 31–32, 174; F-14
    Tomcats, 51; intelligence services in
    Iran, 41–42; Iran border problems,
    37; Iran expansion intentions, 17,
    18–19; Iranian domestic understand-
    ing of, 59–60; on Iranian revolution,
    132; Iraqi-Soviet Friendship Treaty,
    45; PGOI and, 11; RH-53Ds and,
    188–89; U.S. surveillance by, 190–91;
    WWII and Iranian alliance, 21–22. *See
    also* KGB; National Voice of Iran

Vance, Cyrus, 85, 86, 87, 93, 200; on
    arms sales, 58; on coup potential, 91;
    military force dissent by, 176–77; on
    Operation Eagle Claw, 184; on shah,
    57, 95, 96, 97, 186; Swift's call to
    Washington, 120; visits released hos-
    tages in Germany, 216, 217–18
Vaught, James B., 127, 189
Vienna Conventions on Diplomatic
    Immunity, 171
Vietnam, U.S. commitments in, 44, 45
villa, hostages moved to, 182

Waldheim, Kurt, 63
West Germany: SAVAK and, 41
Wiesbaden Air Force Hospital staff, 214
women hostages, 130–31
World Court, 198
Wright, James, 200–201

Yazdi, Ibrahim, 98, 114, 115, 121, 122

Zahedi, Ardishir, 77, 89

ABOUT THE AUTHOR

William J. Daugherty was born in Oklahoma and educated at Oklahoma Military Academy, the University of California–Irvine, and the Claremont Graduate School. He holds a bachelor's degree in social sciences and a Ph.D. in government.

Currently an assistant professor of government at Armstrong Atlantic State University in Savannah, Georgia, Dr. Daugherty served eight years in the U.S. Marine Corps, including a combat tour in Vietnam. Following his military service, Dr. Daugherty worked for seventeen years in the Central Intelligence Agency as an operations officer where he was posted to Iran, the Caribbean, and Europe, specializing in Middle East affairs and counterterrorism. Prior to his retirement in 1996, he focused on the areas of resources management and covert action policy, serving in a liaison capacity to the National Security Council staff.

A licensed pilot and avid tennis player, Dr. Daugherty resides in Savannah.